STRANGE WAY TO LIVE

A Story of Rock 'n' Roll Resurrection

DUNDURN
TORONTO

Editor: Allister Thompson
Design: Courtney Horner
Printer: Webcom
Cover design by Laura Boyle
Cover image courtesy of Dimo Safari
All photos © Carl Dixon unless otherwise indicated.

Library and Archives Canada Cataloguing in Publication

Dixon, Carl, author
Strange way to live : a story of rock 'n' roll resurrection
/ Carl Dixon.

Issued in print and electronic formats.
ISBN 978-1-4597-2853-0

1. Dixon, Carl. 2. Rock musicians--Canada--Biography.
I. Title.

ML420.D621A3 2014   782.42166092   C2014-906757-7
C2014-906758-5

1 2 3 4 5   19 18 17 16 15

We acknowledge the support of the **Canada Council for the Arts** and the **Ontario Arts Council** for our publishing program. We also acknowledge the financial support of the **Government of Canada** through the **Canada Book Fund** and **Livres Canada Books**, and the **Government of Ontario** through the **Ontario Book Publishing Tax Credit** and the **Ontario Media Development Corporation**.

Care has been taken to trace the ownership of copyright material used in this book. The author and the publisher welcome any information enabling them to rectify any references or credits in subsequent editions.
J. Kirk Howard, President

The publisher is not responsible for websites or their content unless they are owned by the publisher.

Printed and bound in Canada.

Visit us at
Dundurn.com | @dundurnpress
Facebook.com/dundurnpress | Pinterest.com/Dundurnpress

Dundurn
3 Church Street, Suite 500
Toronto, Ontario, Canada
M5E 1M2

STRANGE WAY TO LIVE

This book is dedicated to my mother Marje and my sister Christina;
my daughters Carlin and Lauren;
and to Helen Parker, who came along at just the right time.

CONTENTS

"He that will write well in any tongue must follow the counsel of Aristotle, to speak as the common people do, to think as the wise men do; and so should every man understand him, and the judgment of wise men allow him."

— Roger Ascham (1515–68)

"For the composers and musicians, when we get a brilliant idea it is like reaching glory. That's why musicians will never retire."

— Israel "Cachao" López Valdés (1918–2008)

"Writing a Book"
(May be sung to the tune of The Beatles' "Fixing a Hole")

I'm writing a book, where my brain gets in
And sorts my thoughts and memories
Where they should go.
Describing myself in a colourful way
And though it may be difficult
There's a good flow.
And to me it really matters that I get it right
It takes so long to write
But moves along.
Conversational in tone
Careful not to whine or moan
Mention those who helped me sing the song . . .
Surprising myself with an excerpt or two
It's funny when I see it now . . .
May it please you . . .

FOREWORD BY LAWRENCE GOWAN

Carl Dixon and I first met in January 1985, when I opened for Coney Hatch at The Misty Moon in Halifax, Nova Scotia. That was the first official "Gowan" gig ever played, and we hit it off well with the fine fellows of the headline act. I discovered that Carl (like myself) was not only a devoted musician but also an overlooked, undrafted hockey player. This cemented our bond immeasurably. We've shared the ice and stage for years since that first meeting, and he's always proven to be a pal who knows how to pass the puck as well as make a guitar do what it's designed to do. He also sings exceedingly well and maintains a head of hair that's well suited to his vocation (see photos on pages 1 through 10,000). He's built a fine existence that could easily have come to a sad conclusion after he suffered a terrible accident but he chose instead not to allow that dark day to redefine him. His own definition and sense of purpose were clearly intact long before fate attempted to shut him down. How he overcame that incident is a remarkable tale, and you should read about it. This book you're holding is a perfect place to start that process, followed by an immediate trip to see and hear him play (either music or hockey, your choice).

If I were to attempt to distill the essence of Carl's story, it would come down to the simple yet complex phrase: *Keep going*. That's likely the essence of all great stories, though I can't be certain since I've yet to hear them all. Keep going, and once you've done that: *Keep rocking*. In the ongoing story of Carl Dixon, that's one of the main reasons he's still alive.

P.S.: He has a legendary set of balls, which I understand are still intact.

FOREWORD BY PAT STAPLETON

My three sons were all into rock music and loved Coney Hatch. It was 1992 and my boys encouraged me to join them at a fun night of hockey with a bunch of rock stars, including Carl. Those rock stars were very competitive on the ice. They were athletic, but being musicians they weren't fighters, they were lovers. As a hockey player I'd describe Carl as "a mean tryer."

I really got to know Carl later when he came to my farm. We walked across the field talking, and he was so engaged; he was like a sponge absorbing everything I said — and it wasn't anything about hockey — it was about life. He was interested in life.

We could have talked for twenty-four hours. I told him "I can't be with you twenty-four hours a day but I'll give you something that can," and gave him some motivational cassettes. The message was pretty clear: "You become what you think about." Two years later he presented me with a new set of cassettes, because he had worn them out. He was starting to expand his own horizons.

Carl is a man of tremendous willpower. He's very humble. He's very genuine. I will have been away from Carl for two years and my boys will say, "Have you called Carl?" When I call it's like we only talked yesterday. Relationships are like oak trees; you grow together or you grow apart and wither. My relationship with Carl has grown stronger — we're probably closer now than he is with my sons, who introduced us.

He is blessed with a strong will. His I-will might be more important than his IQ. That's what I saw, his I-WILL. After his car accident, in the beginning things didn't look that bright. Then he willed himself back on his skates. I know for sure, there's no doubt, it is his positive attitude that pulled him through. It was his internal wisdom that allowed him to do that.

Carl had some immense personal challenges. I learned as an athlete you never let on about your injuries. When you talk about conditioning … there's a mental conditioning: you have to master your thoughts.

Too many of us as we grow up become unfocused. Carl's focus is sharp. Carl knows where he wants to go and what he wants to contribute to society; he's become his own man. He's spiritual and humble but has great belief in himself.

Carl says he comes to me for advice and wisdom, but I think I got my wisdom from Carl.

— STRATHROY, ONTARIO, JULY 2014

AUTHOR'S NOTE

So we have here a book under the authorship of Carleton Anthony Dixon. It was written to the best of my ability and according to my lights at this point in my life. Perhaps next year I might write it better, or differently. However, as I've been pointedly made aware, next year might not come to me (or to any of us).

It is instructive and enlightening to write your own story. I recommend everyone write his or her book. I personally haven't written anything longer than a letter since I was in high school, so it required the marshalling of all my powers of memory, description, and erudition to get my book done. I've read plenty of 'em, though, so I hope I have some idea what one should look like.

'Tis a poor thing, but 'tis mine own. Some of you may find it absorbing; others may find it inadequate to your needs. If you find it's not up to your standards, I strongly urge you to just put it aside. Don't waste time or thought or energy in condemning the writer. He has told his story as well as he could.

We advance our species by sharing our knowledge and our experience. Whether we glean a profound truth, an amusing anecdote, or a repugnant episode from each other's stories, it all adds to our trove of data. It's what we do with our trove that is significant. What I offer you as a writer and an artist and communicator is an interpretation of my set of experiences and received data, filtered through my unique mind. With the words I write I express my truth as I see it.

In summation, I hope you enjoy my book. If you don't, you could try my next one. Or you could write your own.

— CARL DIXON, SEPTEMBER 2014

PROLOGUE:
ALMOST THE END

"Dammit! Idiot! Idiot! Stupido!" This abusive self-talk, accompanied by the pounding of my palm on the steering wheel, rang in my ears in the early evening of April 14, 2008. I'd got lost again during evening rush hour attempting to drive out of Melbourne, Australia. A mere two nights remained of my already shortened visit with my wife and our younger daughter in the small town of Daylesford. We would have no more time together until their scheduled return home to Canada, more than two months hence.

That April day I'd driven the hour-plus in the morning to Melbourne to work in a small recording studio. We'd planned a beautiful evening back in Daylesford, a sort of joyful send-off. Sadly, my return was delayed as I somehow bungled the directions and got turned around not once, not twice, but three times in the attempt to navigate the Ring Road out of Melbourne. I felt keenly the loss of precious time from our special night and was becoming increasingly distraught.

At six-thirty I pulled off the road after another wrong turn and called my wife on the mobile for one more try at sorting out my directions. This time, with her calming voice, it made a little more sense. I think high emotion is a block not only to thinking clearly but to hearing clearly. There was a Bottle Shop across the plaza from where I'd stopped, and it seemed wise to take a bit of extra time to buy a nice bottle of champagne for our little celebration.

The fact was my wife and I had ends to mend. There'd been months of forced separation as she chaperoned our daughter on the Australian set of the TV series *Saddle Club*, as required for our little girl's new acting career. There was also a malaise in our then fifteen-year marriage, partly the result of my endless travelling as a professional rock 'n' roller. This had been keeping me away from home fully half of each year. There was more wrong here than I knew, unfortunately.

I had sensed on my two prior visits to the set that for her, life on the other side of the world away from husband and home was actually a welcome change. When I turned up for those visits I felt, to quote a Fred Astaire movie, like "something of an igneous intrusion" in her freewheeling life around the TV production. On this third visit, though, I thought I had found a hope of renewal for our vows. April 14 was meant to be a tender, loving night to reflect that hope. For this brief time remaining, I just wanted to put everything aside and forget about the career, the ambition, and the spotlight I'd pursued for decades. All my life I'd been swept along by the trade winds of popular music. They were waiting to sweep me away again in a couple of days to the next show in America. This night was to be special ... if only I could find the bloody way there!

Angry self-recrimination was a bad habit of mine. To yell at myself was both an outlet and a form of punishment, to teach me not to make *that* mistake again. I realize now that it actually makes me weak and rattled instead. Though my drive to Daylesford was now finally on the right course, I continued to smoulder in self-reproach as I drove. About forty minutes later, there I was, far from home, this "rock star" in a strange land — a man who'd stood in the lights of thousands of stages around the world, now suddenly confronted by a blinding light far more glaring and ominous.

IN THE BEGINNING

Let me tell you a little about what led me to here. I've been a professional singer and musician since I was sixteen. I've had some success, seen some things, and made a decent living, even a good living at times.

I come from a modest background, born in the northern steel town of Sault Ste. Marie in the last days of 1958. When I grew up in "the Soo" in the 1960s, the temperature always hit forty below in the long winters and stayed chilly in the short summers that came to that thickly forested country around Lake Superior. Idyllic, if you like that sort of thing.

I'm like most white North Americans, descended from Europeans who immigrated here to seek improved prospects or to escape calamity. My father, Ronald Francis Dixon, was born in Sudbury in 1925. Ron was the tenth of twelve children in a family of Irish-English descent, and the seventh son of a seventh son to boot. His father, John Albert, graduated in medicine from McGill University in Montreal in 1907. I was tickled to learn that, among other extracurricular activities, my grandpa was athletic enough to captain the McGill hockey team. Dr. John Albert "Bert" Dixon went on to a long career in medicine, notably as head of surgery at Sudbury General Hospital for twenty-two years. Bert also opened medical practices in the Ottawa Valley and on Manitoulin Island at different stages of his life. For a time, in the early years, he made house calls with a horse and carriage. Unsurprisingly, his role as physician in these small communities gave the family some slight standing.

My paternal grandmother was Agatha (née) Watters of Ireland. Agatha was a fierce Irish Catholic, which helps explain the twelve blessed arrivals to the Dixon home. I'm not sure of much about Grandma Dixon. She was trained as a nurse, but I don't know if she worked in Bert's practice. She was in her seventies when I came along. I was always a bit frightened of her when we went to visit.

My father told me that Dr. Dixon lost a large amount of money, the greater part of the family fortune, on a highly speculative mining stock investment during the Great Depression. This unhappy outcome reduced

the family's socio-economic standing, and on one or two occasions when my father'd had a few drinks, he would complain that he and all the brothers and sisters "should have been rich."

The Dixon parents were strict with their children and kept things going with their huge brood along hard lines in those times of deprivation. They sent Ron to the CNE fair in Toronto, with its rides, midway, and variety shows, with a quarter in his pocket. Even in the 1930s there wasn't much you could do with two bits. "Make it stretch" was the advice offered.

Bert and Aggie somehow found the money to place my father in a Catholic private school called Scollard Hall. They hoped this experience might lead him to God and the priesthood, or at least to taking life more seriously. The Catholic high school had rather the opposite effect, if it had any effect at all aside from instilling bitter memories. Ron used to threaten to send me to Scollard Hall on a few occasions when I showed signs of teenage rebelliousness or lack of seriousness.

Still, there were many stories of happy childhood memories. The task of raising twelve children must have been a strain, but my grandparents both lived long and well (to eighty-six and ninety-three, respectively). The family was a hierarchy; the eldest children were expected to manage the youngest and relieve Mama's burden. Actually, this responsibility fell mostly to the daughters, while the eldest boys were out making their mark. Ron was tenth in birth order, and along with his little brothers Dick and Des was cared for by his older sister Mary. He always had a special love for Mary, as have I.

Many of the "Dixon dozen" served in the military in the Second World War or after. Ron, my father, was in line to be shipped to Europe with his army unit when VE Day arrived, thank God. When the VJ peace was signed on that battleship in the Pacific, my dad's unit was again awaiting assignment.

There were ways in which my father could certainly be considered a sort of wizard, as befitting his seventh son status. Ronald Dixon was a brilliant, interesting, and artistic man who, alas, spent most of his life as the unwitting plaything of his powerful emotions. His working-life career was as wildly varied as his considerable talents and intelligence. Here was a man who was at different times an army officer, a miner, a logger, a steel plant worker, a radio DJ, a TV news announcer, a newspaper writer, an elementary school teacher and principal, a high school math, English, and art teacher, and a university professor in journalism. He was a poet, a writer, and a painter in oils, as well as an athlete and an animal lover. He was a gentleman with a refined sense of manners and gallantry. He would go to any lengths to entertain children. My own children adored him.

Ron's restless spirit and relentless curiosity were part of the reason for his many lines of work. It also seemed to him that most people and most situations grew simply intolerable over time, and his efforts to raise other people to his standards of behaviour were not always appreciated. I guess he was a bit judgmental. This came out in his keen ability to home in on things that just weren't right and then put that thought into scathing words. It was a trait that was to last throughout his life.

From watching my father, and from my own experiences, I've learned that emotion travels much faster through us than does thought. Strong feelings short-circuit the intellect and can leave even the greatest thinker trembling with misguided or misdirected anger. This was a frequent occurrence for my father. As one elderly librarian hotly upbraided him on the day after he'd made a fuss about something with her, "You were *wrong*, Mr. Dixon … and so *loud* about it too!" That line became a classic in our family.

His powerful emotions, which resulted in continual changing of jobs and homes, led my father inevitably closer to the fringe. Ron was well liked by many, and he often gave selflessly of his knowledge and ideas. At the same time he would be appalled time and again by the expressions of human nature and the ways in which people would often not live up to the highest ideals in conducting their affairs. Dad's sharp tongue could be unleashed at unexpected moments, as his beautiful, polished manners gave way to a sudden torrent of outrage. He was a seeker of truth and beauty in a world populated with the unpredictable and unmanageable, the hell of "other people." If I were to ascribe a thought to him, for much of his life I'd make it: *Why do you all have to* be *like that?*

A self-imposed distancing from his disappointing fellow humans led him into near-isolation in his last years. A man of so much brilliance should have been staying highly connected with society. He was unfortunately so frequently misunderstood (or, alas, sometimes understood all too well) that to engage him might turn upsetting for all concerned, including himself. It must have been difficult to navigate a world in which so few people were able to live up to one's lofty standards. As brilliant and loving and sentimental as he could be, dear old Dad marginalized himself through behaviour that he was either unable or unwilling to control. That continues to be an important lesson to me.

Ron sure had a fun side, though. Put together quick wit, intelligence, energy, a desire to please, and a quirky outlook and you get a man who would constantly conjure up improbable things to say and do. My mother often says he made her laugh through their whole life together, and that talent to amuse is what made her stick with him. I guess it may be true when they say that's what a woman really wants in a man: someone to make her laugh.

In his last years Ron was happiest with his books, making corrections to the author's work in the margins, or painting oil on canvas, or working on supposedly impossible math problems. His mind was keen to the end. We lost Dad to a heart attack on December 29, 2009. He would have been eighty-five on the following June 13. I miss him every day.

My mother, Marje (Mar-*yeh*), is the polar opposite of my father in many ways: cool, calm, composed, enduring, stoic, but also extremely intelligent, with a surprisingly wicked sense of humour. She quietly set about making a solid home base wherever my father's fancy led us. Mom also set about becoming a reliable and substantial force for earnings and savings power. Marje is remarkable for her capacity to analyze a situation and find the smartest solution. Her knack of climbing smartly in every new workplace that our travels took her seemed so normal, I thought everybody was like that. An early example of a "working mom," she knew how to budget, cook, raise children, and keep a marriage together while going to work every day and exceeding expectations. I owe to my mother's example whatever I have of sticking to things and of enduring, whatever happens.

My mother's family is Estonian; they fled from their homeland on the Baltic Sea during the Second World War, when the Russians invaded for the second time in modern history, in 1944. My grandmother Hella Magi was born 1911 in Voru, a small town near the Russian border. Her maiden name was Jaason, an educated family we would now call upper-middle-class, with a large lakefront property as well as a farm on the other side of the lake. Her father, Juhan, was a banker and a director of the local arts council.

Estonia had been under Russian rule for two hundred years, but the collapse of Czarist Russia after the 1917 revolution was the chance for the little country to declare its independence, even though Communist sympathizers agitated in their midst for alignment with the revolution. The small but determined Estonian army repulsed a Red Army invasion in 1919. After a year of fighting, Russia signed a peace treaty in 1920 in which it gave up any future claim over Estonia's territory. This left Estonian Communists seething with resentment, awaiting the next chance. Juhan Jaason would pay dearly for his prominence in free Estonia when the USSR invaded in June 1940.

My maternal grandfather, Rudolf Magi, born in 1905, came from a small village called Pormanni. It no longer exists, having been bulldozed during one of the Soviet collective farming or industry schemes. After completing his studies, Rudi made his way to an education in military college, where he became the youngest cadet ever to graduate. His first posting as a young officer took him to Voru, where he met Hella at the local music and dance hall. Married in 1931, they had "three years' honeymoon," in Hella's words, until the arrival of their first son, Rein, in 1934. Then came Tonu in 1936 and finally my mother Marje in 1938.

Rudi went to Officers Higher Military College, where he earned a captain's rank. He served in the Estonian army in that rank until the end of the Second World War.

My Grandma Hella (Jaason) Magi is one of my heroes in this world, a survivor and thriver without equal. In January 2011 I attended her hundredth birthday party and performed a song for her with my daughter, Lauren Hella, the great-granddaughter named for her. My elder girl Carlin helped Lauren read the birthday greetings from the Queen, the prime minister, and various other dignitaries, including the president of Estonia.

Hella often regaled me with stories of the family's escape from the Russian invasion. In 1944 the Germans were losing the Eastern Front to the strengthening Russians. Rudi saw the threat looming, and in concern for the safety of his children he managed to get a secret letter to Hella in the south, urging her to leave Estonia with the kids as soon as possible. While the Russians were entering the northern part of Estonia above Lake Peipus, she gathered up her three children, including my mother (then six years old), and they were able to evacuate on one of the last trains leaving Voru.

Hella could have gotten her mother out before the Russians arrived, but her mother, Elisabet Jaason, felt she was too old to start over in a new country and refused to leave her homeland by getting on that train with them. My grandmother had already seen her father and her brother, Juhan and Juhan Jr., arrested by the Russians during the first Soviet invasion in 1940 and sent to slave labour camps in Siberia, where they subsequently died.

Like most Estonians, Hella knew that worse was to come under a second Soviet occupation. Only Communist sympathizers were pleased to see the Russians return. Hella waved goodbye to her mother and ensured the safety of her children and herself by getting on that train.

In the end Elisabet was not singled out for persecution under the Soviet regime as a former capitalist. Marje tells me her grandmother had been kind to the Jewish people in Voru and helped some of them to live through the Nazi occupation. She and Hella both believed that Elisabet was so kind, generous, and good, she charmed even the Communists.

The Magi family's boarding of the troop train was followed by a week of rough travel on changing trains in order to put safe distance between themselves and the Russian advance. My mother remembers riding in open cattle cars with other refugees for parts of the journey. The family sometimes slept in fields beside the tracks while awaiting the next train's arrival. There's a lovely story of the day when Marje lost her dolly somewhere on the train and all the German soldiers helped her look for it. It is humanizing to think of them that way.

South from Estonia through Latvia and Lithuania, then to stops in Poland and finally into Germany: this was the course their journey followed over the next months. My grandma got her children into refugee quarters in southern Germany, just as the collapse of the Third Reich began all around them. From their town they could see the distant flames of the firebombing of Dresden. The family bounced around a number of German towns as refugees in the next years, while the chaos that followed the surrender of Germany slowly turned the corner to recovery under the Marshall Plan.

Then my grandfather Rudolf re-entered the stage. He'd somehow survived the fighting and by stealth escaped Estonia ahead of the Soviet invading armies. He searched the refugee settlements for his family until he found them. Rudi was reinstalled as head of his family. Having him back in place meant that the Magis could now apply to leave Germany for North America. This possibility had until then been denied them while Hella was the sole provider without an adult male. At first they applied to go to the United States, but the application was rejected because my grandfather, who'd started the war as an officer in the Estonian army, had technically, albeit unwillingly, also served with both the Russian and the German armies.

After six years of hardscrabble refugee life, the reunited Magis were accepted as immigrants to Canada. They arrived in 1951 to start life over in peace. We who have always lived in North America, where there's been no large-scale conflict in almost a hundred and fifty years, can't truly appreciate the profound importance of that idea. Peace is a primary component of happiness. Without peace, there is no security, no prospects, no planning for the future. If you don't have it, it's all you seek. People will leave behind their precious things, friends, and familiar surroundings just to have a chance at attaining peace for themselves and their families. This is why so many Estonians after the Second World War wanted to get as far away as possible from Europe.

The Magis landed at Halifax with their possessions in a few sea-locker trunks. Once processed at the government of Canada immigration docks, they again made a long train journey, inland to the fertile farmlands of Southern Ontario. A family of willing workers, they established their first household in their new land in the town of Fruitland. It was a one-room shack, provided by a farmer to the fruit-pickers who laboured there in the harvest season. Rudi, Hella, and the three children all went to work in the orchards to earn a little money to get them started.

My mother was enrolled in the local school and was humiliatingly placed in the grade one class at age thirteen because she knew little English. She made a supreme effort to catch up and within a month or so was promoted to the age-appropriate level.

It was my mother's lot to have the same limitations placed on her as on most young women of the time. She was expected to go to work as soon as possible to help the family, while her two older brothers were to go to university and take on professional careers as engineers. This they all successfully did. Marje began part-time in the workforce at thirteen and full-time immediately upon graduating. Her intelligence did ensure her rapid advancement through a long professional career. She never was without a job until her retirement from Employment Canada after many years.

There was also an expectation that my mother would meet a nice Estonian boy in their émigré community and stay within the culture. This did not interest her; she found those boys dull. Along came my father during one of his many job stops, this time as an inspector for the Workmen's Compensation Board, where my mother worked as a secretary. She was eighteen, he was thirty-one. They were both smitten. Some people were agog at the difference in their ages, and the Magi family had their doubts about the wisdom of the union, but Ron made Marje laugh, and he was *not* dull.

They married a month after Marje's nineteenth birthday, and I was born thirteen months later. Fifty-two years of dedicated matrimony followed. I have a sister, Christina, a little over thirteen months younger than me. My sister's birth apparently made things a little awkward for my mother. The males of the Magi family had been prepared once already to fetch their daughter and sister home on the train from far-off Sault Ste. Marie, convinced that Ron was proving unreliable as a husband. Marje was certain her mother, who had already questioned her daughter's choice, would now tell her that she'd only compounded the mistake by having a second child. Marje didn't want to hear it, so she didn't tell her.

In later years Grandma Hella would tell the story of going to the Soo to visit her daughter and grandson in spring only to discover this unknown newborn sleeping in the home. "My goot-niss, who is *thiss?*" Grandma exclaimed. Her anger at being deceived must have been softened by the joy of seeing the newborn Christina. Perhaps Marje had counted on that.

I was probably a typical older brother in my treatment of Christina. As wee ones we were great playmates, and then as I got to eight or nine, I grew very self-conscious that I couldn't be seen with a girl. My poor little sister had to put up with her mildly mean old brother. I had to take her on the bus every week for a year to the doctor's office in Sault Ste. Marie for her allergy shots when I was nine and she was seven because Mom was working and Dad was off in some other town. I'd make her sit in a different seat and then tell her to walk far behind me, as if we didn't know each other.

As we matured into high school Christina followed a similar path to me in her own way with music, athletics, and the arts. In time I was able to more openly show the love I'd always had for her, and she has always been an enormous supporter of my music career. Christina is the kind of fan every artist needs.

THIS IS HOW IT STARTS

"The way you see me when I am playing, that is the way I really am."

— Israel "Cachao" López Valdés

My path to being a musician was really a series of unconscious decisions driven by my compulsion to organize my thoughts and my reality around musical sound waves. Growing up in 1960s Sault Ste. Marie, I was continually pulled toward music as the expression of my inner self. When I was three, I started playing along on our piano to the early morning national anthems, Canadian and American, which began each broadcast day. My parents signed me up for piano lessons when I was four; I still have that first method book, *Teaching Little Fingers to Play*. My kindergarten report card was the first of many to describe my strong aptitude and response to music. It was also the first of many to describe how "Carl would do much better in school if he would only pay more attention."

When I was a boy, my father dreamed I'd grow up to be a concert pianist. He played a little himself and was something of a frustrated artist. There's no doubt he was an intellectual with enormous artistic gifts. Under my father's expectation and my mother's supervision I practised the piano almost every day, when I wasn't outside playing "army man" or riding my bike or playing in the snow. For five years I progressed through the levels of Conservatory music study. The springtime recitals put on by the Kiwanis Club were my first public performances, and I remember them as a terrifying three-minute climax to months of preparation.

Why terrifying? Well, to become a performer I battled shyness and self-consciousness, which are really forms of fear — the fear of being laughed at or judged unkindly. I finally realized that shyness stood between me and getting better results. Fear is a big bully, but if you stand up to it you'll scare the bully away. In time, I grew quite comfortable standing at the front of a room with everyone looking at me.

I think many people would look at the path of my life and assume I had dreamed of being a rock star, and my dream had come true, more or less. That's not how it happened.

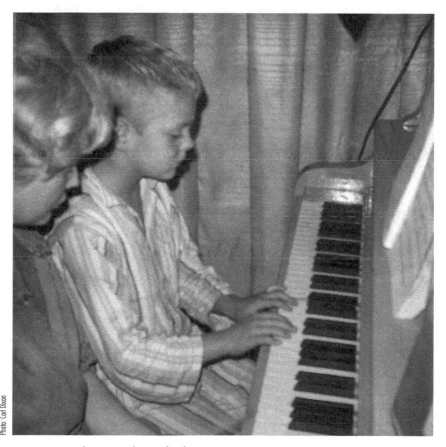

My mom ensuring that I practised piano after dinner.

I don't know if the word "dream" is equal to the weight of the concept of having a goal or a need or a compulsion. There must be a more accurate word to describe the all-encompassing, untiring effort required to reach a difficult objective. In fact, the record indicates that I could not have been other than what I have always been; my character would neither acknowledge nor accept any obstacle.

* * *

Sometimes, as we look back, a certain experience at a young and impressionable age seems to have had a formative effect.

My father kept a piano. Though he played infrequently, when he did tickle the ivories, it was a sound of gentle grace and elegance. Dreamy things like Debussy were among his favourites. I suppose I was following in his footsteps when I started picking out the tunes of the national anthems on the piano keys when I was three. Sometimes as a young lad I'd wake in the wee hours to the sound of symphony albums playing on our old Grundig Majestic record player. I'd stumble out sleepily and find my dad in the living room, ferociously conducting the orchestra. There was unreleased passion for music in him.

When I was about nine I didn't like my piano teacher, Mrs. Shumpski, for some reason. Probably she was trying to make me work harder. I got mad one summer evening and started walking the three or four miles home without telling her. My parents found me, after searching the streets, and that was it for lessons with Mrs. Shumpski. Nightly piano practice had become intolerable. I knew my friends were gathering to play baseball and ride bikes, play army man, have rock fights, or arrow fights with pulled bush ferns ... all kinds of great stuff. My childhood was just "go, go, go" from morning until night. Every minute outside was a good minute. Besides, I couldn't see how the piano music I was learning related in any way to the music on the radio, which had me fascinated.

A conflict brewed as my mother tried to get me to stick with piano. My dad wanted this, they saw my natural ability, and they'd invested in years of lessons. The breaking point came one night when my mother tried to make me sit down and practise after dinner as usual, and I yelled, "F*** off, Mom!" A chill went through the house in response, with my sister and our babysitter in the background. My mother calmly told me to go to my room. My piano lessons tailed off after that.

In those days all children gained valuable musical experience from singing in school. Music class really meant singing class, and though there wasn't much focus on technique, there was an expectation that every child could sing and should sing. This notion has largely been abandoned now, along with other aspects of an arts-based educational system.

School choirs were obligatory when I was growing up, and most children eagerly took part, singing from the songbooks that school boards purchased in bulk. I loved hearing my voice blending in as we'd sing "Aura Lee," "The Church in the Wildwood," or "Red River Valley." When I hear these old songs now they put me in a sentimental mood. Singing them can still make me happy.

My first guitar teacher, Mrs. Tallon, seemed ancient. I suppose she must have been in her forties, but I thought of guitars as something for young people. My mother dropped me off every Saturday morning at Mrs. Tallon's home for a group lesson in which I was the youngest. Almost eleven when I started, I kept at it for about six months. We had a Dick Bennett method book, and then, to "liven things up," Mrs. Tallon would hand out typed copies of songs for us to play and sing: "Little Boxes," "Jack Was Every Inch a Sailor," "Windy," "This Land Is Your Land." I guess she was a folkie.

"Windy" reminds me that there was a girl named Wendy in the class, a bit older than me. I had a little crush on her. That helped me to persevere, even though two things were chafing. First, my beginner guitar was an el cheapo model my uncle had given me second-hand. It had raised-action strings that required more strength to press down than my child's hand could comfortably produce. Second, I felt very little closer to my goal of making the kind of sounds that were bursting all around me. I'd ask if we could play Creedence Clearwater Revival or Beatles songs; I think Mrs. Tallon disliked the "mod" sounds pushing out her favourites.

Getting closer to the magic music wasn't going to be easy. I could increase my knowledge through devoted Top 40 radio listening (this was before FM rock radio was widespread), by borrowing records from friends, or by using my allowance to buy 45s. When I turned eleven, my allowance went up to a dollar a week, so every Saturday I'd go into town on my mother's grocery shopping trip. I'd try to bring a friend, and we'd stand before the record display at Woolworth's, scanning the riches that lay before us. What a thrill to see the latest from The Beatles, the Stones, Creedence or The Guess Who. Sometimes I'd be enticed to buy something I hadn't heard because I knew the artist: James Brown, The Youngbloods, Elvis (who was already way passé to kids by then). It was as if those perfect black discs contained a key, offering admission to the great exciting world beyond our little northern town. Picture sleeves on the 45s added to the appeal: "Man, they look so cool! I wanna look like that. I'm growing my hair! Maybe my mom will get me a pair of those bell-bottoms." You have to wear the proper gear to show the world where your allegiance lies.

I was keen to somehow become a performer. My dad had a portable record player with a speaker in the lid that you propped up to play discs on the turntable. This resembled the guitar amps I'd seen on TV, so one day I took it into the back yard and lip-synched to a 45 with my neighbour. We convinced the little girls next door that we were really playing and singing as we held our crappy beginners' guitars. At least, they said they believed us.

My first real performance singing and playing guitar for an audience was at age eleven, the father and son banquet night for my Manitou Park Boy Scout troop. Our Scout leader heard I'd been taking guitar lessons and enlisted me to perform "You Are My Sunshine." I practised for a few weeks and then that night shyly sang the song, seated on a chair on the stage with some of my patrol standing behind me to add their voices.

This was one of the many years that my father was living away from us for his teaching job, but it was my greatest wish he be there with me that evening. I didn't want to look like I had no pa.

I was well used to only seeing my dad at Christmas and summer holidays. Still, I couldn't help wishing.... And then, when I got home from school on the day of the banquet, there was my dad in the kitchen, waiting for me with a big smile. He'd booked the day off and driven across the province to do the impossible and be there with me. I'll never forget the pride at having my father there watching me perform, on one of the rare occasions that he was able to see one of my childhood events. I hope I thanked him properly.

So there I was, this kid in Northern Ontario in the '60s, when the sounds of The Beatles, The Rolling Stones, The Byrds, Creedence Clearwater Revival, The Guess Who, Simon and Garfunkel, and the dozens of other great bands we still hear to this day first washed over the world. I can't describe adequately the thrill as those sounds grabbed hold of my cerebral cortex. Loud, brash, unafraid, and strong was how the music felt coming over the radio. I was instantly hooked, and from then on the beast awakened inside me had to be constantly fed.

Soon after the father and son banquet, my guitar lessons were done for the summer. A couple of years followed in which there was no music instruction or practice. We'd moved to Haliburton, where it wasn't offered, and I'd given up for a time the idea that I could learn what I needed from lessons. What I did instead was take my record listening and buying to the next level.

The beauty of the vinyl LP was in the very limitations of the medium. Each side could only carry seventeen or eighteen minutes of music grooves; more than that and the sound quality would deteriorate. The result was that you could listen to any artist's full piece of work, the best they had to give you on that release, in thirty-five minutes or less. This time constraint meant that the artists could turn out albums more frequently and give more attention to the details of each project. Many of the classic rock LPs ran no more than thirty minutes in total. With albums, you could give an LP your

Twelve years old in Haliburton, looking like the kid in *Almost Famous*.

full attention and still feel fresh to slap on a different one after that. It wasn't the much-discussed "warmth" of their sound that made vinyl LPs great; it was the time limits built into them. The nature of the listening experience, and the meaning of that experience on a personal level, has been altered a great deal since my youth. Maybe the idea of the "album" as a discrete artistic statement is what made it marvellous.

✳ ✳ ✳

It was a non-playing musical life I had as a pre-teen in Haliburton. I read music magazines and talked about music and bands constantly, assuming that everybody was like me and cared about these things as much as I did. I had some very patient friends in those days who cheerfully went along with my obsession. It wasn't just me, though. Back then music was more central to the culture, a real movement. It seemed important, and for a too-brief period it really did reflect the changes going on in the world. A singer could be a leader to many simply because of the lyrics to his song. We all wanted to believe in the virtue of the people who made the records. It was easier to believe in The Beatles than, say, Richard Nixon.

I spent every penny I could get on new records, and when I didn't have money, God help me, sometimes I shoplifted them. My need was insatiable.

First piano, then guitar, then drums in school band and finally singing; it was a broken but steady path forward. I'd kept playing guitar a bit, teaching myself as I could and, singing along with records or the radio. I eventually found other musicians to play with when I was sixteen and started performing in bars. I got that job, playing with twenty-five-year-olds, because I could sing. The catch was that I had to be able to play guitar as well. Never mind that I'd neglected my instrument for a long time and only remembered three chords; I bluffed and said, "Oh yeah, I can play guitar!" and then ran home to practise madly and catch up a bit. I was prepared just enough and had the accompanying desire that got my foot in the door. I'd lied, but I was in my first band! That was the start of everything.

In time I moved on from that band to others and kept on working and improving. Yet for all this low-level emulation of my musical heroes, I didn't really believe that I could be one of "those guys." It seemed as if they must all dwell in a magical dimension on the other side of the radio/record company machine, far removed from the world that I inhabited. I imagined they'd be thinking great thoughts and living sun-kissed lives of bringing joy to the world. (That's what music means to me: bringing joy to the world.)

Being from the woods of northern Ontario, I couldn't imagine myself in that magical dimension. I didn't ever picture making a career out of music. It may seem odd, but I never thought of a musical "career" at any time. I just wound up having one because I kept on doing musical things.

SIBBY RULES BY BATON

A big part of my development as a musician and as a person came through my involvement with the high school concert band. After my ninth-grade year in Collingwood, where the emphasis in music class was on the marching band, my family moved again to Barrie, where I began school in September. Being new in town, I could choose which of the town's three high schools to attend. I chose Barrie District North Collegiate, luckily, as it turned out.

An energetic young woman named Sharon Sibthorpe taught the music program at North. "Sibby" was the guiding light of the music room. Her keenness and enthusiasm for music in all its facets and details was contagious. She touched the students with her zeal for accomplishing things together as a band as well as individually. It wasn't necessary to hard-sell us on improving our playing skills; a mood of freedom and possibility accompanied all things "North Music." As a new program, North Music was free to be anything it wanted, not constrained by years of tradition or habit. We were the under-dogs in town, the upstart school band with no history, no awards, and no traditions. That left it up to Sibby and the kids who signed on with her to blaze a new trail.

* * *

A word from the music teacher

As a new teacher in the early 1970s who was asked to resurrect a dying music program, I depended on my students to get me through the long days. Their spirit, determination, and talent continued through those early days and over the thirty years that followed. Carl exemplified the student who made each day memorable.

I think you have to know that every girl at Barrie North, especially the flute and clarinet players, had a crush on Carl. The long blonde locks, the athletic good looks, and being a member of the track team, Carl had a winning combination. However, it was Carl's gentle and caring spirit that really made him special. He always had his opinion but was willing to hear yours too.

He played drums in all of the ensembles and over his years at North worked and received first class honours on his Grade 8 Percussion exam. Carl in his last year was Concert Master of the band, a position elected by the students.

I think it is safe to say that in band, through the trips, the rehearsals, the concerts, you learn skills for life. Working as a team towards a goal, travelling across a country together, laughing and crying, struggling through and then mastering the music, were all part of the music experience. I, and the band of the early days, will never forget when a band member died suddenly. Carl and his friends were the pallbearers at that funeral. It went beyond the music, but the music is what brought them all together.

The memory of switching an entire concert program so that the track team could be there to perform is one for the books. The switch from track uniform to band uniform can be done in five minutes flat, I believe.

Every teacher is proud when their students do well in life. Watching Carl's career soar, watching him come back from the horrific accident, listening to him play last year in his community wind ensemble; all proud moments.

Intent on the timpani part, 1975.

Thank you, Carl, for being such an important part of my musical adventure.

Sharon

✼ ✼ ✼

I wasn't sophisticated enough then to give it a name, but I can now recognize Sharon as the first positive-thinking role model I'd encountered outside my own family. Sharon swept her students along with her toward a "never settle, always keep improving" approach to music education. I thrived in that environment as my latent musical ability was expressed through all manner of percussion instruments. I've observed over the years that every organization is a reflection of the man or woman at the top. The organization's methods, strengths, and weaknesses all result from the energy of the person in charge and from the worth of the central idea. In this case the idea was for young people to improve themselves through playing music. With that powerful idea in place, all our organization needed was the right person to encourage those young people toward the worthy goal. Miss Sibthorpe was the right person.

Under Sharon's influence I blossomed and grew in confidence and leadership. She encouraged me but also didn't give me a skate when I screwed up. I missed turning in a major essay in second term one year and watched my report card mark drop from a 90 to a 67. I learned that lesson. It's not enough to play the instrument well; you have to know the history and theory too. Oh yeah, and *do the work!*

MAGIC MOMENTS, OR HOW I TIED THE THREADS TOGETHER

Important formative moments occur in all our lives; some swim into view for me as I cast an eye over the years. In my experience, the learning that comes from the pursuits of music and sports/fitness crosses over in complementary fashion.

Sault Ste. Marie was a nice place to grow up. My parents bought a little bungalow in a subdivision, still in the building stage, and my dad asked the developer please not to bulldoze the trees in our lot the way all the others had been. We had the most popular yard in Manitou Park as a result. Around us were many young families, and we lived across the street from the newly built school, so I had many friends to play with, along with access to a playground, safe streets, and nearby forests where we'd run around all day long. Lakes were close by for summer swimming and snow fell in legendary amounts in winter. There was a reasonable degree of prosperity in the little city of seventy-five thousand because of the Algoma Steel mill and its unionized workforce.

There was an outdoor skating rink a block away every winter, which lasted for months in that climate. It had a wooden shack with benches where you'd sit to tie up your skates and a woodstove with a grill where you'd put your snow-encrusted mittens to dry while you got in from the cold for a few minutes. There was a homemade broad wooden snow scraper for clearing the ice, and all would take their turn in pushing it. The rink was a great little gathering place. I wanted very much to be a good skater like so many of my friends, but my dad was discouraging about hockey; he thought it was for the lower strata of society.

Thus I fell behind my chums and for a time would only go when the rink was empty because I was embarrassed. My grandparents flew up to visit us, and I recall Rudi going out on the ice in his galoshes to take up the goalie stick and tend goal in a pick-up shinny game. I was very proud of him. Grandma Hella bought me my first hockey stick, to my dad's dismay, from a gas station on our way to drop her at the Sault airport. It wasn't until I moved to Haliburton at age eleven that I got to sign up and learn to play.

When I was in grade six our school was sending a team to the Sault school "field day." They decided who would be on the team by having all the kids in the school line up at one end of the schoolyard. Whoever got to the other end first was on the team. I was first or second, so I got to go to my first "track meet." That began my lifelong interest in running.

Again in grade six, a bunch of us were fooling around at recess. I had no concept of my own strength in relation to any other kids. A guy named Todd, one of three tough St. Louis brothers, got me mad and I became interested in wrestling him. He put me on my back, sat on my chest, held my arms firmly by the wrists, and sort of laughed at me. I was shocked at how easily he accomplished this, because up until then I'd thought we were all about the same in physical development. After that I set to work on learning how to get strong.

In a magazine article a year or two later I read that singer Tom Jones did *fifty* push-ups every day "to keep his sexy body supple and strong." That became my benchmark.

The Haliburton school track was covered in fine white sand when I was young, and I ran races on that barefoot. That was my first experience of winning races in the 100-metre, the 400-metre, and the relay. I was a fast runner before I had any upper body strength.

* * *

In high school music, the concert band would exchange trips with other school bands. One time a Peterborough school band came to stay, and a young man named Danny brought his guitar on the trip. On a Saturday afternoon Danny sat in our music room and sang and played Gordon Lightfoot's "Bitter Green" to enchanting effect, right there, sitting on a desk, without artifice or hesitation. It hit me hard that somebody who was about my age could sound so good and was so easy about it. I was envious, but I marked it in my mind as something to try.

We had our turn on the exchange to Peterborough. I had long hair, so the guys from the other school brought me along to their rock band rehearsal. I didn't know what to expect. My memory is clear as day of them set up outside next to the swimming pool, playing the Doobie Brothers' "China Grove." I was excited and awed. How was it possible for guys just a little older than me to sound so much like the magic men on the radio? It made me feel like maybe I could get there too.

Creem, Crawdaddy!, Rolling Stone, and *Hit Parader* — even Canada's short-lived *Grapevine* — were music magazines I devoured from the time I was twelve, learning about new bands and their music. There was a huge amount of information and detail to be gleaned, not only musical but societal and political. I'm sure that much of what I took in then still informs my thoughts and actions. The tone of those magazines was irreverent, but it was also committed to the idea that music *matters,* and so do the people who make it.

(I'm sad as I recall that in the '80s, while on tour with Coney Hatch, we were asked by *Creem* to do a photo shoot in Detroit for the legendary "Boy Howdy!" beer. This repeating feature was a spoof, offering a goofy bio of a different band each month to accompany a photo of the band holding cans of the imaginary brand being "promoted." I was in a bad state of mind at the time from stresses on me and on Coney Hatch, which I will describe elsewhere. These worries made me scowl my way through the session rather than having fun. It all felt wrong to me at the time. The Boy Howdy! feature on Coney Hatch never ran.)

✳ ✳ ✳

Nineteen years old, a campfire night at my girlfriend Gwen's cottage. Her dad Harry and his WWII vet buddies were sipping beer around the fire and someone mentioned, "Carl's got his guitar here. Get him to sing!" This stirred the interest of the veterans, but I was unsure. I was very new at performing and a little uptight. I feared this wasn't really my crowd. I was persuaded by Gwen to sing a nice little song I'd written for her called "By My Side," so I strummed the intro and set about carefully singing my song as sweetly and nicely as I could.

When I finished, there was silence around the campfire. Harry muttered "Well ..." and then one of his army buds set about chastising me.

"Why did you sound like that? That's no way to sing! If you're going to sing, lad, then *sing*, fer chrissakes! Why is he so quiet, Harry?"

"Well ..."

"Exactly! You've got to let it come out, lad. Here's how you sing properly. What about it, boys?" and the man started into a loud, rousing version of one of their wartime favourites. The other men quickly joined in with their "outside voices" and it was pretty impressive. I was feeling my timidity acutely. Five minutes earlier, I'd sort of fancied myself musical hot stuff. Compared to these *men*, I sounded small and afraid.

When they'd finished ringing the air, the old boy turned to me and said kindly, "If you're going to sing, lad, let them hear you." So after that night, I did. Embarrassing lessons last the longest, don't they?

* * *

I graduated high school thinking I would go to university and be a phys-ed teacher. Music was my preoccupation, but it wasn't a job, was it?

That plan went up in smoke when I discovered that all phys-ed students had to dissect a cadaver. No thanks. I took the classic "year off from school" instead. Worked some and put time into playing more gigs with a band I'd formed with school chums: Boots.

My father started to be really concerned that I was now fixin' to be a musician. "You'll end up playing spaghetti houses for fifty bucks a night ... or backing up strippers!"

Unsurprisingly, to an eighteen-year-old that didn't sound too bad. A spaghetti house would mean good eating, at least. As for strippers, they used to perform *before* the bands in the old rock bars, so — nyah, nyah — I never had to back them. Well, maybe once.

My early work history wasn't all musical and in fact took me through a very mixed bunch of low-skill jobs, such as babysitting; collecting roadside beer bottles on my bike; a bit of farm labour; working at a summer lodge; office cleaner; chicken catcher; brush clearing; groundskeeping. As I got older I had a stint as a city parks worker; some ditch digging; temp mail sorting at the post office; night shifts at Sears shipping terminal, loading and unloading the trucks; more brush clearing on Base Borden in winter; anything to make money, really. Later on, in lean spells I did dry-walling, electrical work, some light construction, painting, renovating, concert system set-up and tear down, running laser light shows, and various manual labour calls.

The only career I've ever considered aside from being a performer is to become a teacher or coach. My favourite job in my youth was as a youth counsellor at a teen drop-in centre.

Being a coach and a teacher is very appealing to me; the feeling of passing along knowledge and skills to eager young people is very fulfilling. In addition to mentoring and teaching music and singing, I've also coached youth soccer and hockey. The energy of youth is great to be around, and before my car accident I could keep up just fine. I may have to let them win more often now (just joking). I sincerely hope that I have helped some young people gain confidence and learn some things.

Boots at Kempenfest, Barrie, 1978. Blair Duhanuk in the background.

FOLLOW THE BOUNCING BEAN

So what does an eighteen-year-old music-compulsive reluctant student do with a year off school? At first, finding more gigs for my band became the imperative. I'd joined with fellow Barrie North students in a group we called Boots for no particular reason. We got going with a small number of beginner-level shows. We had no idea about anything except learning our favourite songs; an example of the sort of job we'd get in those days was to play for the Barrie Dog Show for $100. By the third song people ran from various points of the park to scream at us to "Stop, stop! The dogs are all freaking out!" Critics.

I was working two "straight" jobs and, despite Boots, getting impatient with the pace of my music career. In the pursuit of a steadier gig I kept my eyes open constantly.

I found an ad in the *Toronto Star* classifieds seeking a "singer for a steady-working rock band." That was exactly what I thought I needed, as opposed to the occasionally working band that I had with my friends. This could be my big step up to the level of the real pros, I thought excitedly. I called the number and wound up auditioning for a group called Olias. The name was drawn, obscurely, from Yes vocalist Jon Anderson's solo album title. I don't remember the audition but they asked me to join. I was elated.

Olias asked me to come to their hometown of Owen Sound to rehearse for a week before commencing their next slate of one-week stands. The band was popular in bars and worked constantly.

That rehearsal week is gloomy and dark in my memory. Only three of the four musicians attended; the keyboard player was almost thirty (!) and lived in another town. It wasn't worth his while to leave home for unpaid rehearsals. I heard the stories about Dave, the singer I was replacing, a very good singer and frontman but who just didn't like playing with them anymore. He'd given them a month's notice. I thought I was working hard in the rehearsals, but I realize now I hadn't a clue about preparing a repertoire quickly. Ah, I was so green!

We finished our week of practice, and I drove home to get ready to meet in Orangeville a few days later. The band was nervous but I didn't notice. I told the boys in Boots that I was off to join this full-time group to build my experience and my reputation, and maybe we could do something again in the future. I told my girlfriend Gwen the news and promised I'd come home as much as I could and I'd bring her on the road as soon as I was settled in. My dad was out west teaching, but I arranged with my mom to take care of my car and things while I was away. I would also need a ride to Orangeville the next Sunday with my suitcase, guitars, and amplifier to join my new employers. It was an exciting couple of days, filled with anticipation.

Sunday arrived, and my sister came with my mom and me on the delivery trip. The Grand Hotel in Orangeville, in all its faded Edwardian glory, beckoned me inside. I said my prolonged goodbyes to the family and went in with my gear to begin the "Grand" adventure of life as the singer of Olias. Five days later I was on a Gray Coach bus headed home to Barrie, tail between my legs. Released from further obligations.

How had it unravelled so quickly? It was a combination of my inexperience and singer Dave's veteran savvy. He was there to begin the week as part of the transition process, and I was to ease into the role by week's end. Improbably, and unhelpfully, the band had me room with my soon-to-be-predecessor, on a cot in the corner of his room. They had a set number of rooms provided by the hotel, and I was an extra guy, so there was no other place for me. Maybe Olias thought he would coach me toward being ready to fill his shoes. Not so. Dave eyed me shrewdly when I arrived and then set about exposing my un-readiness for the job. He was a typical road dog, staying up smoking and drinking until three or four in the morning every night, inviting the strippers from up the hall into his room for parties. I was unfamiliar with this lifestyle. My presence was not going to stand in the way of his fun, and I never knew whether Dave was intentionally wearing me down or just carrying on as usual. When I think about what I learned in my years on the road that followed, it seems likely he was doing what he would have done anyway and *I* was the oddity, with my wussy desire for a good night's sleep. A memory that I can't shake was of a stripper prattling on drunkenly one night at 3 a.m., moaning about how the hotel management didn't appreciate the great sacrifices she'd made by doing her "*danseuse*" shift on the stage even when she had diarrhoea. Yeoww. Now there's a sexy image I'm wishing I hadn't heard while I was clutching a pillow around my head to shut out the noise and the lights.

It wore me down very quickly, the endless chatter and Dave's eight-track tape player carrying on into the wee hours. The band resumed rehearsals with me in the mornings to get me up to speed (rousting me while Dave slept in blissfully), but that preparation was too little, too late. They got me onstage for a few songs in front of the audience on the fourth night, but it wasn't good enough. I just didn't know how big the gap was between showtime and myself. Increasing bleariness was setting in from my sleepless nights, and it was becoming apparent that I was no road dog.

From the other side, Olias was no doubt panicking, thinking I wouldn't be ready fast enough. They told me Dave had changed his mind about quitting when they let me go. Maybe he had, or maybe they begged him to stay. Either way, it was off back home for me, with egg on my face and lessons learned: be prepared and don't room with the competition.

BACK TO THE BOOTS

Once back home in Barrie, I made the most of the band that would have me. Boots, with Hal Hake, Blair Duhanuk (a.k.a. Duke), and Chris Bastein, with their neighbour Brad Noble on sound, was now the proving ground for my unfocused ambition. With fresh determination, it was time to get serious. A name change was in the works.

I still remember the heat of the day when I returned from Toronto, with our faithful roadie Brad clutching a copy of our new band photo, which now styled us as Primecut. Astro Talent Agency, which had agreed to represent our fledgling unit, had made up the new name on the spot as we stood in their office because they said "Boots" would make people think we were a country band. Stompin' Tom Connors had his Boots Records label, for one thing. Astro's staff quickly printed up promo photos for us to take away. Our drummer, Chris, was the first band member we saw on our return, so we unveiled the great new name. Chris's eyebrows shot off his forehead in surprise. Then he swore at us, said this was idiotic and the worst name he'd ever heard, and jumped into his Trans Am to tear out of his driveway in a fury, tires squealing. Brad and I looked at one another and said, "Maybe this wasn't such a good idea."

Once we'd come to our senses, nobody liked the new name, but we needed an agent to like us and get us jobs. We swallowed our distaste and convinced Curly (as Chris was called) to just go with it for a while until we thought of a better alternative. In the month or two that followed we played as Primecut.

Then one day Astro called. "We have a gig for you in Parry Sound at the Kipling Hotel, but it's this week, can you guys do it?"

"Wow, great ... yes, thanks! I was hoping something would come up."

"There is one catch."

"What?"

"You have to tell them that you are Hollinger."

"What do you mean? Why? Who is Hollinger?"

"Hollinger is a group from Timmins. They were booked to play there this week, but they had an accident on Sunday. Some of them are hurt. They can't play but we don't want to lose the booking."

"Wait a minute ... we have to pretend we're some other band? How will we do that?"

"It'll be okay. Hollinger play kind of the same music as you guys. The trick will be that they're a five-piece, so you'll have to make up a story why you're only four."

"We'll have to make up a lot of story to pull this off. I don't know, this all feels kinda weird."

"Do you guys want to work or not? Just say you're Hollinger when you get there and it'll be fine."

So we were Hollinger for a week. It would have been fine too, except on the second night one of the bar owners started asking us things about Timmins. We deflected. Then he suggested we must have been named after the big Hollinger Mines up there. "Uh, Hollinger Mines? Umm, I don't know about that. It's just a name." We'd never been to Timmins, didn't know the first thing about it. He looked at us quizzically.

The week was a moderate success but we weren't as good as the real Hollinger. We also drove back to Barrie after the 1 a.m. closing each night because the guys had jobs or school. On one of those drives our new name came to me, as I felt the pressure of a return to the detested Primecut name after our Hollinger masquerade.

The band name we chose, finally, was Alvin Shoes, after a shoe store I'd heard advertised on a Parry Sound radio station on the drive home, but I'd misheard it as "Elvin" Shoes. After our beginning as Boots it may have looked like we were fixated on footwear, and then it turned out the store really was called Alvin Shoes, so we were in fact named after a shoe store. It was just a silly compromise born of desperation. Could be worse, I suppose, and probably an improvement on being named after a steak (hey, The Guess Who *hated* their name, which was a promo guy's idea).

After a short time we left Astro Talent Agency, who hadn't been very successful at shepherding us to the big time. I used the contacts I'd made in my short stint with Olias to get us taken on by a company called Pizzazz Productions, an agency that mostly specialized in "show bands." You don't really see show bands anymore, but they were once a big-earning fixture of the live music world. All the starving rockers considered it "selling out" to join a show band, a fate worse than backing an Elvis tribute. A show band was where you'd go once you'd given up on the rock 'n' roll dream and wanted to make some decent money (three hundred dollars a week instead of the seventy-five to one hundred that bands like us were left with; three hundred dollars sounded like all the money in the world back then).

After watching us perform, Dan, the agent, told us we scored almost a zero on his checklist of attributes for selling a band. We were pretty green, and there were no bad boys among us who knew the ropes, who'd been around a little bit.

"Four nice guys from a small town" was the way agent Dan described our identity — that is, our lack thereof. He made us go to Honest Ed's discount shop in Toronto to buy ridiculous new stage clothes. I had a misguided notion that we were supposed to look crazy or outlandish in our new stage get-ups, and among other regrettable purchases I got a pair of heavy blue-felt paratrooper pants with suspenders, genuine army-surplus items, which were huge, hot, and clownish when worn under circumstances that did not involve dangling from a silk parachute at ten thousand feet. Between that costume and other unguided choices, I did not present a fetching image.

We Alvins now set out together for wherever Dan and Pizzazz Productions sent us. In a mood of what we thought was witty silliness (williness?) we decided to have a gimmick, à la the Ramones. We all were named Alvin, and that crazy coincidence was what led us to form a band together. We had Alvin Slicker, Alvin Duker, Alvin Boomer, Alvin Dick Leroy (me), and Alvin Herb Elroy. People were mainly unconvinced and only mildly entertained by this yarn. It became a short-lived test of how gullible or willing a girl was if she believed any of this malarkey. Not that we took advantage of any girls, gullible or otherwise. We were nice boys with girlfriends at home. The fabled rock lifestyle remained veiled to our naive eyes.

So we set off and took all of road life's blows square on the chin. This resulted in a fair amount of stress, but I managed to convince the others to keep their chins up and plow ahead. I had to; they were all unwitting pawns in my undefined quest.

Our first round of hard lessons was a tour of northern Ontario in the winter of 1979. Schumacher, Dryden, Schreiber, Marathon, Hearst, Timmins; one hot spot after another played host to "The Shoes." In Hearst I was amazed to find a completely French-speaking town in Ontari-ari-o; it's more common than you'd think. I also learned that sometimes men thought I was a pretty boy, possibly gay, and wanted to hurt me for it. This mystified me because I've always been a very hetero guy with macho leanings. Someone threw an ashtray at my head in Hearst and barely missed doing damage. There was no market for rookies like us in the bigger towns like Sudbury, North Bay, Sault Ste. Marie, or Thunder Bay. We set about earning our wings wherever they would have us.

To an unbiased observer it would have looked like a fiasco. At the end of the run we felt we had emerged bloodied but unbowed. I was the band's money manager for no reason other than that my mom had lent us the money to buy a used cube van for getting around. I did not possess any business acumen or experience. One of my first moves was to drive away from Timmins on a Sunday morning with our entire week's fee forgotten in my hotel room.

Our cube van was a two-seater, with a couple of our parents' old armchairs set up at the front of the box and a folding lawn chair set up between the cab seats. This was to carry five people plus our gear. Short straw drew the lawn chair, which wasn't much fun on a five-hundred-mile drive. The heater wasn't adequate for the forty-below temperatures we sometimes encountered, and we'd be so cold as we drove that on one trip Duke had ice forming on his beard inside the van as his breath condensed and froze there, like those photos of Antarctic explorers. Duke remembers having moose stew at the bar and watching the Super Bowl with the Dryden locals. Near the end of the tour somebody in the North finally took pity on us and shared the trick of placing cardboard inside the engine's front grill to create more warmth in the car's heating system.

On our final night we were so keen to get home after six weeks away that we lit out driving after our Saturday night load-out only to find there were no gas stations open for over a hundred miles, and we hadn't filled up. The gas gauge dipped below the empty line for our final very nervous fifty miles, and the temperature was once again dipping below the minus-thirty mark. Just as our engine coughed its last combustion, we crested a rise to see a Husky service station several miles in the distance. In my excitement and relief I roused everyone from icy fitful slumber and shouted, "Get out and push the van while we're still rolling so it's not a dead stop! We can make it to the station!"

Poor Duke responded to the alarm cry before he was even awake. He rolled out with the rest of us onto the frozen tarmac under the starry northern sky in running shoes and no jacket but gamely took up a corner of the van in the frosty night. Four strapping young men set to work pushing the five-ton load two miles up the highway with every ounce of their strength. It was like a bizarre dream we were caught up in together, as a final kick in the arse from the North.

When we at last rolled the van across the deserted highway into the Husky station, a man who'd been watching our approach with interest wandered outside. He offered this helpful thought: "Why'd you push your truck all the way here in the freezing cold? You should have just jogged down here and I'd have taken you up with the tow truck to put some gas in it." If our heads hadn't already been flushed bright red with freezing, he would have seen us blush with embarrassment. It's funny now, but at the time it all seemed kind of normal, part of the experience called "being on tour."

Performing four shows a night, six nights a week, and then driving all day on Sunday to get to the next town; staying in seedy hotels and eating every meal in cheap diners: that was the routine. We'd try to save money by keeping a loaf of bread and a jar of peanut butter in the room, maybe bananas or hot dogs on the window sill to keep them cold; learning to live on seventy-five dollars a week. The quest for cheap food occupied a great deal of our time, and many touring musicians' idea of heaven was to be invited home by a local girl who could cook. Everyone in travelling bands got skinny.

So, if you overlook the hunger, the living conditions, the cramped travel, and the low pay, what is left for the aspiring musician? What's left is the opportunity to perform on your instrument for an audience, and if you're any good at all, to entertain them and feel their approval. That is a powerful intoxicant, powerful enough to keep people persevering through unbelievable stuff. However, if what you're getting from the audience is hostility — or worse, indifference — the whole thing starts to look pretty bleak. That's when musicians start to reassess their prospects, decide it's not too late to go to law school, and chuck the whole thing. For many that's a sensible decision. Many are called, few are chosen. At some point later, though, people always regret putting down their instrument.

PREPARING FOR LUCK

In those early days of touring with Alvin Shoes, I would find my voice giving out by mid-week. Something had to change if I was going to keep singing, so I found a singing teacher in my hometown. She kept an ad in the classifieds that said, "Miss Jessie Bradley, vocal instructor." I went to see her one weekday afternoon in her Edwardian brick house. Miss Jessie herself appeared to be of the same vintage because it was a very old, stooped lady with a smart reddish-brown bobbed wig, be-rouged cheeks, and a circumspect look who greeted me at the door. I stepped around the stacks of old music method books and song sheets as she led me through to the drawing room, where she kept an upright piano.

Jessie put me through my paces with a series of scales and sounding-out exercises and then some kind of a song. I was twenty and this was my first singing lesson. What she decided after these preliminaries was that I had a nice natural voice but I didn't know how to manage it, and I sure didn't know anything about technique.

The kindly old vocal coach then proceeded to reveal to me the mysteries of diaphragm breathing, the basics of note placement and "vocal production." She taught me about the Italian vowel sounds and about warm-up exercises. I heard the word "diphthong" for the first time, and I liked it. I got stronger and more reliable as a singer after one or two classes, but I was still prone to colds and the like until I learned to eat better and get more sleep. Miss Jessie also advised against the use of cough lozenges while singing, a common bit of self-medicating that singers often employed in those days to fight a sore throat from over-singing.

Vocalists then were often ill informed about their instrument. Maybe many still are, although there is so much more information easily available now. In the early years of my career, almost every singer I met was fearful and superstitious. They had to have a certain kind of tea onstage or they would cack out, or else they had to have Hall's Mentholyptus or Fisherman's Friend lozenges, or they needed certain incense sticks burning on the stage; there was no end to the tomfoolery. They'd need something to "coat their throat." There were those who felt that their special style was dependent on having a certain kind of cognac or brandy before the show, and if it weren't available, they'd squawk and fuss and throw a tantrum. Southern Comfort was seriously talked about as something that would "coat the throat" effectively.

In the Coney Hatch days singers on the circuit discussed the details of Scorpions' singer Klaus Meine's lost voice and his vocal nodes surgery as a "this could happen to any one of us" cautionary tale. I was once told by a credulous music fan the tale of one of the supposed up-and-coming singers in a bar band who one fateful night "went for it" and sang full strength on a high C-note, whereupon he promptly "burst the blood vessels in his throat, man" and saw his career come to a premature end. Uh-huh. I still meet singers who have sworn off all dairy products because they fear they cause phlegm in the passages and the dreaded "mucus build-up." Blechh. Singing is such a beautiful thing. Terms like "mucus build-up" should not infringe on the same domain, should they?

One famous Canadian singer, whose life was on the highway, believed that the special nature of his voice would best survive the rigours of touring if the environment around him was kept quite cold. He insisted that the tour bus temperature be set to near-freezing conditions. This, along with some other interesting ideas, did not endear him to his bandmates as they bundled in ski jackets and froze each night. Gee, that sounds familiar.

A singer I've worked with has recently given up smoking after almost fifty years. The reason he persisted all those years? He's the kind of guy who thinks to an obsessive degree about his musical presentation and is very uptight about how he's perceived. He kept smoking, against all advice, because he liked the rough, dry sound it gave his singing voice, something he felt he needed to overcome the "sweet" sound of his natural, unharmed air passages. To his mind "sweet" doesn't *rock*. To this singer's amazement, after quitting a fifty-year smoking habit, he found that his voice now remained very rough without the daily application of carcinogens. Miraculous!

All of these misguided measures are in my opinion the result of a sad lack of knowledge. The people who study vocal technique and apply it know that none of these things are necessary to produce good sounds repeatedly. The reason it happens is the same one that's behind every wrong-headed thing: fear.

Many unschooled singers are convinced that their raw, untrained sound is the key to their presentation. They don't think they need some hokey, old-fashioned, uptight "teacher" to tell them what to do. What often happens with such singers is that whatever early success they gain can be based on other factors such as being young and pretty, or wild and unrestrained. Of course they'll believe that the "natural" voice they brought to the party can't be tampered with. That's what got them attention in the first place.

On the other hand, when their untrained voice goes raw and hoarse and then cracks and loses the high notes from strain, misuse, and abuse? When it actually causes pain in their throats to make a sound? That's when they feel embarrassed, exposed, and alone. They'll start dropping difficult songs from the set or run from the stage in tears mid-song. They'll blame the soundman for making their voices too quiet or the band for playing too loud. They'll blame the songwriter for making the song too difficult, or the caterer for making the wrong kind of sandwiches or the management for booking too many shows. Most of all, they'll tell you, "Nobody understands how difficult it is for a singer! All I've got is my voice, which is a fragile instrument, while the musicians just have to move their fingers around! If you think it's easy, you're wrong! I'd like to see you try it!"

One '90s-era singer recently disclosed to me that he called the cops on his partying bandmates down the hall in their hotel because they were keeping him awake. "All I could think was *I'm the singer and nobody gives a shit!*" You're probably right about that, friend.

All this argy-bargy goes on simply because the poor singer gets trapped in a few small fears. Their rampant insecurity leads them to make excuses not only for notes muffed but also in anticipation of notes they haven't muffed yet. I was guilty of that one, for sure. Enter the room sniffing and utter a cautionary "I've got a bit of a cold, guys; might be a bit dodgy out there tonight," and you've got a fair imitation of the vexed and wary vocalist. You set up your excuse in advance so that if you mess up, it's not your fault. And if you don't mess up? Well, you toughed it out bravely and overcame the odds. Hoorah for me! It's a bit pathetic, really, but the band usually just buys in to keep the peace.

I was cured of that little habit during the making of the first Coney Hatch album. We were having trouble with a key song, and the label called in legendary producer Jack Richardson to help out. Jack, who'd produced every album by The Guess Who as well as a wide range of acts from Alice Cooper to Poco to the Bay City Rollers, was all business. I was in awe but also intimidated. The first day was spent getting the instrumental bed track to tape. Richardson stood out in the studio and conducted the band with a pencil, waving it about six inches from my nose. Scary. In the record you can hear me start out a hair too fast from nerves and then relax slightly.

Day two was reserved for the lead vocal. I came to the studio that morning kind of nervous and worried. A few of those excuse-in-advance phrases started escaping my lips: "Hi, Jack. Yeah, I'm a little tired today, and my voice feels sorta funny. I'm not sure if I'll be that great." I gave a nervous laugh.

Jack took this in for a moment and then boomed, "What is this talk, these ex-*cuses*? Don't you know a lead singer is supposed to be strong and powerful, and lead the band with his voice and his energy? Let's hear no more of this weakness. Come on, get in there and work!"

I was embarrassed and ashamed. I had always aspired to be strong and to be a leader, but fear of looking inadequate had made me aim for smallness to lower people's expectations. Jack shamed me into recognizing that in myself, and I never forgot the lesson.

FOLLOW THE HIGHWAY 'TIL YOU HIT THE OCEAN, THEN KEEP GOING

A tour of Newfoundland in the spring of '79 proved to be the Waterloo for the band with the stupid name Alvin Shoes. Somehow, at the end of our knucklehead's tour of northern Ontario, we'd come out feeling pretty good about ourselves, thinking we were now battle-hardened veterans. We were full-time touring musicians, and everyone in the band had quit jobs or school courses to do it. Then Dan the agent set up six weeks of spring gigs in Newfoundland. Ominously, he warned us that this, the Eastern circuit, was the real "trial by fire" of new bands. Dan had no idea....

It seemed simple enough. We were to pack our cube van with instruments, amps, PA system, and lights and drive from Barrie to North Sydney, Nova Scotia, where we would board the Newfoundland ferry. On the other side at Port aux Basques we'd resume driving, crossing the entire length of Newfoundland to begin our tour at the Atlantic Place Strand bar in downtown St. John's. We had a vague understanding of the task before us but did nothing special to research or prepare. We had a cash float of a few hundred dollars for fuel and ferry toll, and my mom loaned me my dad's credit card for emergencies. How hard could this be? We had always just gotten in the van and started driving, and things had always turned out okay. Figure it out as you go: that was the plan.

Photo: Carl Dixon

Alvin Shoes 1979 in full regalia. Left to right: Hal Hake, Chris Bastein, me a.k.a. "the girl," and Blair Duhanuk.

Well, the trip began badly and went downhill from there. It's actually kind of a big deal to make a journey of 3,150 kilometres, but you wouldn't have known it by watching Alvin Shoes in action. Hal and Blair had once driven straight through to Fort Lauderdale, Florida, for spring break, so that was our yardstick. I'd never driven even half the distance we faced. It seemed to us in our collective wisdom that if we left on Friday night and then drove straight through, we'd make the ferry to Port aux Basques by Sunday. Landfall on the Newfie side would put us in position to drive the eight hundred and fifty kilometres across the island and set up to play our first night Tuesday. There was no margin for error needed because what could go wrong?

This is the story of what could go wrong.

We were three hours late for the scheduled departure while we worked at prying Brad, our soundman, out of the Queen's Hotel disco and the company of a young lady he'd fallen for that same night. So compelling were her charms that he changed his mind on the spot about going to Newfoundland. Somehow we eventually found the right combination of persuasion and threats to get Brad into the van.

Once under way, we discovered after driving only fifty of the initial two-thousand-kilometre run to the ferry dock that we had an oil leak. This now required us to stop every hour, then half hour, to add another bottle of oil.

We hit Montreal around midnight in a rainstorm, now five hours behind schedule. The highway interchanges on the Décarie Expressway in downtown Montreal can be confusing at the best of times; Blair at the wheel and me navigating somehow put us on the southerly route toward Sherbrooke, a wrong turn that took us two hundred kilometres out of our way.

Our ship of fools pressed on, stopping every so often to pour in fresh oil from the stash we now carried, but every service station on our secondary highway route through rural Quebec was closed for the night. Running on fumes in the pre-dawn hours heightened our choking anxiety. I was sustaining a hope that we could still make it on time for our first night in St. John's, in spite of our errors, if we could just nurse the cube van along somehow. Running out of gas, though, now? How idiotic would that make us?

The possibility of missing our gig was unacceptable, inconceivable, and I shifted into marshalling all my thought, resourcefulness, and courage to forestall that unhappy outcome. I was going to get us there, period.

We reached a small town in Eastern Quebec at about 3 a.m. There was an old-fashioned service station, one where the owner lived upstairs. This was our chance to keep alive the spark of hope that we might still reach the ferry on schedule, if we could just get fuel and keep moving. If we parked until morning we'd miss the boat, literally.

For some reason I believed that gas station operators held a sacred trust to aid travellers in distress. Armed only with a smattering of grade seven French, I decided to address the house. Dim memories of "La Famille Leduc" ("*Peitou manger le rôti d'bœuf,*" etc.) led me to holler up at the apartment, "Ah-Sée-Stawnse! Ah-Sée-Stawnse, Sill-Voo-Play!" My urgency was not felt by the people who lived upstairs, and I tried repeatedly to make my meaning clear. There may have been a language barrier. In any event, the only sign of life was a slight flutter of the curtain; otherwise all remained dark and quiet.

I think it's fair to say that a kind of craziness took me over at this point. I was bitterly frustrated. I left the guys to wait with the van at the service station while I went to scout around. In full confidence that I was being clever and resourceful in a crisis, I started darting around the lawns and driveways of the sleeping town, prowling through people's back yards in the hope that someone's full gas can might have been left out for me to "borrow." No luck.

I was roused from this little fantasy by a mustachioed Quebecker in a muscle car, out cruising at 3:30 a.m. for some reason. He spotted me emerging from someone's yard just as he drove by, so he applied the brakes and swiftly began to turn around. Instinct told me to run. I cut back through the yard where I'd just been, over the fence, and through the next neighbour's yard to the street beyond. My souped-up pursuer was speeding around the corners to try to intercept me, tires squealing. I sprinted across the open street and through another two back yards. The driver probably imagined being feted as a local hero for catching a "*maudit anglais*" in the act of doing suspicious stuff. I recognized that I would have a hard time explaining my decisions to the law, so I went into full evasive action. Cut hard right for two back yards, jumping fences, then double back to the spot where I began running. Flat on the ground behind someone's garbage cans, I lay very still as I heard the car speed around the streets close by for maybe another five or ten minutes. Monsieur Muscle Car gave up after a time, and the sound of his engine faded.

A different approach seemed prudent. Getting fuel somewhere was still the only thought I could hold. We must get to the gig! As I cautiously walked back to the service station, I noticed a Quebec Provincial Police outpost a block or two from the highway. *Great! They'll help us get fuel.* The doors were locked but there was a call box. I picked up the receiver; it quickly auto-dialled and was answered by someone whose main language was, of course, French.

In time I was able to make him understand why I was calling, and he told me that my location was a satellite station, only open in the daytime. He was speaking to me from the nearest station, half an hour away. I thanked him, hung up, and started to think about this new information. I thought about the QPP car sitting parked and untended until morning in this little town, about how all the cops on duty were in that town half an hour away and, God help me, about how that police car was bound to have fuel in the tank.

I hurried back to the service station where the guys remained waiting. "Okay, does anyone know how to siphon gas?"

They say craziness is contagious, and I guess we were all so tired and stressed that I was able to overcome the good sense of my fellows and convince them that this could work. It seemed awfully clever in the moment.

It was agreed that you need a hose to siphon gas out of a car. Then you have to get past the awful taste of the gasoline. Who volunteers? Ha-ha. Now let's find a hose. I'd seen some in the yards where I'd been skulking, but I didn't want to go back down there. Hey, there's an air hose on the tire pump of the service station. *Scoop.*

Now, off to the police station and the lonely car in the lot. We pulled the van up at an angle so our gas tank was near the police car's. Their gas cap was standard issue, no locking device. Stuff one end of the hose down into the QPP gas tank and have our tank open at the ready. This'll be great! Chris had a try at sucking hard on the hose, to no effect. I fancied that I had extra lungpower, so I tried. Nothing. Someone pointed out that the hose was at least twenty feet long and had a very narrow opening, as befits an air pump hose. It would be impossible for even Hercules to siphon gas through that. Man, we were the world's worst criminals.

We began frantically searching now for something to shorten the hose, but what to use? Hey, here's a pop bottle. Break the glass and use the jagged edge to cut! I smashed the Coke bottle to reveal the thick glass of any standard issue Coke bottle, sans jagged edge, but tried sawing away anyway. The futility of this finally sapped my remaining belief in the idea. In disgust I lifted my head, blew out the pent-up air in my lungs, and took a step toward the street. At the same moment a QPP cruiser roared up the street right past us.

There were two officers in the front seat, one at the wheel and the other holding a shotgun upright ready for action, but neither one looked to their right, where we were standing. They likely never expected to have a crime scene unfolding right in the police station parking lot. I barked, "Back up the van away from the car! Close the gas tank!" It was now critical to hide the evidence. In early April in Quebec there were still high snowbanks, so I grabbed the air hose and the broken pop bottle pieces and heaved them over the snow banks, where they'd be hidden. Just as I completed this task, the police pulled up abruptly on the sidewalk to face us with the patrol car and block our exit.

They got out of the car with shotgun still at the ready and demanded to know what we were doing. I turned on the innocent-kid-from-small-town-Ontario charm and glossed over the unpleasant parts of the story. I explained our predicament: that we had a long trip ahead and we were almost out of fuel, and said we had come to the police station hoping to get help but found it closed. That much was true, just a few gaps in the tale.

The police relaxed a little, and I think they even liked that we were a band. One checked with the call centre to verify that, yes, someone *had* called from the outpost call box asking for help maybe an hour ago. The two officers told us they were in town responding to a local complaint that there were strangers in town doing some funny stuff, but they felt sure now that our actions had been misinterpreted.

Unbelievably, they now took it upon themselves to help us get on our way. There was a Shell station maybe ten miles up the highway. They called the owner and asked him to get out of bed to come and pump gas for these poor musicians. They even gave us a police escort. They were such nice guys that I felt bad about fooling them. However, the pulse of our mission was still beating, faintly. That was all I cared about that night.

We now had a full tank to resume a run for the ferry dock, but there remained the oil leak problem. None of us was a mechanic but we could hear well enough that our engine was going da-da-da-da-da-da-da-da-da-da, louder each hour. We were stopping every fifteen or twenty minutes now, and that wasn't good. The engine was overheating over and over, but we had no idea what to do except drive on grimly and see how far the doomed vessel would carry our weary crew.

Just about the time I was beginning to see double from being up all night, a ferocious pounding din broke out as if someone had crawled in under the hood to wield a ball-peen hammer. There was shouting and steam and fumes and hissing as we pulled off to the shoulder and then … silence.

Within a few miles of the New Brunswick border, but still only halfway to the ferry, we had created an immovable object. That cube van was dead.

I know it will seem like I'm always at the centre of the story, but I think I just clamoured to be there because it always seemed as though that was where I should be. In this case I decided that we had to find help to continue our quest. I believe I still hadn't quite surrendered. Somehow, I got a tow truck involved to pull the van into the next town, a little place called Dégelis. We were exhausted. We got the local mechanic to look it over. His diagnosis was swift: blown gaskets had led to oil leaks, which led to overheating, which led to the pistons seizing and the engine block warping when we kept driving. A rebuilt engine would have to be dropped in, to the tune of four hundred dollars. Was that a good price? We had no idea. It had to be done, though. We couldn't stop there, and we weren't going home. Good thing I had my dad's credit card.

We had to cool our heels for a day or two in a little motel at Dégelis and spent most of our pocket cash. Poor Brad tried killing time by kicking a soccer ball around with Curly in the parking lot, but he gave the ball such a hoof that it flew up and smashed a hole in the motel's neon sign. Brad had to cough up a hundred and fifty dollars to pay the bill and was now just as broke as us.

With all this aggravation before we'd even played a note, you might expect that the story would now settle down, that the band would figure it out and get in a routine once things got going a bit. In fact, the start was only a harbinger of one unlikely event after another.

Obviously, the goal of arriving on time for the first week in Newfoundland was not achieved. We did get our new engine and the van running well in pretty short order. Meanwhile, our agent, Dan, contacted the Kirby Agency in Halifax to ask them to help find us something on an emergency basis; he'd been able to salvage our second week of two in St. John's. They got us a weekend gig at the Red Lion Pub in Dartmouth, which seemed a bit rough to me, but the Red Lion was willing to let us play and pay us for it. We were directed to the Inglis Street Lodge in Halifax as a place where musicians often stayed while visiting that city, so we paid for rooms there and in fact did meet some of the East Coast bands going through the place.

Unfortunately, all was not uneventful. I'll quote from a letter I wrote home from Newfoundland when the memory was fresh. It went like this:

... The night I spoke to you on the phone from Halifax an arsonist struck at our lodgings at about 3 in the morning. The story is that a long-time tenant had a falling-out with the owners and decided to have his revenge. Brad, Blair, and I were sharing a 2nd floor room while Chris and Hal were in the basement. The fire was set in two places: just outside our door where some highly flammable curtains were hung, and in the bathroom which opened onto the only stairs. I awoke to a muffled commotion of human voices and an odd hissing sound. I sprang from my bed to see what was the matter.

The hall, when I peered out the door, had a strange white light in it. I then realized that it was smoke-filled, which muffled the voices. The hissing sound was the automatic sprinkler spraying down. I turned and yelled at the others and we skedaddled out. Luckily I had slept in my grey track pants, but Blair and Brad were in their underwear and it was a very cold night. We were all barefoot and shirtless, wondering where the fire department was.

Blair ran back inside to get his leather football-team jacket at possible risk to life and limb because he refused to stand out there freezing any longer in just his underwear. He returned swiftly wearing the coat. After a minute I looked over to where our van was parked and saw a girl trying to climb out a window about seven feet above it. She felt trapped by the fire but was afraid to jump, so I scrambled onto the top of the cube-back and helped her and a guy friend get down. The fire department showed up in a couple of minutes and they found that the only real damage was smoke and water damage....

Before we could leave the Red Lion, our music store demanded the return of our rental lights to Ontario. We left them behind in the bar for the Halifax agent to ship back for us on Monday. Agents don't like those jobs.

We drove up Cape Breton in fine sunny weather to North Sydney to catch the night ferry — a week late but, by gar, we were getting there! We'd never been to sea, so the crossing was exciting. Hal and Blair got a berth and took turns sleeping in there.

At about 6 a.m. our vessel emerged from the fog to our first sighting of "The Rock," at Port aux Basques. On one hand I felt an exciting kinship with the first Europeans who landed there centuries before. On the other hand it looked to me like we were approaching the end of the earth. Was this a hint of foreboding?

The Alvin Shoes band disembarked and started driving across the entire island to St. John's to begin our delayed conquest of the Rock. Hoorah! Only, as it turned out, the Rock conquered us — or more accurately, *we* defeated us.

We got into the Atlantic Place Strand, right downtown, for set-up and began the week's run. Our lack of lights was embarrassing, and the musical performance was leaden and amateurish. Everyone had been traumatized by the journey to get there, and we had no idea that we were supposed to be this "hot new band" from Toronto.

I thought we were doing "better" after the first night, but our dispirited show was still bad enough to provoke an outraged article in the local newspaper's entertainment guide the next week, in which the reviewer asked the priceless question, "Does the mainland think they can send us any old crap like this Alvin Shoes band and we'll just take it?"

On the Thursday night everyone in the band came to me to tell me they were quitting, only agreeing to finish up our existing booked commitments till summer so we could pay my mom back more of the cube van purchase price. I felt very guilty about the band collapsing after convincing my mom to help us out financially.

As I wrote to her:

> *I guess I should tell you the main thing which motivated this letter. Last night things fell apart and everybody (me included, but last) announced their intentions of quitting when this tour is over.*
>
> *Anyway, you're now up to the minute. I had better get to bed soon or that will make three nights in a row I've watched the sun come up.*
>
> *Love to everyone, Carl*
> *P.S. Not to worry.*

"Not to worry." Right. Mothers don't worry much.

That was Good Friday and we had the night off because of the religious holiday, so we all went out and got drunk and smoked cigars. It was actually fun to blow off steam. Out on the town I must have cut quite a wasted figure, but a petite young lady in her mid-twenties with long blond hair showed a keen interest in me even so. She suggested that we could go somewhere, and somehow a room was rented. When we got there she removed her very high heels, and even to my double vision it was obvious she was in fact not only petite but tiny, like maybe four foot eight. Probably something ensued. I don't remember. In the morning she was gone and my pockets were empty. She must've needed the cash more than I did.

Next day most Alvins straggled into the Atlantic Place around dinner-time in search of food, badly hung over and with "the big quit" fresh on our minds. That's when we discovered that we were supposed to have played two matinee shows that afternoon. We had now made our disgrace complete by failing to appear for this time-honoured Saturday afternoon whoop-up. A long night followed as we wore our failure. *Please let this end*, we prayed, *so we can get on to the next town and start fresh.*

Harbour Grace and its Pirate's Cave club was next. Mercifully, it was a fairly short drive on Sunday, just an hour or so. We pulled up to the building and the owner, Sam, a great big fella, and his bartender came out to greet us with broad smiles and friendly handshakes. Nice welcome. Then they peered past us into the van and said, "So, where's the girl?"

We soon realized that when the Alvin Shoes promo photo had arrived from Pizzazz, they'd mistaken *me* for a girl singer. Hoo, boy! Must have been the hat. Their disappointment was plain as we left them to go claim our rooms in the band house.

We had the night off, so we wondered what to do. There was a public swimming pool in Carbonear, a town about ten miles away, so we decided it would be fun to go make a splash and change up the mood. After some paddling about and silliness in the water, I thought it would be goofy and fun to have a dog paddle race, and everyone greeted this idea with enthusiasm. A harmless bit of play, you'd think, and so it was until I reached the end of the pool, about to win, and reached up with my left arm to touch. Trouble was that I'd dislocated that shoulder twice in the previous year and the joint now slipped off the bone again from the water resistance. I yelled in pain as I started to sink in the deep end, and the lifeguard came running to pull me up by my good arm. Off to the hospital now, me still in bathing suit, where they were not super quick in the emerg ward. With that particular injury, shoulder dislocation (I've had seven of them over the years), the area is numbed a bit at first by the shock, but after half an hour or so it begins to go into excruciating spasms as the joint demands to be restored to its proper position. By about an hour after the injury, I was failing to suppress a few gasps and moans in the waiting room, and a nurse came out to scold me in stern Newfoundland tones.

"You just be quiet now with all your noise, there's pee-pull in here who's really hurt! Hush!"

Eventually a doctor twisted my shoulder back on and applied a body brace to immobilize the arm. Well, that was just great. How would I play guitar now?

"The singer's got a broken neck!" Big Sam the club owner complained as he called the agent to fire us. It was bad enough the singer wasn't a girl; now I was sporting a sling from a major injury and awkwardly playing rough guitar with my arm immobilized.

Next day we woke up fired. I'd never been fired before. I was called in to the Pirate's Cave office to receive the news and learn how little we were going to receive of our pay. A one-eighth portion was all we'd get because weeknights are worth less than the weekend. Also, we had to move out of the band house, *now*. A band called the Rhythm Method who had the week off happened to have turned up looking for somewhere to stay, and they'd now take over our week. I got mad and frustrated and was ready to physically contest Big Sam, even with my dislocated shoulder, for a greater portion of our reduced fee until he warned me that he used to be a pro wrestler and I should just drive off now, like a good lad. I took his meaning. I actually shook hands with Sam as we left. It was nice of him to give me the warning instead of just flinging me about.

Well, we had to stay somewhere, so we moved on to Corner Brook, and I rented us some rooms with the credit card. We just had to hang on until the next week at Grand Falls-Windsor and Stephenville after that, tightening our belts for a few days, and we'd still get some cash to take home.

I got my own room and the others doubled up because we were now on opposite sides of the who-quit-who divide. How excited I was to get a slip of paper from the front desk of the Corner Brook hotel saying I had a telegram. Wow, receiving my first-ever telegram, like a scene from an old-time movie! What could it be?

I went to the office to claim it. It was an official notice that we were fired from our tour-ending week in Stephenville because of "false advertising." They'd read the reviews from St. John's and monitored our faltering progress. Hit me again, bartender. Wow, fired twice now.

There was a nice lady in Grand Falls who owned the club we were booked into next, the Loggers Lounge. She permitted us to come in a day early to take up rooms at the Cloverleaf Motel, where all the bands stayed. That night we went in to watch the band that was finishing up its week. Cool name on them too — Firefly — from Montreal; strong presentation, good singing, good playing. I acutely felt the contrast between us and them, and I wanted to feel like them, not us.

Our turn now at the Loggers, and over the following nights it was a forlorn bunch of Alvins who were releasing flatulent performances to the patrons who stuck with us. The feeling of surrender was following us like a bad smell as we played out the string. I didn't know yet how to summon up the good stuff when I needed it.

We finished up on the weekend, got the money (which was enough to get us home, at least), and moved on. We stopped at the Lorelei Lounge in Stephenville to see Steve Butler, the guy who had fired us by telegram. I don't know what I thought would happen. Maybe he'd relent and give us a week if we were there anyway? He gave us all a shot of whisky in mid-afternoon, the civil thing to do, and sent us on our way. We got to the ferry boarding dock back at Port aux Basques, where the bands Firefly and Rhythm Method unexpectedly would share the crossing with us after completing their own tours. I befriended people in both bands, presciently getting names and phone numbers. The next contact with Firefly lay just around the corner; playing with Mark Severn from Rhythm Method lay many years in the future.

All that was left was to drive all the way back to Barrie with no stops. All the guys grew happier as we neared home. Still sporting my shoulder brace but back to lifting dumbbells to build strength as we motored along, I was convinced I had to be hard to get through this change. Over the following two months Alvin Shoes would play out the string of remaining shows around Ontario before grinding to a halt.

The story seems unbelievable when you take it in whole. If luck is the moment where preparation meets opportunity, this misadventure was the precise opposite. We didn't know how naive and unprepared we were, even when it was over. For my part, I didn't understand how badly we'd done until I learned how to do it better.

Four of the five people who experienced all this took it as a sign from the gods to go home and return to regular jobs or school and a quieter, more sensible life. One of the five took it as a sign to search for his next band.

ODE TO A FIREFLY

Firefly's soundman, Chris Chamberlain, has remained a friend over the years, and remembers our first meeting: "We could all see that you were something special and a gifted performer."

Firefly watched us somewhere, and we in turn had watched Firefly in Grand Falls on one of our nights off; they had really impressed me. After I'd spent a couple of months back at home, licking my wounds after Alvin Shoes' final death throes, I called Richard from Firefly just to say hello. It was now August 1979. He shared with me that Darryl, their drummer, had decided to quit. Feeling my pulse quicken, I blurted out, "I'm a drummer. Can I audition for you?" Richard wasn't sure at first, but I talked him into it, and the next day I was on the highway to Montreal in my parents' second car. Firefly was set up for auditions with Darryl's kit in their rehearsal basement. I slept on Richard's couch and then got ready for my tryout the next afternoon. Before we got started, I locked myself in the bathroom and stared in the mirror, psyching myself up by whispering, "You can *do* this … You *can* do this … *You* can do this … You're meant to be in this band … You've got what it takes…." I'd never played drums for a rock band in my life.

All through high school I'd done well with drums and percussion in the marching band and the school orchestra, but propelling a rock band forward is a whole 'nother thing. Well, we banged through some of the Firefly song list, and though I gave it all I had, I really have no idea how I did. Probably more spirited than skilled. Their expressions were inscrutable as they thanked me. After thirty-six hours in Montreal I turned around for the seven-hour drive home with no clue what to expect. A couple of days later the phone rang and it was Richard. "Our drummer decided not to quit after all, but we'd like you to join Firefly as another singer-guitarist. We'll be a five-piece instead of four." I leapt at the offer, and a few days later I was headed back up the highway to live in Montreal for the next year and a half.

Richard, Dave, Bryan, Darryl, and now Carl: Firefly gave me a chance to learn a lot from some more experienced, talented guys who knew how to take a band on the road properly and do well with it. We travelled in a converted school bus, driven at moderate speeds, and compared with the Alvin Shoes' cube van it felt like the *Queen Mary*. I got very skilled with the gearshift on the iced, hilly winter streets of Montreal. It was my first experience working with a road crew and playing in a popular band. I didn't even mind that our first big trip together after a couple of months was back to Newfoundland for eight weeks; Firefly was big there. Richard Kurek on keyboards was the oldest; in the '60s he had been in a Montreal group called Wizard, and he was now back in music after a hiatus. Darryl Bagley on drums was a good-natured guy who did his best with limited experience but added big personality. Bryan Hughes on lead guitar was a really strong, schooled musician who went on to form recording acts Beau Geste and the Bryan Hughes Band. Nice player.

Singer/bassist Dave Marleau was skinny as a hockey stick but had a huge voice. He was a big reason for Firefly's popularity. Dave was not completely in favour of my joining, I think, and warily attempted to manage me once I was in the group. He correctly viewed me as a threat to his status before I even knew I was a threat.

Firefly was known as "The Little Beatles" in parts of Quebec because they favoured Fab Four tunes when they first began. When I joined, we branched out into heavier stuff, and the result was really strong with all the good singers we had. With Firefly I learned how to stay healthy for the stage, how to dress better, and how to deal with an audience more effectively. We had lots of laughs, too. Quebec and the Maritimes were, and are, fun places.

In those days a record deal was still the Holy Grail. There was no indie music scene, and the only way to get your music heard was for a record company to sign you and then pay for everything. Everybody thought if we could just get signed, we'd have it made, and if we didn't get signed, we'd end up playing in Holiday Inn lounge acts or out of the business altogether. (When I later got a record deal, I learned that it was just the beginning of the hard work, not the end.)

The most important part of preparing for that opportunity was songwriting. I had begun at age fifteen when I realized that all the musicians I liked wrote their own songs, so I should too. To make a record you have to have songs — fairly obvious, right? This made me pretty focused on writing new material, and I hoped Firefly would be the popular band that would bring attention to my songs.

Not everyone shared that view. The bass player, Dave, was sure that we were going to get discovered and signed because of our version of Elton John's "Your Song." As lead vocalist he had arranged the song to a painfully slow tempo and then insisted on singing, with long-held notes, the line "… that I put down in w-u-u-u-u-u-u-u-u-u-u-u-u-u-u-u-u-u-urds" with wide vibrato as the whole band paused. I was torn between annoyance and envy at this blatant look-at-me tactic.

The singing bass-man believed that we just had to keep playing and polishing our show exactly as it was, with no changes and no songwriting. When the show was sufficiently polished, somebody surely would someday come along and sign us to a big deal because of our sheer brilliance. And the songs? The big-deal people would find songs for us. Well, that sure didn't happen. Maybe our show-polishing lacked sufficient elbow grease, but I didn't believe in the strategy anyway. I didn't give it much time either, but when you're young things seem like they're taking forever.

Two details from my time in Firefly were telling of my personality and of my future ways of dealing with things. One day I was chatting with Dave Marleau about my habit of fussing over other people and always trying to help them.

"I think I have a strong mothering instinct," I offered with a smile.

"There's no room for a mothering instinct in rock 'n' roll!" Dave barked as he turned on his heel and left the room.

That left me wondering for some time about whether, for all my effort and desire, I was actually in general terms a misfit with these musician people (in time I became certain that I was).

Onstage with Firefly in St. John's, Newfoundland, at the Atlantic Place Strand, 1980.

In 1980 we had some personnel changes, and I have to admit that my powerful need to do things my way led to some people leaving Firefly or being pushed out. Some were sorry they ever let me in, I think. At the time of my arrival poor Bryan thought I'd been brought in specifically to replace him. I wasn't. Personnel changes notwithstanding, the band wasn't destined to get to the next level the way I'd hoped.

For one thing, half of "The Little Beatles" were now out. The band had a different character now than when I joined. For another, the writing progress just wasn't there. In Alvin Shoes we'd played about ten different songs of mine, but in Firefly I had to fight to get even two of my songs into the show.

I also found life in Montreal difficult after a time, subsisting on the low wages of a musician far from the support of old friends and family. I had to start selling off guitars just to eat and pay my rent, even though our pay was sometimes reaching a dizzying one hundred fifty dollars a week. Unfortunately, that wasn't every week. Eventually I couldn't see any more to be gained by remaining in Montreal, even though it had been like a college education. At some point you finish college. Soon after a New Year's Eve 1980 show in Quebec City, I packed my things and headed back home to Barrie.

THE ASYLUM BECKONS....

I wasn't sure what to do next after leaving Firefly and Montreal behind, but my respite lasted only a few weeks of January and February, time enough for plenty of road hockey and for pacing the floor of my parents' house, wondering how I would get back into the music game.

The *Toronto Star* classified ads section used to have a category 635, "Dramatic/Musical Talent," which in those days was thickly populated with ads saying things like, "Band seeks drummer. Must be into Black Sabbath," or "Piano player seeks steady lounge gig close to subway." One fateful Saturday morning I scanned the ads and saw, "Touring rock band needs an experienced guitar player/singer. Call Bruce Wilson Management at blah-blah-blah for details." Whoa, a band with management? This was another potential step up.

I phoned and got the manager on the line. He told me the band was called Coney Hatch and their specialty was AC/DC music. Two months earlier I had ranted at a Firefly gig how much AC/DC bugged me. "Great!" I now told the manager. "That's cool!" You have to be adaptable sometimes.

I went to their show and learned why AC/DC music works well in a rock bar. The twist was that the guy who was quitting, Paul, was the real AC/DC nut in Coney Hatch, but that was their identity now. They played other stuff too and played it well: "Drugs in My Pocket," "The Cradle Will Rock,"

"Walking on the Moon," "Crew Slut" ("Don't make a fuss, just get on the bus") ... all kinds of songs. It takes a lot of music to fill three hours a night. I was more impressed that Coney Hatch also played a bunch of their own songs — maybe the oddest songs I'd ever heard, but definitely original. We met on the break, spoke, and got on fine. They told me a few songs to learn, and the next week I met them at the Village Inn in Bradford.

The audition went great. Having beat out the other candidates, I was told to meet Steve Shelski, Andy Curran, and Dave Ketchum at Steve's parents' house, where we would rehearse for a week while the parents were in Las Vegas on holiday. The rehearsal mode we followed ever since was established that week in Steve's basement: fifty percent of the time devoted to hard work, the other fifty percent spent laughing our heads off. Vastly amused but not over-prepared for the show, I found myself on a stage in Aylmer, Quebec, on February 28, 1981, to begin life with Coney Hatch.

The first week actually reminded me of Olias. I wasn't ready, and each night I walked onto the stage scared of failure. I was again sharing a room, with three others this time, and the party commenced each night after our 2 a.m. finish. I was down to my last nerve. By end of the third night I was feeling choking failure onstage. I raced ahead upstairs to get in bed and shut the lights off, hoping for some badly needed rest to do better the following night, hoping the other guys would take the hint and move the party to the strippers' rooms instead. No such hint was taken. They came in, turned all the lights on, and fired up music on the cassette player good and loud. Not mean, just oblivious. It was party time!

After stewing in my own juices for a couple of minutes, I got up without a word, walked over to the cassette player and shut off the music, removed the tape, and detached the power cable. I then went back to my bed bearing those items with me in the stunned silence, swore, and stuck the pillow back over my head. They all left, grumbling, after a minute, but I'd struck a blow for the inhabitants of Planet Carl. It was sometimes a lonely planet.

Once we got properly rehearsed, Coney was a charmed band. We had a perfect four-way balance of personalities and skills, and everything was clicking in our favour. For those with an interest in astrology, it helped that we had one each of earth, air, fire, and water signs in our quartet. In a short time we were working productively and cooperatively writing new music together. Quickly we sorted out roles in the group dynamic. Crowds formed when we played, and a feeling of being on the rise attached to us. Girls liked how we looked, kinda pretty, and guys liked how we sounded, loud and heavy. A team spirit was forming. On one memorable night we even emerged unscathed from a barroom brawl.

That was an incident from our first summer together, up at the Empire Hotel in Timmins. We'd been to Timmins before, and I've always felt at home in northern Ontario. On this week-long gig, we were starting to permit ourselves some excitement. The demo that would land us our record deal was done and being shopped around, and the future looked bright. Too bad a small gang of four guys decided to give us a hard time; their reasons were unclear. It was suggested that they didn't like the way the Timmins girls looked at us. As four long-haired, good-looking guys who were projecting confidence and testosterone, we seemed like a threat to some locals, not for the first or the last time. That's just the nature of being a travelling musician, and it always has been.

The first part of our stay was enlivened by a mid-show fire. On the Tuesday night we'd been rocking away with our heads down in the second set, pounding out the tunes at pretty high volume. Lost in the moment I was, until my focus was broken by a surprising and vigorous tug on my arm. I opened my eyes and looked up in annoyance to find a girl from the audience gesturing wildly and yelling something I couldn't hear. I thought she was over-refreshed and attempting to request her favourite song at an inappropriate time. I brushed her hand off my arm and said, "Not now! Ask me later!"

She grabbed my arm again and screamed, "Look! Fire! Fire!" while pointing off to stage left. I was very surprised to see one of our large PA speakers pulsing flames out in time to the music. In those days we used to keep our water on stage in those plastic sports bottles with the fixed nozzle on top, so I put my guitar down fast, grabbed the bottle, jumped off the stage, and started squeezing water onto the fiery speaker box. Before long the flame was extinguished and all was dripping wet. The band had stopped the song and now everyone was gathered in front of the stage. Our soundman, John (Reptile) Belrose, was very upset because he owned the PA and quickly busied himself drying everything off with a towel. I think he was mad at me for getting his other speakers wet. Our very high output had caused a voice coil in one speaker to sizzle and fry, which ignited the paper cone. The flames shooting out in time to the music occurred because the huge kick drum sound was continuing to bang through the speaker as it burned. Very scientific and unexpected, but exciting, of course; this was spontaneous pyrotechnics we couldn't duplicate every night.

Over the next few nights those local lads I mentioned earlier decided to provoke and test us by heckling and intimidating our road crew. Our light guy, Marcello, who was not big physically but normally a brave kid, started to get uptight and told us he was getting a bit worried by these antics. They were goading him and throwing lit cigarettes at his head as he worked. I'd already marked one of them, a very tall guy, as the probable leader. It seems a girl he liked had said that she liked us. That was all it took.

By Friday night's show there was tension in the room, and we could see that they were badgering our crew again. When the set ended we walked toward the gear set-up in the back of the room to check on our boys; really, I guess it was to assert our presence in some kind of display of tribalism. Some bands might have bought the local guys beers and befriended them to defuse the situation. Those are the smart bands. We were young and aggressive, I suppose. As we approached I saw one of the Timmins boys throw something again at Marcello. One of those moments of powerful impulse for which I'm known filled me up, and to the surprise of Coney Hatch and the Timmins boys — and even myself — I climbed up on a railing and dove, Zorro-style, down into our group of tormentors to knock them all down like bowling pins. Beyond that, I didn't really have a plan.

The tall leader got up and decided that I was now a good candidate for a proper fight. He came at me fists flailing but I managed to get a grip on his arms and prevent the punches from reaching me. I had good arm strength at that time, but he stood at least six inches taller. As he tried to position himself to advantage, I hung on for dear life, and we grappled for some time. We danced around the bar a few turns, and to my surprise some other spectators to the event darted in and gave my ribs a few good punches. An unseen interloper then tripped me, but I fell against the bar and stayed upright. I'd got twisted round facing the bar in my awkward fall, and my opponent took this opportunity to grip the back of my head firmly. He pounded my forehead smartly down on the bar several times. *This can't go on*, I thought and somehow pushed off the bar, back into my partner's waiting embrace. I held on grimly, daring to hope that this set-to might still end in a stalemate, until another bar patron helpfully stuck out his foot to trip me and down I went with the big man on top of me.

This could have been very bad. What saved the day for me was that Dave Ketchum, our drummer, who is mild-mannered but very tough, was also involved in the fracas. Having quickly followed my lead, Dave waded into the fray with his own fury. He had just finished mopping the floor with one of the gang until he cried uncle and now squinted around the room without his glasses to see what had become of me. He was able to make me out after a second or two, flat on my back with the biggest guy in Timmins sitting on my chest. I was still trying to keep a grip on my opponent's arms but was struggling at a distinct disadvantage. The big man got his right arm free of my grasp and was cocking his fist back to plough me a good one. In the milliseconds that it took for me to comprehend that the flattening of the Dixon face was the probable next event, my rescuer was already approaching. WHACK! Dave came up and booted the guy across the throat. He was out cold instantly. It was eerie to feel the strength and consciousness drain out of my assailant as he rolled off me and onto the floor in a heap. I got up, dusted myself off, and thanked Dave for saving me. I would have been beaten badly or even killed if Thumper hadn't intervened in that decisive fashion. We all need people to save us from ourselves at times. Impulsivity got me into that scrape, friendship got me out of it. Coney played on.

It would be nice to say that this rout brought an end to the unwanted attentions of the Timmins bad boys. Unfortunately, it didn't quite end there. On Saturday night we were packing up when we were visited by members of the local constabulary. They told us that they were aware of the bar fight, and our adversaries were "known" to the local lawmen. They'd also become aware that a small group of four local males was lying in wait for us outside in a car. The police had the sensible solution: they would stay close by until we packed and then give us a police escort to the town limits. So it unfolded. We left Timmins under escort and made it safely out of town. I didn't fancy a second rumble with four incensed hostiles.

* * *

Immediately upon my joining Coney Hatch, we started putting in extra time to write new songs. Andy and I were both working on ideas, performing at night and getting up to rehearse the new songs with the band before the bar opened. Within two months we were playing at the famous Gasworks in Toronto, the dream gig for all young bands in those days. Rush, Moxy, Triumph, Max Webster, and the cream of Canada's recording acts had all played there on their way up. We were introduced to Kim Mitchell, who soon helped us do a demo tape, and six months after I joined Coney Hatch, we were negotiating a record deal with Anthem Records. It was considered Canada's coolest label because it was the home of Rush and Max Webster.

The head of Anthem and their management arm, SRO, was (and still is) Ray Danniels. He was an impressive guy and he sure knew how to make "the grand gesture," that move that gets everyone's attention. I was on the fence about Ray and actually resisted signing the contracts that he was offering. A lady who knew him well had warned me not to sign. Ray now identified me as the Coney who must be won over, and together with Tom Berry and Mike Tilka, his top record and management guys, he took me out to a lavish dinner at Bigliardi's Steakhouse, a gathering spot for Toronto's wealthy. The honchos buttered me up with assurances of all they could do for the band and for me. When the waiter brought the tab Ray made sure to let me know that "This is costing me more than my first car. Not kidding!" That sort of thing impresses a hungry young musician. I agreed to consider his deal favourably. I'm afraid that in hindsight it sort of looks like I was bought for the price of a nice meal.

When it came to record-contract signing day, we gathered at our lawyer's office for the formality. Ray once again made the appeal to the musician's stomach by going downstairs with Tom to a McDonalds to bring back a celebratory feast. Ray said, "I just bought up everything in the place that they had ready to go for lunchtime." We were so knocked out. We didn't know you could even do that.

(Recently I saw Ray at a Rush concert and thanked him for giving me my start all those years ago. He smirked a little, said, "Hey, I got paid!" and laughed.)

Kim Mitchell was present at the signing because he was to be our producer. Being "discovered" by Kim was the best break Coney Hatch could have gotten. He was cool and down-to-earth. His time with Max Webster had made him a star in Canada, and he was known and respected around the rock world. He really did take us under his wing, teaching us how to make recordings and to play tightly. He even let me live in his apartment in Toronto for a time because I had no place to stay.

I've already mentioned that Kim helped us record the demo that landed us a deal with Anthem. Andy's dad paid the studio bill, and we had some music managers interested in signing us in on those sessions. They dropped out of the picture, though, after Kim shopped our tapes to various record labels and it became clear that Anthem was the most interested. Kim was signed there himself. As the negotiations went on, we continued to play shows and also got some studio experience, preparing for our real album recording.

As the deal-signing day approached, cool reality began to set in. We knew that there'd be a $10,000 signing advance, more money than we'd ever seen. We'd have to pay our lawyer bill out of that, but we started dreaming about the great guitars we might buy or cool stage clothes or maybe even a van for the band to travel in. After we "inked the pact" at our lawyer's office, I was handed the advance cheque along with our lawyer's bill. The advance was $10,000; the legal bill was $9,634. I was in shock as I handed the papers to Steve, who turned white. His expression will be forever etched on my memory. We were left with $366, enough for an expenses float to get us to our next gig in Quebec. That was our first lesson in the economics of the real music business.

MAKING CONEY "HATCH"

We had done several demo sessions with producer Kim Mitchell prior to the start of the real album recording, including a bleary all-nighter in which the label asked us to record every original song we had. This meant doing seventeen songs in one day, and though there was some ferocious playing, some of the throat-shredding vocals we were churning out by three and four in the morning would have done Lemmy proud. That rough sound didn't endear the "B" songs to anybody (upon hearing the tapes, Ray Danniels said, "All those other songs, you can have 'em"). That narrowed the focus to ten main songs to constitute the album. Very late in the game we came up with two new songs — more on them later — and so two of the original candidates, "Dreamland" and "Where I Draw the Line," were bumped.

Kim was a legendary, iconic player even then, but he was new at producing. He kept things fun for us and as pressure-free as possible. The recording was done in the winter of '81–'82 at a sixteen-track studio called Quest, in Oshawa, thirty miles east of Toronto. We'd gather every morning at "The Goof," a funky Chinese diner in the Beaches area of Toronto where the Chinese waiters all knew Kim. All of us would pile into Kim's van after breakfast for the drive to Oshawa, to laugh and talk about music and girls.

Coney Hatch, likely late 1981: Andy Curran, Dave Ketchum, me, Steve Shelski. Unused first album photo shoot, soon after signing with Anthem.

I have many nice memories from that time. On the last session before a break for Christmas, we had a bit of a party and recorded some goofing-around songs. Among them were our "disco" number "Toujours l'Amour" with drummer Dave Ketchum on vocals, a snarly instrumental called "Ants on the Move" and some Christmas songs I sang to the stylings of the Coney jazz trio under the direction of Steven Shelski. We laughed like fools, drank too much ouzo, and then toddled off home for Christmas. Man, I wish we still had those tapes.

Working on "Stand Up" was a tough go. We had real trouble getting the right feel for the bed track, no matter which way we approached it. After a fruitless day or two of playing it over and over, Billy Wade, the late drummer from Moxy, happened to drop by the studio. He volunteered to have a try at playing the song with us in case a fresh approach might help. Dave Ketchum stood down from his drums like a good sport and Bill took the chair. The rest of us stayed out there to play with him. Well, none of us knew that Billy had a funny habit of sort of "moan-singing" along as he played a beat. It was a loud, kind of baritone-ish "Mmmm-mAHH! Mmmm-mAHH! Mmmm-mAHH!" which he sang in time to the kick and snare. After our initial surprise, Steve, Andy, and I started to get the giggles. We tried to avoid eye contact but inevitably we did look at each other and lapsed into hysterical laughter to the point that we could barely carry on playing. I think poor old Billy must have noticed because he looked displeased when he got up. Anyway, he did help us out indirectly because we relaxed after the laughing fits and soon got the keeper track for "Stand Up."

One night we all went out for fish and chips and had our usual laff riot. As we walked out of the restaurant to return to Quest Studio, a long-haired Oshawa punter was hanging around in the parking lot. He spied Kim and, visibly trembling with excitement, pointed and blurted out, "Oh, wow! Geddy Lee!"

With all this exposure to quality studio recording, I began to think about music and sounds in ways I'd never done before. The lively sound of that room where we recorded the drums, all plaster stucco with wood panel wainscoting, jumps right off the grooves, a unique tone. We learned from Kim about doing the intonation on guitars to perfect their tuning, about auditioning lots of speaker cabinets to get the best tones for recording, about hearing the difference in tone between nice new speakers vs. the beat-up amps we used for gigs, and about the way that changing the combinations of amps, speakers, and guitars can make huge tonal changes and enhance the feel of the whole song. That was guitarist stuff like I'd never had it, straight from a master — what an education!

When I listen to the *Coney Hatch* album now, I'm struck by the energy and exuberance. Beyond just laying down our songs in a studio, we captured something: the power of being young, fresh, and unafraid is all over that album. Kim was a big part of that, and so I thank him from my heart. Engineer/Quest Studio owner Paul "Steamer" LaChapelle worked tirelessly to come up with creative solutions to deal with some of our technical shortcomings. The other component was the unique combination of people and talents in Coney Hatch.

I couldn't have wished for a better start.

HEY OPERATOR

After a couple of months the album was completed and we got back to playing gigs while waiting for it to appear. There were still details to be attended to for the release; for instance, we were having trouble getting a good cover photo. The record company thought we looked too "posed" in the first sessions, so they brought a case of beer to the next photo shoot. What they got this time was photos of four *drunken* rock guys, but it was felt that this shot at least had a good "attitude."

During this waiting period we continued to write new songs, already thinking ahead to our next album. One night after a bar show in Thorold, I went outside to make a 1:30 a.m. collect call home to my girlfriend. The operator was fun and sympathetic at first, redialling the call a couple of times as I insisted, "She promised she'd be there!" but there was no answer. The operator shut me down after a while, her patience at an end. I stomped away from the phone booth in the rain, frustrated and angry. By the time I got back to my hotel room I had some words in my head, so I picked up my guitar and in about twenty minutes I'd worked out most of "Hey Operator." The lyrics are a classic transference-of-blame story, in which I suggest that the operator has it within her power to connect us if only she will try a little harder.

The next morning at rehearsal I showed it to the band. We roughed out the parts, and that night we put it in the show. When our record company guys came to see us play a few days later, they said, "Wow, what's that?" I told them it was a song for the next album, expecting to be patted on the head for my diligence and forward thinking. They said, "No, it's not. That's the single we've needed for the first album. You've gotta get back to the studio and record that." Everything was put on hold until "Hey Operator" and "We Got the Night," another new song, were completed.

Although "Hey Operator" was written after we thought the first album had been put to bed, we returned to Quest for sound (and budget) continuity. On this production we went for more "spit and polish" since it was now the intended single. We soon used up almost all the available sixteen tracks. We had one track left open when I came up with the piano part in the choruses. Kim decided that it must be doubled to sound right, and the only way to make this fit was to play and record two pianos simultaneously to one track. Steve and I were the keyboard guys, so I played a "tack" piano in the downstairs room and Steve played a grand piano in the upstairs room. Lining our playing up in tight unison was the most critical listening I'd ever had to do and needed a few takes, but Kim was right. It turned out great.

That's how "Hey Operator" came along and broke Coney Hatch open on the radio, taking us Top 20 across Canada. In all there were five songs on that first album that got serious radio play across FM rock radio and AM hit radio, including "Devil's Deck," "Monkey Bars," "Stand Up," and "You Ain't Got Me."

The arrival of the *Coney Hatch* album into the world took us on a rocket ride, shooting to one thrill after another. One memorable moment came from a simple pleasure. I was hanging around in Toronto's Earl Bales Park with wife-to-be Stella and a bunch of her friends on a hot summer afternoon with a transistor radio playing 1050 CHUM, the biggest radio station in Canada. Suddenly the guitar intro for "Hey Operator" came on. The big deejay voice announced, "Here's Canada's own Coney Hatch!" This was the radio station that I'd heard since childhood, and now there I was, coming over the airways from the "magic kingdom." It was the greatest exhilaration I'd ever felt, hearing myself on the radio for the first time. My spirits soared as I danced and whooped and jumped around. Three minutes, thirty seconds of a dream come true.

Coney Hatch soon started playing more high-profile shows to get the new album greater exposure. Our first time opening for another band was with Trooper on a tour of small-town arenas in Ontario and Quebec. Trooper

Sam the Record Man Yonge Street autograph session, 1982, with Kim Mitchell. Left to right: Andy Curran, Steve Shelski, me, Dave Ketchum, Kim Mitchell.

was still considered a big deal in 1982, and it was important experience for us. Make a great impression in forty-five minutes or less and then get off the stage: that was now the challenge.

Trooper spotted us for the rookies that we were. On the first day everyone was seated at the crew meal tables at the arena after the sound check. Brian "Smitty" Smith came over to "welcome" us in his own unique way: "So, you boys think you've been around a bit now?" Yeah, I guess, we hesitantly replied. "Seen some things, done some stuff?" Sure, Smitty. "Well," he shouted, "have you ever seen this?" and with that Smitty popped out his glass eye and smacked it down on the dinner table, where it stared up at us. I think he got the freaked-out reaction he was after.

Another good story from that summer tour with Trooper takes place in Kincardine. There had been some late-night carousing the night before, and our band arrived a bit green around the gills. Our tour manager announced that he'd forgotten to book us hotel rooms, so the search was on for a place to flop. We pulled up to a motel on the edge of town, and I got out of the van with one or two other guys to inquire. I rang the front desk bell until the owner came out, eyeing us warily. "Yeah, wuddya wan'?" he mumbled.

I said, politely as I could, "Hi, we've just arrived from out of town. Do you have any rooms available for tonight?"

He looked us up and down for a moment. He's seeing young longhairs, unshaven, hung over, and hardly dressed because of the summer heat, maybe looking like trouble. He says, "Are you guys a ball team?"

A bit bewildered, I replied, "No, we're a rock band."

"Oh, all right, I'll give *you* guys rooms, but we're not having any more of them *ball teams* here!"

Trooper got us started, and our next big deal of that summer was a show at Exhibition Stadium in Toronto as opening act to headliners Ted Nugent and Cheap Trick. It was to be our triumphant return, playing in front of our hometown crowd and also our record company and agents down front in the VIP section. Our tour manager arranged a limo for us to go across the football field out to the stage (which I foolishly declined because my wife wasn't allowed aboard). Once assembled backstage, we were *sooo* ready to rock the house.

The time came to begin our thirty-five-minute set, and the crowd of twenty thousand welcomed us with a roar. I can still feel my scalp tingling at the memory. We launched in with confidence, and the amazing big sound on the stage made us feel sure we had it going on ... only there wasn't the expected crowd response at the end of the songs, and our business people in the front rows wore concerned expressions. All we could do was plow ahead and get to the finish line. When we were done, we found Bun E. Carlos and Rick Neilson from Cheap Trick in the backstage rooms, and they were friendly and nice, although complaining about hangovers. Suddenly Terry, our giant soundman, burst into the room, babbling incoherently and throwing things around. The Cheap Trick-sters excused themselves quickly, and then Terry began ranting that Ted Nugent's road crew had intentionally gotten in his way and saddled him with a bunch of restrictions on the volume and on sound system gear that he wasn't allowed to touch. They threatened to shut us down if he broke any of their rules. The Nugent road crew wanted to make sure that we, as the puny opening act, didn't look too good and possibly overshadow their boss in any way. It may also be that they were just bullies who liked to push around the little bands for sport. Terry was embarrassed that we sounded quiet, muffled, and tiny to the big crowd. It was another lesson for us: not everybody is nice.

Road crews of some headlining acts go out of their way to make it difficult for opening bands. In recent years I've been surprised to learn that some Coney Hatch crew were occasionally mean when we were headliners. We in the band had no idea, and frankly I don't get it. Maybe it's an attitude that develops from being treated poorly when you're at the bottom, like the hazing that's given to freshmen and then they pass it on to the next crop. I apologize to anyone who was treated badly on a Coney Hatch show.

The next month we crossed over into the U.S., where our album was released on Mercury/Polygram Records. Our first show in America was at the Cleveland Agora for radio station WMMS on their coffee-break concert series. Eleven a.m. was not a time we were used to rocking full tilt, but we did a good promo for our new release.

We bounced around the eastern states, playing either on our own or with headliners like Eddie Money, Edgar Winter, and Peter Frampton. Frampton was nice and friendly. Although he's quite a small guy, at the time we looked a fair amount alike, which may be why he gave me a funny look as we shook hands. It was amazing to think that just six years earlier I'd been a high-school kid in a crowd of thirty thousand watching him on the "Frampton Comes Alive" tour. (I didn't see him again until twenty-five years later, when I was with The Guess Who. So many years, and Peter remains a brilliant guitar player with a nice smile, though now very little hair. He still mostly stands there like a load of wet washing onstage; for him it's completely about the guitar playing.)

After a few weeks in the States we received the news that we'd landed the opening slot with the Judas Priest tour that was just getting started. We had three days to get up to Quebec City and meet Priest at the Colisée. That first night, as we stood backstage waiting to play and watched the lights go down, the crowd roared in anticipation and then got their lighters going by the thousands in the darkness. It was an unforgettable sight, and this time nobody messed with our soundman. It was the most excited we'd ever been, and we ran around the stage and jumped in the air and played all our songs too fast. What a great time! Later we went out to watch the mighty Judas Priest show and were bowled over at how good they were that night and then *every* night of the tour. We began to learn about the importance of delivering a top show every night, in every town, in the same way, no matter how you feel.

The tour took us across Canada, first the east, from Quebec City to Montreal and then into Maple Leaf Gardens in Toronto, where we got to do a proper show for the hometown crowd this time. A triumphant little foursome we were, playing a venue we'd hardly dared *dream* of playing, in front of many of the people who'd supported us in our rapid rise. No funny looks *à la* CNE stadium that night.

And on through to the west, where I'd never played before: Winnipeg Arena, Edmonton Northlands Coliseum, Max Bell Arena in Calgary, and then the PNE in Vancouver, working our way across Canada. Our nerves were conquered. It's amazing how quickly you begin to acclimatize and feel at home at the top. (Oscar Wilde: "I have very simple tastes. I'm always satisfied with the best.") We were still making some rookie mistakes, as in Vancouver, where Dave Ketchum and I decided to walk around and see the sights. We'd been inspired by witnessing K.K. Downing and Glenn Tipton of Judas Priest returning to the hotel in their nice golf sweaters and slacks after a morning round of whack-fuck (although it was disconcerting for us to see them out of their rock regalia for the first time).

The B.C. climate was turning chilly and damp for autumn, but the afternoon sky cleared, and we thought it would be a great idea to circumnavigate Stanley Park on foot. No idea that the park could be miles around ever entered our little musician brains. What began as a lark in the sunny, brisk mid-afternoon became a grim windblown slog home in the evening darkness alongside Vancouver's rush hour traffic. By the time we returned to the hotel I was whipped, and onstage that night I had easily my worst outing of the tour. The lessons never end: even if you only have an opening set to deliver, you still have to conserve energy in the daytime. At least, that's what I do. It's all about the show; there's no other reason for you to be in that city.

SCREAM FOR ME, SEATTLE!

Next we headed south into the western United States. First it was Seattle and Spokane, Washington. Portland and Eugene, Oregon followed. The Seattle show was staged on the grounds of the 1962 World's Fair, in the Coliseum. The location was significant on this occasion.

On the day of the show Dave and I, who always roomed together, got to the Coliseum a bit late because I'd had one of my forgetful episodes. That morning, still sleepy, I'd taken off my wedding ring and set it on the toilet tank while washing. I then checked out without it. We'd walked down the street about three blocks when I glanced at my hand and noticed the ring was missing. Poor Dave ran frantically after me as I galloped back to try to reach the hotel room before the ring was either thrown out or taken. Often my good luck prevails in these situations, and on this occasion that was the case. I bounded into our room just as the maid was discovering the forgotten gold band, and I expressed my *gracias* with relief.

It was now slower progress we made in retracing our journey to work, as the energy bite from the run caught up with us. I believe I bought Dave a coffee as a conciliatory gesture, and so we walked into the parking area of the Coliseum later than scheduled. It was early afternoon, and the crowd was already milling around outside. As we approached, great walloping bangs of explosive noise were audible. A security guy was watching over the scene, so we asked him what was going on.

"Those are M-80 firecrackers," he said wearily. "They're the equivalent of a tenth of a stick of dynamite."

"Isn't that dangerous?" I asked.

"Yeah, but we can't do much. The World's Fair was created under federal jurisdiction, so city police aren't allowed to search or frisk people on this property. Keep your head up in the show because people carry those firecrackers in there and throw them around, and we can't prevent it. Those things really could take out your eye."

That gave Dave and me something to think about as we went in for sound check, and even in the centre of the cavernous arena you could hear the M-80s going off in the parking lot. It was an idiotic hobby but an even more idiotic technicality that allowed it. The no-search rule made showtime pretty hot for our pesky opening act from Canada.

People go to a show to see the headliner. That's who sells tickets. Opening acts are rarely an attraction and are often barely tolerated. You have to deliver up red-hot tamales in your short stint onstage to win over the mostly indifferent crowd. On bad nights the reception can be hostile. In Seattle that night, there awaited the most whipped-up, spoiling-for-a-fight crowd I've ever encountered.

For comparison, one time in Allentown when we played there with Iron Maiden, we heard the crowd chanting before the show. All I could make out was "something-Coney Hatch, something-something-something" over and over. *Cool, they like us!* I went closer to the stage to bask in the crowd's welcome and from that vantage point I heard clearly, "F**K Coney Hatch! We want Saxon!" (We'd replaced Saxon on the tour.) A bit disappointing, but we put on our best hockey game-faces and went out to try to win them over.

Another time, at the Kabuki Theater in San Francisco, we were opening for Accept, and the front rows seemed to want to bring a metal-punk vibe to the event. The crowd's mood felt more malevolent, darker, than the mainly good-time crowds we'd been used to. The more extreme edge of heavy metal — speed metal, death metal, goth metal — was beginning to influence young listeners. We got out there and played it as tough as our music permitted, but I felt the aggressive energy. Something I often did over the years was to hold my guitar forward, arm's-length in my hands, to let the people in the front row play and bang on it with their hands and make the big guitar sound. On this night I'd been braving the aggression, almost daring them, to show I wasn't afraid. I extended the guitar at the end of one song. Suddenly I had people clutching at my legs, hitting my hands, grabbing my arms, trying to pull me into the pit, where who knows what would have happened. I instinctively started kicking out hard, whacking with my guitar and punching to get them off me. As soon as I got free, I stood back from the edge where they couldn't reach me. Prudence told me to avoid further interaction.

The night in Seattle with Judas Priest, though, was in a class of its own. As we stood backstage, waiting for the lights to go down, the crowd sound that night was a roar, different and shriller than the one we were used to, punctuated by intermittent blasts of M-80s. Our name was announced and we hit the stage to a chorus of boos and hysteria from at least the front rows. The enormous sound of our opening number, "Stand Up," rather than quelling the malcontents, only served to inflame them.

Many young people at that time believed — or pretended to believe — and acted out the "Satanic" piffle that was going around about heavy metal bands like Judas Priest, Iron Maiden, etc. Yeesh! Those bands seemed tame compared with the ones that came along in the years to follow. We were faced with a bunch of kids waving upside-down crosses and screaming their dislike for *us*, the unwanted opening act and obstacle to the arrival of their adored "Priest." I suppose they thought that if they could scare us off quickly, then Judas Priest would take the stage sooner. (Note to concertgoers: It doesn't work.)

Almost immediately, baseball caps flew through the air at the stage and began to pile up around our feet. Coats and other garments came flying in as we soldiered on. Somebody threw a wad of wet chewing gum and it stuck to my guitar strings.

A coat flung at Andy landed over his face while he was singing, and he shook it off. Another landed over the neck of his bass and he had to stop playing to pull it off. A tennis ball hit him and bounced around the stage. From every angle people were throwing those green glow-sticks, standard issue at concerts for years, in a seeming deluge. Our crew guy, Sluggo, was running onto the stage every few minutes to clear away more debris so we wouldn't fall over it. I've never seen so many hats. People must have just brought them to throw at the stage, because I hadn't seen that many covered heads out there at the start.

The climax of all that mayhem was when somebody threw a homemade stink bomb in a half-pint milk carton. It landed on the drum riser and started belching yellow sulphurous fumes, while poor Dave drummed away with his eyes watering, unable to escape. What a reek! Sluggo ran again onto the stage to remove it.

Now, there were pockets of people who were just trying to enjoy our music, but from the start I'd had a little cabal of wannabe Satanists parked right in front of me. They jumped up and down, screaming their disaffection for us with great energy and really working it. Two of these characters in particular got quite excited, screaming at me: "Fuck off!" "Get off the stage!" "We hate you!" They shook their little crosses upside-down and vigorously gave me the finger over and over. At first I laughed it off, and then after a while I smirked at them in a taunting way. Next I tried looking menacing, but they weren't buying it. It wasn't like I would jump off the stage mid-show to go after them. (Umm, right. I'd done that to death in Timmins.)

Stuck in between the two maniacs was one little guy, maybe fourteen years old, who really liked us and tried to show me his support with encouraging eye contact and enthusiastic applause. That gave me something to work with, and I thought Little Guy and I were really bonding, even in the middle of the non-stop barrage. M-80s continued to explode in mid-air above the crowd.

At some point the stress of feeling all that hostility directed at us started to wear on me. I got fed up with the two nuts in front of me and decided to get those little bastards ... but how?

I looked around the stage floor at all the thrown objects and saw some of those glow-sticks around my feet. *I'll kick one of these things in their faces and that'll shut them up*, I told myself. I had a powerful kicking foot from my years of soccer and track — powerful, but not always accurate. As the demon children worked themselves into another frenzy, I hoofed the glow-stick as hard as I could. In horror I saw Little Guy, my only friend in the front row, take the glow-stick right in the middle of his forehead. Thank God it was the flat side and not the point or it would have split him open. As it was, it left an angry red welt. L.G. staggered back in pain and confusion for an instant and then resumed his position at the barricade, though with no trace of his former supportive expression. I think he now hated me too. The devils either side of him realized I'd been trying to hit them and were roused to new heights of fury.

I felt so guilty at this point that I just wanted our show to end. When our last song was finished, the lights that went up for the interval revealed a huge collection of hats, coats, shirts, and other garments that had been thrown at us piled in a mound by the stage. The house crew joked that they could divvy up the haul and not need to buy clothes for years.

I still retain a bit of a bad taste about Seattle.

The guys from Priest were friendly and we got to know them all (K.K. Downing let Steve try his Flying V guitar back at one hotel and sadly, Steve dropped it to the floor), but singer Rob Halford was the nicest. He was always friendly and made sure we were being treated well. Rob jumped in with us to ride in our motor home going back to the hotel in Vancouver and joked around, self-effacing and unpretentious, just like he was one of us. He even picked up my dumbbell weights during the ride to clown around with them and test how strong he wasn't. He was able to laugh at himself and just be one of the guys.

It was amusing as the tour went on for us to see how a man who was openly gay in his private life was able to project a public image of macho, leather-clad biker ferocity. He was accepted by the legions of young, no doubt generally straight males who worshipped the band as the embodiment of their self-image. It did not surprise me when I later learned that he'd started his career in England as a decent Shakespearean actor. Rob knew that perception is reality.

Even though he was open about his sexual orientation, it was still jarring to my sheltered experience when Rob said to me one day backstage, "Oh, Carl, have you met my lover, John? He's flown in to visit," and then introduced us. Very nice they were together, too. I felt that I was growing in sophistication in such moments, moments that were pretty unguarded for 1982.

On we went through California and Nevada, one town after another, through heat in Death Valley and snowstorms in the Rockies. Whenever we did radio promo interviews, every damn announcer wanted to do "hoser" jokes with us because we were Canadian and the Bob and Doug McKenzie record based on the TV skits had just taken the charts by storm. I never thought the "Great White North" shtick was that funny, but America loved it. It took no time at all to get tired of radio guys asking "Canada, ehhh? So, where are your toques?"

Famous rock people turn up around any tour. In San Francisco we played at the Cow Palace for promoter Bill Graham. Neal Schon and Gregg Rolie from Journey turned up, and that was kind of exciting. That's just the biz; guys go out to each other's shows. It made us feel cool to see them backstage. For the shows in Long Beach, California, our tour manager, Neil McDermott, set us up with three nights' stay aboard the *Queen Mary* in Long Beach Harbor — a treat, but maybe too posh for the likes of us. The cabins were smaller than I expected.

The famous people effect worked to our disadvantage in Long Beach. It was the closest the tour would get to L.A., and Judas Priest had many friends there, showbiz and otherwise, who wanted to attend. What that meant for the pesky opening act this time was that all the front rows were bought up by or reserved for the guests of the mighty Priest. For the two nights at Long Beach Arena, those rows were almost empty when we played our set. When the lights were down, it was like playing to an empty house. We thought we'd have Hollywood watching us, but whatever Hollywood element was there was busy swilling free booze in the hospitality suite during our set.

Unfortunately, for our final six shows of the tour I was in a body sling again, unable to play, after severely dislocating my shoulder in Las Vegas. This injury, aggravating the remnants of an old hockey wound, was the result of my overly enthusiastic arrival at the backstage entrance of the Aladdin Theater. Neil, our tour manager, had driven us to the top of a grassy slope that led down to the stage door. I was pretty pumped up about our first show in Sin City, so I yelled out "Hello, Las Vegas!" executed a perfect somersault down the hill and jumped up saying "Ta-dah!" I was so pleased with myself that I did it again, evidently a bit carelessly. As I tumbled I heard and felt my shoulder fall out of the joint with a sickening crunch. I struggled to my feet and said in a choked voice, "Neil, take me to the hospital." Poor Neil thought it was part of my little performance and began to laugh, until I roared, "Now! I'm not kidding!" Band and crew then had to figure things out for the evening's show while Neil hustled me off to the nearest emergency department.

The performance was a blur to me. I returned to consciousness from a general anaesthetic after complicated shoulder relocation treatment. Completely groggy and disoriented, I was hustled straight from an emergency ward gurney to the stage of the Aladdin. I was high on Demerol, the injured arm bound to my chest with a sling, but somehow I walked out on

Las Vegas, 1982. Out of the ER and onto the Aladdin Theater stage, doped up, arm strapped to my side.

the stage with Sluggo or Neil leading me. I sang my lead vocal parts in a daze and then, when it was Andy's turn to sing lead, I was led back to side-stage before I fell over. I perched on a spare guitar amp out of sight of the crowd and sang my harmony parts into a waiting microphone (kept hidden because of course being injured *doesn't rock*). I later wondered how anyone could play music when stoned, especially in front of an audience. It was a completely disconnected experience.

The remaining four or five shows I performed with arm strapped down to keep it still for healing, but at least I was now clear-headed. Andy milked the crowd's sympathy every night by claiming I'd just been injured the day of each show. "C'mon! This guy's gotten up from his hospital bed tonight just to do this show for you. Give it up, people! C'mon!" In San Diego, Phoenix, Tucson, Santa Fe, and Albuquerque, they all dutifully gave it up.

Our time on the Priest tour ran out in Albuquerque. It was strange to think that they'd be continuing on without us, but their crew made our last show memorable in a way that left us unsure of our standing. Mid-show, in the middle of a song, the Priest crew somehow contrived to have our amps shut down so that we were left with only drums and voice. It was meant to embarrass us so their roadies could have a laugh at our panic. I turned to Dave at the drums and yelled, "Play the beat for Gary Glitter's 'Rock and Roll'!"

I had envisioned getting the crowd to do a big arena-sized sing-along, "Rock and Ro-o-oll, HEY! Rock and roll," to fill the time until our gear was working again.

Dave yelled back, "I don't know it!"

"Whaddya mean, you don't know it? Everyone knows it!"

"Well, *I* don't know it!"

I was incredulous but gave up on pushing the idea. We were left with me talking to the crowd like a game show host while our crew scrambled around the stage trying to get things working again. The Priest crew took pity after about five minutes and turned us back on. They'd had their fun.

I flew home to meet with a shoulder specialist, and so I was spared the cross-country long haul in the motor home. I was told to have surgery. I declined. The shoulder hung on unhurt for twenty-two more years after that as a result of smarter limb management.

By the end of 1982 the band and everyone around us had heightened expectations of where we "should" get to in the ranking of rock groups, if we played our cards right. It had been a year filled with new experiences: recording and releasing our first album, hearing ourselves on radio, giving interviews, touring in the U.S., and working as a support act for the first time. After years of working hard and long into the night in Canadian bars, the single forty-five-minute opening-act set required of us felt like "hardly working" as we played second fiddle to Trooper, Cheap Trick, Ted Nugent, Eddie Money, Edgar Winter, Peter Frampton, Saga, Kim Mitchell, Streetheart, and most notably, Judas Priest. What an education for the Canadian rookies! Rob Halford's vocals and theatrical showmanship and the twin guitar power of K.K. Downing and Glenn Tipton were a definite influence on us as we soaked up all that we could of the "big time" experience.

For New Year's Eve 1982 we again played Maple Leaf Gardens in Toronto, this time with Kim Mitchell and Saga. Just months earlier we'd been working up the street at a rough bar called The Gasworks. No wonder everyone expected so much from us in 1983. For Coney Hatch, 1982 had been like hanging on to a rocket going straight up.

THE EVILS OF DRUGS, DRINK, AND ROCK 'N' ROLL

Caring about fitness should not automatically confer "fanatic" status on a person. It's simply a matter of choosing what you do with your body and your time. It is a fact that even when pushing fifty I was choosing to swim lengths or use the hotel gym after gigs on the road rather than joining in on the pursuit of Scotch or dope or hot fudge sundaes. It didn't make me better than other people; it just made me healthier. We always have a choice.

There have been countless occasions when I've been swimming against the popular stream. It wasn't contrariness. I simply believed I was choosing the best thing for me at that time. People might say, "Carl's here, now the party's over," simply because I didn't like drugs. I took a perverse pride in being the only sober guy and therefore the only one in shape to drive us to the next town, night after night.

Drives of ridiculous length were common for a band at our level that didn't have a lot of money. Saskatoon to Chicago, Toronto to Austin, San Francisco to Milwaukee, Halifax to Toronto, etc. Driving for a day or two straight was just part of the deal. Because I was the strait-laced one, I took the wheel a great deal of the time. On a public-perception level, being sensible probably doesn't "rock." The fans who think it must be great to be a musician so you can just party all the time wouldn't really want to live that way themselves, month after month. You know, I did get hammered every

Me in 1977, on the 4 x 400 relay team. Trumpeter and third man Rob Campbell is receiving the baton. We set a regional record that year.

six months or so as a cleansing ritual, and an occasional beer was enjoyable, but mainly it was about keeping control, being *ready*.

I thought maybe I was demonstrating to the world that I had clarity and energy to burn because I kept to the straight and narrow. My dedication to health probably didn't register with onlookers in the way I had hoped. One memorable moment showed I might be making the opposite impression.

We were out on the Iron Maiden tour in '83. Our budget didn't permit us to have a tour bus, so we were touring North America in a Shasta motor home, the kind a family would rent to go on vacation. Night after night we'd play our opening set and then the backstage party would commence, usually not including me. Often the festivities would continue on after departure in the Shasta as I manned the wheel deep into the night. It began to feel like my role had morphed into that of chauffeur for the rolling party wagon, not lead singer for the recording act on tour. Yet for reasons suited to my character I kept stepping up for the job.

After three or four weeks, the pace was beginning to take its toll on me. I was getting a bit resentful. Sometime after midnight of one night's party on wheels, our tour manager, Neil McDermott, took a break from the fun in the back and came up to check on me in my solitude at the wheel.

I decided to take the opportunity to vent a bit, or maybe get some praise for the responsible, stand-up job I was doing. I replied, "You know, Neil, it's starting to get to me a bit, doing all this driving night after night for so many days. It's wearing me down."

Neil looked me up and down in disbelief for a moment and then retorted, "You? You look after yourself. How do you think we feel?"

I had to laugh.

My old guitar tech, Jon Dalby, recently reminded me of a time when the band stopped for lunch and I decided to skip the meal and instead go for a run up ahead on the highway. I'd calculated they'd take about a half hour to eat and that after about forty-five minutes of me running they'd catch up to me. The only problem was that I didn't confirm the route they planned to take; I just took off. There was apparently some pretty good cursing attached to my name when the guys had covered some distance on the resumed drive only to realize that they'd have to double back to find me. For my part I just kept running and running, assuming they'd gotten deep into games of *Ms. Pac-Man* and hadn't left on time. It was a very run-out Carl who was finally picked up by his disgruntled pals after an hour-plus.

Strangely, that didn't stop me from making that exact mistake on more occasions, once outside Lubbock, Texas, where this time the boys feared for my safety. A long-haired pretty boy in shorts alone on the roadside might attract unwanted redneck attention. It had never occurred to me that there could be danger.

Neil was larger than life, a character whose lively "party leader" disposition was at that time aided, not hindered, by the liberal application of mood-enhancers. Professionally, he knew how to talk the talk, but he could also walk the walk, and that rightly convinced people of his experience and knowledge. The music biz is filled with good bullshit artists, many of whom can be unmasked over time. This guy brought a lot to the party in every sense. Neil could run the whole show and then organize a great celebration afterward, keeping up with the most dedicated "party-hearties" — a formidable combination of traits in the music business.

I had decided back in high school that drugs weren't for me. The most I had ever done was to try a puff on someone else's joint a couple of times. I did inhale. It didn't impress me. None of my friends in school were druggies, and the musicians I knew in Alvin Shoes and Firefly weren't either.

However, once I was in Coney Hatch and immersed in the higher-level touring life, I entered a world where everyone seemed to think it was normal to put unknown chemicals from a stranger into their systems. Acid, dope, mushrooms, cocaine, even heroin — okay, gimme. I was the odd man out.

I like fun, but I just couldn't see the connection between drugs and fun. We all know somebody, musician or not, whose life has been seriously affected, ruined, or even ended by drugs. Where's the fun in that?

I can remember the period where open discussion of drug use entered the mainstream media and the general consciousness. It was particularly focused on the fear of "what the young people are doing to themselves with their reckless shift to casual drug use." Since the late '60s I was seeing and hearing media discussion of drug use. Often it came up nonchalantly in the interviews and articles contained in music magazines, which I constantly devoured. The references came from an implied "of course, everybody's taking drugs, right?" perspective. As a boy I watched in confusion, along with the rest of the "straight" world, as one music idol after another crashed to earth through drug use.

I thought, *Why would you do that to yourself? Aren't you having enough fun without that?* I felt bad for them.

In high school in the '70s, many of my peers assumed that because I was a long-haired guy fanatical about music, I must also be a dope smoker. I had no hesitation in hoisting a few beers at a party, but I didn't even know how one would go about acquiring dope, or what it would look like if you could.

Years later my wife once strongly urged me to try a joint to loosen up a bit. I took her advice and wrote a complete song that I really like, but the lyric doesn't make strict sense. I didn't feel enough benefit to make it something I'd want to pursue.

Even though I didn't take them, drugs have still affected my life. Sometimes it was funny to be the straight guy looking on. On a night drive with Coney Hatch, from Montreal through the Adirondacks to Pittsburgh, a couple of the guys took magic mushrooms. The altered reality kicked in as we were driving in a snowstorm.

Mushroom Man 1: "Why are you staring at me?"

MM2: "Man, you've got brown stains like gravy all over your face. It's freaking me out."

"No, I don't! You're freaking *me* out! Stop staring at me!"

A minute goes by.

"Ha, I caught you! You're staring at me again!"

"Sorry, man, it's freaking me out! Lemme wipe your face."

"No, I'll wipe *your* face! Stop it!"

Several silent minutes later, MM1 is looking out the windshield at the swirling snow.

"Carl, I think we're in a tunnel."

"We are not in a tunnel."

Silence.

"Are you sure we're not in a tunnel?"

"We are *not* in a tunnel."

Silence.

MM1: "Aaaahhhhh! Look out!"

Brakes slam on, van slips and slides to a fishtail halt.

"What? What? What is it?"

"Oh, sorry, man. I thought the tunnel was ending."

Here's a memorable exchange I overheard during our tour with Iron Maiden. The Maiden crew were all on lunch break backstage, some thirty or more people, all told. One of the riggers started griping about the quality of the food just as the group's tour manager came on the scene: "Look at this catering we have to eat, man. It's crap, I tell you, *crap.*"

The tour manager curtly retorted, "What's wrong with it? It's fine."

"*It's crap!*"

"There's no need to carry on like that, y'know."

"Look, I'm just tired of the same kind of food being served up to us day after day. We need a change!"

"Well, you can *buy* something different if you want a change. What do ya think your per diems are for?"

"Why, drugs, of course!"

Coney Hatch once employed a soundman nicknamed "Tiny," a massive guy and a character. He'd bring acid on road trips and take it before going to sleep, with the rationale that if it was good quality, it would awaken him and he'd get up and enjoy the trip. If it was low-grade, he'd stay sleeping but have great dreams. He had the hair-raising habit of taking acid if he had to do a long night drive, to keep him entertained. It seemed everyone who took acid really liked it.

It's easy to see the funny side of the effect of drugs when you're watching it on other people. As my former wife Stella once said, "I guess small tits are okay ... on *other* girls!" Life already offers so many opportunities for ridiculous behaviour that it's hard to believe we need drugs to get us there at all.

An amazing drummer named Tim once had a thought to audition for Coney and spent a few days with us so we could get to know each other. One evening everyone was gathered at the tour manager's house. We sat in a circle in the living room and Tim started to roll joints for everyone. I got up and excused myself.

Apparently Tim asked the others, "Hey, where's Carl going?"

He was told "Carl's not into this. He doesn't take part."

Tim's eyes grew wide and he told them in complete seriousness, "I don't trust *anyone* who doesn't do drugs."

We'd met Tim at an outdoor show near Quebec City where we'd performed with Mahogany Rush and the Joe Perry Project. Joe Perry was in the period of his career where he had quit Aerosmith to pursue the making of solo albums and the taking of more drugs. His drug of choice at the time was cocaine, which he somehow smoked. His manager asked Andy and me if we'd like to meet Joe backstage and, eager fans that we were, we said sure. We were led to a change room in the little community centre. There was Joe, alone, sprawled on a bench, and evidently passed out.

"Hey, Joe, wake up! There's someone here to meet you."

He groggily raised his head and then sat up.

"Who is it?"

"These guys are a great young Canadian band that opened the show."

"Oh, yeah? Hey, man, how ya doing?" he sleepily croaked.

I give him credit; he was quite civil even though half-gone.

"We're good, Joe."

"Yeah, well, I've gotta get ready for the stage. Catch you later."

He must have had some kind of magic to summon the energy to perform shortly thereafter.

His band members were all journeymen from Boston, Joe's hometown. The bass player was a big black guy, muscle-bound, front teeth knocked out, wearing a do-rag and for some reason a big Bowie knife on his belt, both onstage and off. He was scary but he was a nut too. When the show was done, Joe's manager again offered visits to the dressing room, this time to

Andy and Steve. There's Joe sitting semi-wasted again on the bench, and Steve reaches out to shake hands. Now, during the show Joe had somehow completely ripped out the crotch of his leather pants. As Steve starts to speak, he realizes that Joe's pink parts are hanging out of the huge tear. Sitting next to Joe was the scary bass player, who had now undone his pants in solidarity with the boss, and was also just hanging out of them. Steve spluttered incoherently and the big bass man started howling with laughter, saying, "Come on, man, show us your meat. Come on man, siddown and join in. Show us your meat!" It was hard to know whether Joe was in on the joke.

The last we saw of the bass player was next morning as we pulled away from the motel where all the bands had stayed. He had his room door open and was bouncing on the bed like a little kid, all 250 pounds of him, head thrown back in wild laughter.

Drugs were a costly influence. After a show in Chicoutimi, one of our first tour managers got good and stoned on a joint for the long drive home. He forgot his briefcase with five thousand dollars of our money on the counter of a convenience store when he stopped for munchies with the road crew. They drove a hundred miles before he realized it was forgotten and then raced back in a panic. When they got there ... all gone. (Our management company made us sue the poor bugger years later to get that money back. Not our finest hour.)

Another tour manager disappeared completely with many thousands of our dollars from gig proceeds. When he emerged a week later, the money had been spent on a massive cocaine binge. He proposed that we treat the missing money as an advance, which he'd work off by putting in extra hours. Incredibly, there were sympathizers who wanted to agree to this. Perhaps they were at the party. I insisted he be fired. After a lengthy debate, he was gone. Nobody aside from me at the time seemed to see that once that money we had worked for had been thrown away like that, the effort we'd expended to earn it had also been wasted.

We'd often end up with shady characters in our dressing room or at social events who had wormed their way in solely because they offered drugs. These were people you wouldn't want to spend two seconds with, but cocaine gained them access through many closed doors. They felt cool because they were hanging with the band. It began to seem as if drugs were the magic key to any door.

We had a roadie who used to say, "For best results, insert drugs here," pointing to his nose and mouth. Now, John was a sweet, hard-working guy. That line made people laugh until he turned into a full-blown heroin addict and his life was ruined. He was later stabbed to death on the street in a random act of violence, just after he'd emerged from cleaning up his heroin addiction. We had other friends who died in the '80s of cocaine-related heart failure, similar to the way young basketball star Len Bias perished in 1985. Bias's story brought to light the little-known fact that every time a person takes cocaine into their system, even the first time, that drug has the potential to interrupt the involuntary messages from your brain to your heart. This can then result in the heart stopping. All in the pursuit of a little fun.

LET'S NOT GET OUTA HAND!

For Coney Hatch's second album, Anthem Records hired a producer from England named Max Norman. He had worked with Bad Company and Ian Hunter, but most impressive was the fact that he'd recorded Ozzy Osbourne's first two solo albums with Randy Rhoads on guitar. Max was both a producer and an engineer, so he ran the whole show of technical and creative decisions. The making of our second album was, as is often the case, nowhere near as streamlined as the process of recording album one.

January of '83 was the beginning of rehearsals and writing time for our next album, finally titled *Outa Hand*. There wasn't much leftover stuff from the first album, only a couple of tracks that had been bumped. Some early writing efforts that had been deemed unworthy once already were the only other crumbs in the cupboard. We had to get to work on new songs, and fast. You often hear about the "sophomore jinx," based on the fact that bands spend their whole lives preparing for their first album and then have just a year to make the next one. In our case the lack could be attributed to the new demands of touring. Our songwriting changed because we were no longer spending entire weeks living together at one gig, focusing on the band and the music. We were more productive when we could get up and rehearse together each morning and get fresh ideas cooking right away. There's more energy in the songs that way.

A rehearsal space was rented and we dutifully started going in there every day to generate songs. There was a large difference this time, though. The pressure was on to take everything "up a notch" from what the debut record had accomplished. This attitude led us into a situation that still makes me squirm to recall.

We were young and didn't know much about business, and we were in awe of all that was happening around us. We began to hear suggestions from our label that we change things up: "You did the first record with no experience, in a low-budget demo studio under a producer who'd never produced a record. Think what we could accomplish this time if we change to a better studio and a real producer!" The problem with this idea was that Kim Mitchell had discovered us, gotten us signed, and produced the first album. He was also expecting to produce the second album, a fair assumption. The record company, however, had their eye on Max Norman. Somehow Anthem had made contact with Max or his people, and he was available.

Now, if this had all been worked out amicably with Kim, and his role in our rise had been suitably honoured and compensated through future royalties, then fair enough. Somehow, to my everlasting shame, we agreed to a plan put forth by our management and label to audition the two producers and see what we thought. I guess they wanted us to feel like going with Max was our idea.

Kim came to that rehearsal room to go through the exercise of hearing the five or so songs we had to date. He said simply, "I like 'em all." He had to be both nervous and furious that he had been put in that position. At the end of the session, God help us, one of us even said, "I think we can almost guarantee that you'll be getting it." He didn't.

It could be argued that we should have stood up for the guy who'd got us there. We didn't. Sorry, Kim! I think we were manipulated to come to a preordained decision. Sure, we were ambitious, but we had stars in our eyes. We weren't about to rock the boat.

Max came to his "audition" and somehow endeared himself by making it clear that he did *not* like most of our songs. Max is a kind of bantamweight Cockney with a generous helping of sarcasm in his conversation. Brilliant in flashes and smart in general, Max was trained as a recording engineer before becoming a producer, which made him much more oriented to the technical aspects than Kim was. A verso, he was not a musician, so it would be a large adjustment for us to work with someone who didn't speak quite the same "muso" language, or who couldn't play an instrument better than we could.

It's hard to overstate the importance of a producer to a young band. In most cases they are so naive about "the big picture" that a producer can steer them down whatever path he pleases. The lucky artist is one who gets a producer who can be sympathetic but also motivate.

I no longer remember what made up our minds. Probably we believed this was one of the hard decisions we had to make to get to that "next level." Go big or go home.

The pre-production went on for a few weeks with Max while we tried out arrangements and wrote additional songs. He brought in a four-track reel-to-reel recorder to make demos of four works in progress, two of which ("Fly On" and "Too Much Too Soon") were held back for many years (until the CD reissue).

The pre-pro was also memorable for an afternoon session in which Max decided to "show [us] how it's done." After yelling at us for being too polite, he reached for my Les Paul. The guitar looked huge on his small frame. "'Ere, lemme show you." He lit a smoke. "A'roight, play tha' again." He then proceeded to pick out some truly horrible "rhythm" guitar over the band's backing whilst slouching like Keith/Ronnie with the ciggy hanging out his yap. Song completed, he handed me back my guitar and snapped, "Do it like that." We were mystified as to what aspect of this performance we should emulate.

Max did get the band's attention, particularly that of lead guitarist Steve Shelski, with his stories of working with guitarist Randy Rhoads. One story in particular that Steve loved was the trick of using a tape loop to rehearse solos. Max had gotten this idea as a response to Rhoads's desire to perform very intricate and difficult solos. To create and then perfect the parts, Randy would have Max, who was the recording engineer, play back the twenty-to-thirty-second piece of multi-track tape over and over again, perhaps a hundred times — great if you're a hyper-focused player on a mission; not so much fun if you have the task of pushing the rewind and play buttons over and over. Recording sessions become exhausting and demoralizing if you get caught up in time-sucking repetitive tasks. It was also bad for the two-inch tape, which, in those pre-digital days, could be degraded and lose sound quality from being run over and over.

Necessity is the mother of invention, yes? Max made a copy of the backing tracks for the solo segment on two-track stereo tape and then spliced and edited the tape into a short loop so that Randy could run it over and over to his heart's content. Max and Ozzy and the band were now free to go for dinner, go for beers, go home to bed if necessary, and then return to record the part on the real master tape after Randy had rehearsed on his own time.

After Steve heard this story, he used the same technique to great effect, creating some really brilliant guitar parts.

Through this time we kept working up more song ideas. "Music of the Night" began as a bass-and-drums groove that Andy and Dave launched into spontaneously, drawing inspiration, I suspect, from some Dio song or another. Steve and I started playing some guitar over it, and a shape emerged. I got a glimmer of a lyric idea and wrote the verses at home that night. For some reason I thought a wordless chorus of singing "Naa-na-na-naa-na-na-naa" would be very evocative of some great but indefinable feeling. The only reason I came up with the words that became one of my favourite choruses is that Max came along and said, "Ya can't go 'na-na-na' for your chorus. Go write us a proper one!"

"Don't Say Make Me" was an amalgam of guitar bits from me, Andy and Steve, to which I added the first "angry" lyric I'd ever composed. Andy or I wrote all the Coney Hatch lyrics, and they were often written from the viewpoint of our utter confusion about getting along with girls. Pete Townshend once said that pop songs were meant to ask questions, not answer them, and I think that describes our efforts fairly.

The lyrics of "First Time for Everything," "Too Far Gone," and "Fallen Angel" are cut from that same cloth of confusion, annoyance, or resignation. Yet in other songs there was a leavening of hopefulness here and there. "To Feel the Feeling Again" is an example. It came from me writing in a little basement apartment in the wee hours, by the light of a Pioneer stereo tuner, about my desire to recapture the feelings of hope and joy that accompany new love or new adventures.

"First Time for Everything," the single from the album, began life as an instrumental demo that Steve Shelski worked up alone in his home studio. The music was almost identical to the final version on the album. He gave me a cassette copy to work with, and with music that good it was almost absurdly easy for me to think of the melody and the lyrics. Who's for a sensitive story of innocence lost, hmm?

The album title, *Outa Hand*, came about when Tom Berry took the band out to the Pink Pearl Chinese restaurant to celebrate the conclusion of the recording sessions. He asked "What are we going to call this thing?" and a near melee ensued as we loudly flung ideas and maybe some foodstuffs around. We were getting nowhere when after one rowdy outburst Tom scolded us, "Hey, let's not get outa hand here!" I seized on that phrase and the others quickly agreed.

In a different sort of radio climate "First Time" might have done well. It was quick out of the gate with ads on about two hundred radio stations in America, but after a few weeks it fizzled and dropped from the charts. It was a similar story for our video at MTV. I didn't really understand how these things worked for a number of years until I read the book *Hit Men*, which details the story of the sleazy promotion methods used in the music business to make a song into a "hit." It's not a pretty picture, but when big money gets involved in things, it's often not quite cricket, is it? You can accuse me of sour grapes if you like for suggesting that it was someone else's fault we didn't get a hit. Of course, I'm not an objective judge of my own music, but I think if "First Time for Everything" had the same kind of promotional money backing it that some of the other hard rock bands of the time received, we might have had a medium-sized national hit. Of course, it could also be argued that if we'd received promo money and had a bigger hit, it would only have happened because of the money. You could say "Coney Hatch sucked," and some people have, but sucking has never been a barrier to success in the music industry. Ever wonder why really bad songs get played so much that they become hits? Someone was getting paid.

As it happened, we were out on tour for *Outa Hand* in the U.S. just as Def Leppard was out touring to promote *Pyromania*, which had been released at about the same time. Def Leppard was on our label, Polygram-Mercury Records (outside Canada). It was most instructive to see the opposite directions in which our two new releases were going as more resources were diverted away from us and toward *Pyromania*. Somebody decided, correctly, that Def Lep's album was a better bet for a home run. That was a smart call by Polygram. Leppard's album was better than ours.

Outa Hand was popular in the UK and other parts of Europe. In North America it was considered by some to be a letdown after the first album.

GIT ON YER BIKES AND RIDE!

It was a coup in 1983 for us to once again land the opening slot with the hottest metal group coming up at the time, this time Iron Maiden. Andy Curran closely followed the news of the New Wave of British Heavy Metal (NWOBHM), and he kept us clued in to the contenders. Once again we didn't know whom we'd be going out with until it happened, but our management must have pulled some strings. We also heard that Maiden liked us and were keen to have us. They're closer to us in age than Priest, and there was a greater connection. A couple of dates out west opening for The Tubes in Winnipeg and Regina had positioned us when the call came to join the Maiden tour, and we had two days to get down to Alpine Valley outside Chicago.

On day one something in our vehicle's engine blew from overheating in the Prairie summer, so we spent a day baking in Portage la Prairie while we waited for repairs. We arrived in Alpine Valley just as our set would have been ending, but after that we got really attuned to life on that tour for months to come.

We had a five-man crew with us: two stage techs, a light guy, a soundman/ tour manager, and our own monitor guy. This was extravagance. To perform a set that would be only thirty-five-ish minutes in America and forty-five-ish in Canada, such a crew was unnecessary. We must have been hemorrhaging money, but somebody in management approved it as an expense against our future earnings. Tour support money would cover the shortfall in the name of promotion, but we'd have to pay it back through earnings. Really, the whole financial end was like running up credit card debt. Everything was based on big expenses now that might possibly be covered by big album sales that might or might not eventually happen. Music was/is a crazy business, a continual gambling habit that makes no business sense unless it works.

With Iron Maiden we made a complete tour of venues large and small, from the Spectrum in Philadelphia to Wings Stadium in Kalamazoo, Michigan (capacity, 1,200) and everything in between — all over the eastern U.S. Lots of fun nights and days. In Cape Cod we played some crazy overstuffed tin-roof shed down on the waterfront. That day we'd gone down to the beach to take our first-ever swim in salt water, and Steve damn near drowned from swallowing the stuff.

After a month or so of one-nighters in the eastern states with almost no nights off, it was back up to the Colisée in Quebec City to start crossing Canada. A promoter in Chicoutimi put up the money to have the tour head up there after Quebec City, and I still have a sweatshirt that the British road crew in their "how-did-we-end-up-here" amazement had made up for the occasion: "Iron Maiden: today Chicoutimi, tomorrow the world!"

The Montreal Forum followed, and then a triumphant hometown show at Canada's Wonderland north of Toronto. I still have people to this day telling me they were at that show and how much they loved it.

Soon we were to play the Winnipeg Arena, where they still kept a portrait of Queen Elizabeth at one end of the ice. On the afternoon of the Winnipeg show we decided to ask Maiden's tour manager, Dickie "der Führer" Bell, if he'd introduce us to the crowd that night. Dickie was like a Monty Python guy to us with his accent and sarcastic manner, and we thought it would be funny or cool if he came out as our emcee to introduce our show. If it worked out, maybe he'd do it every night.

Dickie's eyebrow twitched in response, and then he snorted a kind of laugh, gave us a demonic grin, and slowly said, "Yeh, awright, I'll intre-duce ya." We couldn't help wondering if we'd made a mistake by asking, and when evening came Dickie confirmed our fears. The lights went down over the crowd, which roared in anticipation as he walked out in a spotlight to the centre-stage microphone. He then bellowed, "'Ello, Winnipeg, are you ready to rock?"

Another massive roar ensued.

"Well, too bad, yer gonna have to wait. 'Ere's Boney Snatch.'"

He turned and left a puzzled Winnipeg Arena audience in his wake as we sheepishly stepped forward to overcome.

The tour rolled on to the Saddledome in Calgary and then to Northlands Coliseum. We were starting to feel like this was our circuit now, the level where we were meant to be. We knew we hadn't built this funhouse, but we sure felt at home inside it.

Without reaching the Pacific, we dipped down into the States again to places like North Dakota and Nebraska. On most of our U.S. tour the new/old group Fastway was on middle of the bill. "Fast Eddie" Clarke was the guitarist and leader, and he'd formed Fastway after leaving Motörhead. I say "new/old" because even though the band was less than a year old, it was three-fourths composed of wily veterans Clarke, Jerry Shirley of Humble Pie on drums, and bassist Charlie McCracken from Rory Gallagher's band Taste. Standing in front of these stalwarts to sing was big-voiced newcomer Davey King. We got along with Fastway great for the most part, and I liked the scrawny Irish lad King personally.

The only cloud to mar the blue sky of playing with Fastway came in the form of an ill-judged comment by Steve Shelski. Fast Eddie had taken up with a stern German lady named Barbara, who was recently separated or divorced from renowned record producer Roy Thomas Baker (Queen, Journey, etc.). Barbara was travelling with the tour for some weeks, and Steve, after chatting her up over a few drinks at some backstage party, flippantly lipped off to her that Roy T-B was a crap producer or couldn't produce a kid's birthday party or something. Barbara lost her mind over this dissing and stormed off to demand that Eddie must now come and punch out our Steve's lights in retribution. Meantime, Steve vanished from the scene, and so when Eddie turned up, all hot and bothered to champion his lady's cause, he had only Andy and me to huff and puff at. Eddie turned out to be a reluctant champion, and we soon saw that he was only doing his obligatory bit to keep peace in the bedroom.

I felt bad for the man and thought, not for the first time, that it can be a disruptive influence to have wives or girlfriends on rock tours, and often not for the reasons you'd expect. Andy and I persuaded Steve that he'd better go and apologize to somebody, either Fast Eddie or Barbara. I don't recall if the peace offering was received gracefully.

One minor incident on that tour confirmed my long-held doubts about the band KISS and any claims to coolness or legitimacy that their apologists always make. There are probably KISS Army members reading this, waving the flag or carrying the card in their wallet since they were teenagers. A great number of males born between 1960 and 1970 took their allegiance to KISS very seriously. I was annoyed and unconvinced by their act. They didn't play or sing or write very well, certainly not up the level of The Beatles, the Stones, Creedence, Zeppelin, etc. — the groups on whose music I'd been nurtured. Lame, unskilled posers were what they looked and sounded like to me, playing bubblegum rock music. I know, harsh. I thought they were witless cartoon characters, cynically pandering to the lowest common denominator. It was years before I realized that was the secret of their huge success. The approbation of any KISS Army members who might read this likely awaits me.

Anyway, in 1983 we were playing at the Nassau County Coliseum on Long Island. Our big-time manager and big-time agent were visiting us backstage. The "great" Paul Stanley swept in with a babe on his arm. Our poor Andy was a KISS fan and was very excited. Paul, though, proceeded to make conversation with the business moguls while completely ignoring us. To add to the insult, he also gobbled up a generous portion of our food and beer. After almost a half hour he left without even a glance in the direction of Coney Hatch, his hosts. Manners, please, Paul! We may have been nobodies to you, but you were not to some of us. I was, and I remain, unimpressed.

OLD ROAD DOGS

Just as it's difficult to overstate the importance of a producer to a young band, it's similarly vital to have an experienced road crew on the job once the record's done and it's time to go on tour. Young bands usually get a buddy from high school or a neighbour who's always hanging around rehearsals, or someone's brother who's up for a lark, to jump in the van with them and roadie. Back in the '80s the job usually meant helping with the driving, setting up and tearing down the gear, and standing out front during the show at the soundboard, twiddling knobs. Sometimes the guy with the best stereo in the neighbourhood got asked to do sound because he must know how it all works, right? As you can imagine, there were dubious results from hiring low-wage novices to run the technical part. Like all bands we had to have someone to help us, but we were on starvation wages ourselves.

I've never been able to figure out why people would become roadies (or techs, more respectfully) as a career, except that they like the nomadic lifestyle and the perceived glamour. The reward you get for doing well is harder work, longer hours, and being away from home and your loved ones for extended periods. Wait, that sounds just like being a successful musician! The difference is that the musicians are doing it for the acclaim, the creative outlet, and the potential rewards for their art. The road crew does the grunt work. There is no show without their effort. To be on a road crew, you have to like hard work. You also have to have a love of music, or for the band you're working for, or maybe require a place to hide from the law — we had all of those — to stick with the difficult life of roadie-ing.

Techs aren't always treated very well, but good ones are worth their weight in gold. They can get burned out fairly quickly, and so it's a high-turnover job. From 1981 to 1985 Coney Hatch employed more than twenty-five crew. Imagine any small business going through that many employees over a five-year period. Yet it's a fact that even with an almost bewildering variety of names and faces, I can summon up instantly a personal memory of every one of those men.

It's no doubt something to do with the intensity of the touring experience that events are seared deep into the memory. Perhaps that intensity is another reason why road crew and musicians alike put up with conditions most people would find intolerable, just to feel that feeling again. You work together so closely and under conditions of such intensity that the bonds you form are very close and last forever, like the ones you see with the old-time hockey players who have been through the sporting wars together. I feel gratitude for, and a bond with, those crew guys who have made it their job to get me to the stage or make me sound and look good each night.

As with any other workplace, things go on behind the scenes that the bosses never know about. Lorne "Sluggo" Brown shared a story with me, many years after the fact, about a return to Canada from the U.S., which he'd conducted with our soundman Sonic Smith. A stash of dope was hidden among the amps and road cases by another crew guy who'd flown home, hoping to pick up his stash once they'd smuggled it safely, albeit unwittingly, through the customs officials. Only the unwillingness of the drug-sniffing dog to jump up in the truck saved them from being arrested.

* * *

An experienced road manager is an essential component of successful touring. There are countless details to be organized and personalities to be managed. As with any other profession, you get good tour managers, mediocre ones, and then the ones who are in way over their heads. The one who had the biggest impact on us and who was the best fit was Neil McDermott. Although he could condescend to us or treat us like kids, Neil had the right combination of roots and experience to shepherd us along.

Late in the Maiden tour, after thirty-some shows, we were scheduled to play in Saskatoon. Unfortunately, Maiden drummer Nicko McBrain had in the previous days somehow "stabbed his forearm accidentally with a pencil." That's what he said. This had developed quickly into blood poisoning, and drumming was now out of the question. Any physical exertion would speed the blood poisoning to his heart via the artery, with potentially fatal results. This affliction was diagnosed the night before the show, and so northern Saskatchewan metal fans were denied their Iron Maiden wallop.

Into the breach stepped our resourceful tour manager Neil. He'd already built a strong bond with Maiden, which he was keen to cement. The show being suddenly cancelled meant there was a void in the plans of many Saskatooners. Neil decided to offer Coney Hatch to the local rock bar, the A-4, for a special appearance. It was agreed that we would play for a small fee plus a bar tab for our guests. We'd invite the band and crew from Iron Maiden as our guests. The A-4 owner was excited about the prestige this would bring, especially since he wouldn't have to put up any cash. He put the word out on radio and on the street, and by 9 p.m. there was a packed house. We used the amps and drums from a band that was already set up so that our crew could have the night off, and thus equipped, we played our Coney Hatch show. The Maiden guys, band and crew, did come out and were glad to also have a night off and a change in the routine. Bruce Dickinson got up with us to sing "Devil's Deck" with Steve Harris on bass, and we backed Adrian Smith doing Joe Walsh's "Rocky Mountain Way."

The party was in full swing when the bar owner came to Neil in a state of agitation. He hadn't reckoned on the drinking prowess of about thirty mostly British musicians and crew and was crying poor at the way they were running up our tab. Neil basically told him that a deal's a deal, and that he wasn't prepared to insult our friends by telling them they were cut off. I believe he hinted that it could get ugly if the drinks stopped. The poor owner of the A-4 was left to bitterly comply for another hour or two until someone decided that the party should move locations. I also believe that we kicked our small fee back in to redress a portion of his "losses."

I still meet people out west who talk fondly about that night.

* * *

When you're always highway travelling, you're bound to cross paths with the law eventually. On one occasion we were crossing Ohio in convoy, the motor home and the equipment van. I was driving the equipment van that day, as I often did, just to get away from the band and change things up for a bit. Jon Dalby, the guitar tech, was riding shotgun. Neil was at the wheel of the motor home, and he must have had a lead foot going because we lost sight of it before long. I decided to goose the cube van a little to catch up, and after about ten minutes we went through a speed trap. The state trooper came up to the window and asked for my licence.

"What's your big hurry today?" he asked.

I swear to God, I thought he might let me off the ticket if I told him the truth.

"We're part of a band on tour, and our other vehicle got going faster than us. They took off way ahead, and I was speeding to try to catch them. We need to arrive at the show together."

"Mm-hmm. Are they from Ontario too?"

"That's right, sir. We're all from out of state."

I hoped that might sound folksy and endearing.

"Wait here a minute."

I still had hope that I might escape with a warning.

He returned surprisingly quickly with a speeding ticket for doing seventy miles per hour in a fifty-five zone. He collected cash on the spot then jumped back in his car and sped off up the interstate. I figured he had to get to the coffee shop and so gave the incident no more thought (aside from the dent to my paycheque) until I saw Neil at the gig.

"What did you tell the police?" he demanded angrily.

Turns out the wily Ohio state trooper had used my flimsy excuse as grounds to apprehend the other speeding vehicle from Ontario a few miles up the road. Oops.

* * *

Neil was a firecracker who was always thinking of ways to keep things exciting. Our final show with Iron Maiden was at the Kiel Center in St. Louis, once Nicko's health had been restored. Tour was ending for everyone, so it was already expected to be eventful. It's traditional to plan onstage pranks or gags for the last night. We'd heard that Iron Maiden had cream-pied the opening acts onstage on another tour. Andy and Steve thought it would be a sassy turnabout to get out on the stage and pie the Iron Maiden guys in the middle of *their* show. Unfortunately, they decided it would be even "funnier" if there were cat food mixed in with the whipped cream. That afternoon there was a trip to procure these supplies, which were hidden in our wardrobe trunk until the proper time for their deployment. Personally, I was dubious about the cat food part; I felt that might be crossing the line of good sportsmanship, and the Iron ones could get angry. I spoke my misgivings and then surrendered to the universe.

Neil, for reasons that I leave the reader to judge, decided to secretly visit Iron Maiden in their dressing room and reveal the secret. He next led them to the trunk where the ingredients were stored. The plan was turned back on us, and midway through our opening set the Maiden men appeared from nowhere, each bearing two whipped cream/cat food pies. Poor Dave Ketchum, an easy mark sitting at the drums, had one pie in his face and another stuck on the back of his head by Nicko. Andy and Steve both gamely tried to escape, but they couldn't deke out Steve Harris and Davey Murray. Adrian Smith approached me hesitantly, and with adrenaline on my side I dodged this way and that on his first four or five attempts to hit me. It did suddenly dawn on me that I didn't want Adrian to look clumsy or even fall down in front of the audience while trying to pie me. I shrugged, surrendered, and stood still. Adrian mercifully planted his pies on my chest, where they dripped down my shirt. Through this chaos we had continued to play "No Sleep Tonight." I have a cassette tape of the shambles that resounded as we were under attack.

Somehow Neil escaped anything more than mild censure from us over this treachery. He was laughing his head off as we came offstage and insisted that he'd done the right thing. It could have been bad for us, he said, if we'd "pied" them in that way. Maybe. Turncoat? Yeah, maybe.

I think he escaped censure because the guys were so keen on the next gag that he had come up with, something for the Iron Maiden show. Neil bore a passing resemblance at that time to Bruce Dickinson, the Maiden singer. This was the springboard to the idea behind his gag.

Steve Shelski and Dave Ketchum from our band bore a resemblance respectively to Maiden guitarists Adrian Smith and Dave Murray. Andy had become close friends with Steve Harris, his bass counterpart in Iron Maiden. The gag idea was this: Neil persuaded the Iron Maiden wardrobe girl to let him and the other doppelgängers into the dressing room while her boys were onstage. Each Coney dressed in their corresponding Maiden guy's alternate stage outfit. At a set point in the show (mid-song in "The Trooper," I think) our guys ran out on the stage to stand next to their doubles. Neil strutted beside Bruce, hamming it up and imitating Bruce's expansive stage gestures. The other Coneys were holding their doubles' spare guitars and standing next to them, miming. It was pretty funny, and I wish I had a picture of the moment. The Iron men were good sports about the whole thing, and it got a great reaction from the crowd. Just fun, something special that obviously doesn't happen every night, and which that night's audience was lucky enough to see.

FRICTION

Our run as a recording act led to three albums released worldwide, with videos and tours to accompany them, but toward the end the thrills were becoming fewer. We were learning that being a Canadian rock star didn't always mean you could even pay your bills. The search for the missing break-through ingredient led us to question ourselves and to start reconsidering our roles. A lesson that I took away from being in Coney Hatch was that when everyone's equal, there's no leader. That can work for a mature or wise bunch, but we needed direction. The title of our third album, *Friction*, was unfortunately all too apt. It was the time when we felt the greatest pressure while at the same time all our relationships and methods were in flux. That pressure to succeed weighed us down and worsened built-in conflicts. For instance, there was more competition than ever between Andy and me for the lead singer role, and we were unable to sort it out ourselves by choosing what was best for the band.

A new complication, and an unanticipated result of our parting ways with drummer Dave "Thumper" Ketchum, was the loss of his steadying influence on our group dynamic. That change was one of my greatest career regrets. I suppose we can all act like goofs on the road to wisdom. In that case a lack of wisdom led us to cast our drummer overboard. It's been done by many bands; the drummer gets scapegoated for the band's shortcomings. Dave took the fall for our increasing fear that we were "blowing it." The truth is, when a band is not succeeding, it's never because of how the drummer hits his drums.

I'll quote Carlos Santana, speaking to *MOJO* magazine in 2005 about the breakup of the first Santana: "We didn't know better; one minute you're in high school, the next minute you're on the same stage as Sly Stone and Jimi Hendrix. So what happens is the same thing that happens to most bands — excess, drugs, and not sleeping and not having the wisdom or the knowledge or the common sense to put things in perspective." Dave had played a critical balancing role in the energy of the band; with his ouster things started going awry.

Although I apparently got blamed for Dave's axing, it was our collective folly. However, I will apologize on behalf of all of us now, here in my book. Sorry about that, Dave. I'm very glad you had it in your heart to come back in with us and have many fun times playing together since then.

*** *** ***

After a process of holding open auditions to replace Thumper, Barry Connors was selected to hit the drums. Barry brought with him a near-pathological desire to become a "star" at any cost. Once inside our camp, he began to apply pressure on us to succeed, frequently chirping, "This next album is make-or-break time. If we don't make it big by our third album, we're dead. We'll get dropped by the label. We'll have failed," etc. I guess Barry thought he was helping us take it seriously. I was pretty serious already.

I don't mind feeling pressure to produce; in the right measure it's helpful for focusing one's attention. That negative pressure, however, from an insider who was supposed to be part of the solution, was like having a fifth column sapping our little nation's equanimity.

For two years we'd been trying to find our way back onto the rocket ride we'd experienced during our debut, and for those two years we'd been instead dogged by feelings of letting people down. We hadn't reached the expected target.

At that age, then twenty-five, a couple of years felt like half my life, and I just wanted the pressure to stop. To worsen things, I was bedevilled by the issues that often accompany marrying young and too hastily. When I was twenty-three, just as things were taking off, I had rushed into wedlock as, and with, a notably unprepared partner. The reason for my haste is not clear now, but I think I needed to feel I had a home and to feel loved.

I was travelling a lot, completely focused on my career to the exclusion of almost all else and expecting that would be understood. That view was not shared; other priorities were important to my wife, and she was entitled to them. My bride, Stella, was a French-Moroccan girl and hot-tempered, something I'd never encountered. These factors were not helpful in achieving successful matrimony. The strain was telling on all aspects of my life.

The process of creating our third album was lengthy and arduous. Many songs were written and demoed. Pre-production began while we were still playing shows through 1984 to make our small paycheques. Several potential producers were brought in to look us over, including Eddie Kramer, John Ryan, Aldo Nova, and Lance Quinn. For various reasons they didn't work out. Poor Aldo was set up for a fall by the guy running Anthem Records at the time, Val Azzoli. Aldo had producing ambitions and wanted very much to get the gig for our next album. Val told him, sure, I'll set you up for a day with the band and we'll see how it goes. For some reason Val told us a different story: that his friend Aldo was coming in to co-write with us. We were surprised and put off when Aldo started acting like a producer with our existing ideas instead of helping us create new ones. The day fizzled to an unsatisfactory conclusion of mutual incomprehension. As I drove Aldo back to the office, we discussed the day's events and realized how we'd both been played. Aldo's hot Italian temper kicked in, and my last sighting of the Nova was him bolting up the back stairs of Anthem Records to tear a strip off his "friend" Val. People lie in the record business all the time.

Lance Quinn actually spent a week with us on pre-production, kicking the tires on our songs. He drove his motorcycle up from his home in Philadelphia to make a fun road trip out of it. At the end of that week he determined that we weren't ready to make a record and motored back to Philly to take another job. He told us to call him when we were ready. It was now June and we were feeling the anxiety of these delays in getting a new album off the ground. Desperate measures were called for. Re-enter Max Norman.

Our label hadn't wanted to bring Max in again after the *Outa Hand* results; we in turn were not completely thrilled by the prospect of again bearing his harsh manner. We are all nice guys who didn't harsh back. However, he needed a gig. Max had just been let go from the Ozzy Osbourne *Bark at the Moon* sessions. His version of the story was that he had failed to control the spiralling costs of Ozzy's cocaine, er, *album* budget, and so wore the blame. That's as may be; for our purposes it became a case of "better the devil you know." We had to have someone in place to get us going. The label sent him a cassette of our demos to ponder, a deal was made for Max's services and he was shortly on a plane from England.

I met Max at the airport with Andy. The first words out of his mouth were not, "Hello, chaps. Lovely to see you again." No, they were directed at me: "Ya can't write a song abou' a feck-ing *lobster*!" And so it began.

(One of the songs on the demo tape sent to Max was "The Lobster Quadrille," in which I'd incorporated the poem of the same name from Lewis Carroll plus additional lyrics written by me. At the time I'd thought it clever and unusual. No doubt it was, but Max was probably right. It didn't rock. One of the chastisements I later received from Max, albeit well-intended, was, "The trouble with you, Carl, is you're *too fucking clevah*. You're too smart for your own good." "Lobster Quadrille" eventually became "He's a Champion," which I wrote about Muhammad Ali. No lobster, him.)

Much hard work lay before us, and there were some difficult moments. Max pushed us hard to finish a slate of proper rock songs, and then we moved camp to Le Studio at Morin Heights in Quebec. Normally that place would have been out of our price range, but they'd had a cancellation and offered us a deep discount. There was a nice old *habitant* farmhouse, with staff, for us all to live in for the summer. At the other end of a small lake lay the studio. It was an idyllic environment for a season of focused creative work.

Financially, we were up against it. The budget only allowed us to receive a hundred bucks a week each as a salary, and there was no other source of income. We only got paid when we played. The longer the album took to complete, the broker we got. Even with that additional pressure we couldn't go any faster. As summer ended, we still weren't done after about eight weeks of toil. In the waning days of summer Andy had a couple of hard pills to swallow. On one session he was straining with might and main to deliver a vocal performance that would meet Max's standards. At the start of the guitar solo Max asked Andy to deliver a big scream to add to the excitement. This was not one of the normal vocal tricks Andy relied upon, but he agreed to try. When the moment came, Andy took a deep breath and gave it his all. "Aahhhhhh!" was what came out. Max instantly stopped the tape and yelled down the control room mike, "No, not like that! I asked you for a big rock scream, not like someone just stepped on yer toe, ya prannit!"

("Prannit" was one of a number of terms of roughhouse encouragement that Max used to motivate us. We were never quite sure of the meaning but could judge by the context that they weren't compliments.)

Andy had been pushing hard to be lead vocalist on some of the songs, but Max, after giving him a chance to try, pulled him off the job. In fact, this happened on two or three songs; I can't quite recall. Fact is, I was fed up with Max and ready to head for home while Andy finished up his lead vocals. I was in my room packing when Andy made the call from the studio. Not pleased or delighted to hear the news that I'd have to stay longer and do more work with Max, I also heard my friend's pain and disappointment. That was how I ended up singing all the songs but one on *Friction*.

Max broke camp to fly to Japan to produce Loudness, a Japanese heavy rock group similar to us and to lots of other bands of the day. He'd made the Japan commitment prior to taking our job, so our album had to linger uncompleted for a few months.

With some vocal overdubs left to do and also a few other guitar and percussion parts, we convinced the label to let Steve and me go back to Le Studio for a week prior to Max's scheduled return. The idea was to save time so Max could just get straight to the mixing job. I had lots of vocal harmony ideas, some guitar fills, and arrangement things I wanted to add. We brought Freddy Curci, the singer of Sheriff and later Alias, along for a few days to add some really high vocal harmonies that I couldn't reach, and he was superb. At the end of the final day Steve Shelski and I got him over to the house for some drinks and jamming. We got around the piano and Fred asked to do "House of the Rising Sun" and some other gruff tunes. I launched into my equally gruff piano solo, and my hand somehow became a piano-pounding blur (it wasn't just the drinks). No point to the story, just a fun memory.

That week of working at Le Studio with their staff engineer, Paul Northfield, was very productive, confidence-building, and a lot of fun. What was confidence-sapping and not a lot of fun was the return of Max. He'd been informed that we were doing this work to prepare the album for his return, but he sure didn't seem happy about it. Many pieces of our good new work were disparaged and even erased as we played him what we'd done. It was as if he couldn't like anything that had been done without his input. It was not a pleasure to be in on the ensuing mix days, and I beat a grumbling retreat from Max Norman for the second time that year.

Pardners: me with Andy Curran, Toronto, 1985. The next twenty-five years we played together in a lot more hockey games than gigs.

Over the years we usually let the bad memories fade into the background and remember the nice things. Max was abrasive and even unpleasant to our delicate muso sensibilities, but I understand better now what he was doing. It would have been beyond us to produce ourselves, and competing agendas at work within the band complicated the producer's job. Where other producers threw up their hands and said, "Nah, too much work," Max took on the challenge because he felt he could herd our cats' collective with the right mix of push and pull. He had a vision of what we could create if he could get us all on the same page and buying into a shared vision. That wasn't easy, and I wouldn't have wanted the job. Even so, I still use "Shu'-UPP, Cahl!" to get a laugh of recognition from Andy.

WHY I QUIT CONEYING UP

In a climate of increasing uncertainty, I eventually lost perspective and cracked under the mostly self-imposed pressure. It seemed like we'd been under the gun forever, when it had really only been a couple of years.

What Coney Hatch created with our third album, *Friction*, after much work, turmoil, sacrifice, and several false starts, was a more polished sound. That really captured the attention of European rock fans. Unfortunately, the new sound didn't resonate with our international label, Polygram-Mercury. We made a video in England for presumed MTV play and prepared to hit the road. The album was unleashed upon the world in February 1985, and we waited for things to fall into place as they had for our first two albums, with the radio play, major tours, promo hype, etc., only this time ... they didn't. Our expected U.S. tour was delayed by booking agent and record label politics, and no headlining act was emerging for us to sign on with. This played upon our latent fears. We'd spent more money than ever, taken longer than ever, worked harder than ever. *Friction* had to carry us over the top! Yeesh, talk about yer pressure. It wasn't helpful.

Rather than sit in limbo waiting for America to call, we embarked on a "grassroots tour" across Canada to get something going. The idea was to build up our fan base in the smaller venues and towns, where we hadn't played much in the last three years because we had always gone through western

Canada on the big arena tours. Shows were poorly promoted and attendance ran hot and cold. Our record company promo reps, whose job it was to make the world care about the new Coney Hatch album, always seemed to have either bad news or no news. In fact, the Winnipeg Capitol-EMI rep, "Soupy" Campbell, who'd done good promo there for our first two albums, met us this time with the statement, "I haven't really been around town to see about how your record's doing. Have you guys heard anything?"

Troubling signs of indifference in our home territory began to pile up. "Poor Coney Hatch," wrote a Canadian music magazine about our new album; "they watch as exciting new bands like Platinum Blonde shoot past them on the charts...."

Radio play was more difficult to obtain this time out in the anti-heavy-metal political backlash of the era, and our expensively produced video was only getting limited airings. We returned home from our disappointing spring 1985 grassroots tour a bit downcast, and with our hopes more than ever pinned on that big American market breakthrough.

A U.S. tour was finally offered, third on the bill to Krokus and Accept. It wasn't on the grand scale of our previous American support tours, but it was something. This would take us to new places, albeit smaller halls than usual, and we were determined to make the most of it. A twenty-six-hour drive from Toronto to Texas to join the tour set the tone for the difficult days to come. In Austin we met Ted Mellencamp, the Polygram-Mercury Records rep for Texas. Ted was the spitting image of his brother John (Cougar) Mellencamp, and in fact had for some years worked as John's tour manager. It would appear that Ted was at times volatile in the role of tour manager and could make things a bit hot for John through his behaviour on behalf of his bro. When this was eventually deemed an insurmountable problem, Ted was found a safe sinecure as a record rep. This was happily explained to me by Ted himself. He was a pretty good guy, and we got on well personally as he attended our various Texas shows in his role as our record rep. At some point in the week, though, Ted shared a discouraging story.

"Y'know, Carl," began Ted in his Indiana drawl, "I like your record, but you guys are on a real steep climb down here."

"I know that, but so's everyone," I replied.

"It ain't what you think," Ted replied. "Let me tell you a story. A couple of months ago we had the big annual record company conference in Atlanta, and Gunther, the president of the company, came over from Germany. We were talking about marketing plans for the year and all that, and they weren't saying anything about you guys or a few other bands that I like. I got up at the meeting and asked him, 'What about Coney Hatch or some of those other young bands we have signed? They have good new albums. Why aren't we putting any promo money into them?' Gunther turned to me and said in that German accent, 'Be-causs, Ted, ve haff uzzah priorities!'"

Ted paused for a second and then said, "I knew right then you guys were sunk."

That explained a lot. Since our album release and our subsequent arrival in America, radio play had been minimal, interview requests were sparse, and people often seemed surprised to see us. It began to appear that our management had gotten us onto this tour as a last-ditch measure, hoping for a miracle.

On one of the days following Ted's revelation, I was a passenger in the band motor home, having a little siesta in the hot afternoon as we rolled across the Texas desert. I had a vivid dream in which a great giant was sleeping flat-out on the ground, looking a bit like the one in Bugs Bunny's "Jack and the Beanstalk." He was snoring away, fast asleep, and we four Coney Hatch guys were flies buzzing around his face, saying "Bzzz, please pay attention! Bzzz, please promote us! Pleeease helllp us!" in annoying little fly voices. The giant would grunt about his disturbed sleep and sweep us away from his face with an outstretched hand before returning to slumber. We'd then resume buzzing around and pestering again, "Pleease...." I roused myself from my own nap and thought long about this dream.

The seeming futility of our efforts and dashing of our hopes, merely by the indifference of our record company, was an obstacle we couldn't have foreseen and were powerless to change. As our tour progressed, the shaky beginning turned into a full-on defeat. Days when we weren't playing with the headliner tour were filled in with some truly disheartening gigs. An example was the show our U.S. agent booked for us in Salt Lake City as a "routing date." It had become obvious by then that we were just being thrown any old show to make it appear that an effort was being made. We arrived in late afternoon at a place called the Carrot Snapper. I am not kidding when I tell you that the doorway to this hole-in-the-wall bar was a painted depiction of Yosemite Sam, of Bugs Bunny fame (see giant dream above), with his guns drawn to blast the varmint. You entered the Carrot Snapper by walking through Yosemite Sam. Once inside, we found that our crew had arrived earlier only to find a tiny sound system, inadequate to making us heard above the drums and guitars, and a stage that was barely big enough to hold the drums. For this big tour we had splurged to hire one of the top stage-lighting men in Canada, Steve "Killer" Hill, and the lighting rig available on this night consisted of two pink hundred-watt floodlights with an on/off switch. We turned our stage monitor speakers around to point at the audience to make the sound system louder. Andy Curran told me later that he had gone for a pre-show walk in the streets, depressed at how bad things were becoming. That mood lasted until he came across a guy in a wheelchair who'd had both legs amputated but was selling pencils with a big smile. Andy perked right up, realizing things weren't so bad for us from that sobering perspective.

The final humiliation came when we arrived to play our show. Our dressing room was by day a storage room for the food tins and restaurant supplies. It happened that we needed to share this already tight space amid the pickle jars and pie fillings with our opening band. They complained as they changed post-show from their sweaty stage clothes. "Man, what are you guys doing *here*? When we were asked to open for Coney Hatch we were excited. We thought it would be at the Salt Palace or someplace big. Geez, we turn down gigs like this and we're just locals." We replied dispiritedly that it really hadn't been in our plans either.

There were enough of those nights to make it obvious that our big play for Coney Hatch success with *Friction* was not trending toward success. As the days tottered by I found our situation increasingly stressful and disappointing. Our record company guy at home, Val Azzoli, was nowhere to be found when we were urgently calling home to see what could be done to help us. Val had gone off on holiday with Geddy Lee to watch Blue Jays baseball spring training in Florida; Val was a skilled career-climber. I think he'd assessed that Coney Hatch would not do his career much good, so he was n/a when we were in trouble.

A powerful feeling took hold of me at this time, a sense of what it meant to be ignored. As a result, for a long time I made it a guiding principle never to accept this treatment.

My relationship with the other guys grew more strained than ever. We didn't make much of a paycheque, and I needed every penny of my weekly wage to keep an apartment and monthly bills paid. Steve and Andy still lived with their parents, and they, along with Barry Connors, had credit cards, something I couldn't afford. That spring the U.S. airlines were engaged in a price war, so Steve, Andy, and Barry often elected to pull out their credit cards and book flights to the next city, like the rock stars we were, rather than go through the nasty drive with the vehicles and road crew. It either didn't occur to them that I was unable to join "the band" for this travel option, or they didn't care. As a result I certainly *was* there, along with our road crew, for every mile of every long drive. In fact, our vehicles couldn't have gotten there if I hadn't taken on much of the driving. Now, it was one thing for me to drive as I had in the past, with the band at least sharing the journey together. It was quite another feeling to have them fly ahead to enjoy the hotel, the pool, the sights, and the comfort without me.

What made this really stick in my craw was the fact that just before the release of *Friction*, when we were settling the songwriting credits (and thus the royalty shares), I had made the gesture to Steve and Andy of sharing all the credits on the album with them equally, as a three-way split. My real share was a majority of the writing, but I chose to give that up. With so much at stake for our combined futures, I decided we should all, after the work and sacrifice we'd shared, have the same amount to gain or lose — stand together and succeed equally together. Steve had lauded this as "a noble gesture," and Andy had also seen the point of it. I couldn't help feeling that my "noble gesture" was now being forgotten. This only stopped at the end of the tour, when I confronted them and said something unhappy about it. We were facing a forty-eight-hour drive from San Francisco to Milwaukee in slow-moving vehicles, and the band was talking about flying ahead again. The three credit cards stayed in their wallets that time.

With these factors in play, I felt disaster overtaking us, as we all must have felt in our different ways. We gave name to the fear and talked and talked about it, but we couldn't believe it. We had to still continue putting out a convincing and powerful rock show in the hope that somehow we'd prevail.

The breaking point came after a show in Los Angeles near the end of that tour. I finally cracked under the strain and made a spectacle of myself. It was a display meant to demonstrate my defiant new stance that I would *not* tolerate being ignored any longer.

On the night in question we were playing the L.A. Palladium with Accept and Rough Cutt, an L.A. band that had replaced Krokus for the California dates. Rough Cutt were managed by Wendy Dio, the wife of heavy metal singing star Ronnie James Dio, and this Palladium show was an L.A. showcase for that band. A dressing room area had been improvised in a banquet hall at the front of the Palladium, to be shared by Coney Hatch and Rough Cutt. Dividing our side from theirs, a clothesline ran diagonally across the room with hanging bedsheets clothespinned to it. At first it seemed hokey enough to be kind of funny, just more of what we'd been experiencing on this goofy tour. Then, post-show, it became clear that a large music-biz party was under way on the Rough Cutt side of the sheets (it seems laughable just to write that), to which our band was pointedly *not* invited. On our side of the barrier I sat alone, occasionally chatting with road crew as they came and went, but mostly just glowering by myself. We had no visitors, our record company had sent no reps to the show, and we had no friends. Oh, how I glowered when people from the Rough Cutt party started to slip through the bedsheets to help themselves to our food and beer. Our tour manager, Ross Tuskey, came along to talk to me at some point, and he could see that I wasn't very happy. Ross had to leave me alone and went to attend to business. I sat there and brooded until eventually one of the party people poking into our dressing room treated me like *I* was the intruder. That pushed me over the edge. Making my way into the party side of the room, my sole mission was to raise a ruckus and force people to notice me.

With an unpleasant forced smile I engaged the first people I met, a group of musicians on a couch, in an intentionally bizarre conversation. Suddenly I picked up a huge bowl of peanuts and heaved the contents into the air, showering everyone nearby with them (including Viv Campbell, the guitarist who has since joined Def Leppard, who was pleasant and inoffensive and didn't deserve a peanut shower). I walked away and left musos sputtering in my wake. Next I loudly sang a filthy limerick to the startled assembly, and then I spotted Dio chatting with somebody across the room. The "I will not be ignored" devil was at this point shouting, not just whispering. There was an ice bucket with drink cans on the floor, so I fished cans out one by one and started throwing them — hard — at the wall, with that whip-arm motion that fastball pitchers use. The cans flew behind Dio's back to crash loudly against the wall, first one, then another, then another. Poor Ronnie tried to ignore me at first, maybe not wishing to look unsettled. After the third flying icy can Ronnie excused himself as I reached for the next can with a set, closed expression. At that point Dio's large bodyguard stepped forward and yelled, "Hey! What are you doing? You're trying to kill my boss!"

I replied calmly (and disingenuously), "No, no, I'm just practising my pitching, not trying to hurt anyone."

"F**k that. You're trying to kill my boss and I'm going to f**k you up!"

He stepped forward menacingly, his huge fists raised. Just then wise Ross Tuskey, hearing the commotion, rushed in and talked the giant into standing down and letting me go.

Maybe to all those present the event soon became the story of how some maniac got loose at a party in the Palladium. Maybe, with any luck, it was soon forgotten. For my part, I felt powerfully ashamed once Ross calmed me down on our side of the clothesline.

On a five-mile midnight walk through Hollywood back to my hotel, I played the evening's events back in my mind. I said to myself, "I hate the word 'asshole,' and I'm not an asshole, but I acted like one tonight. The stress is twisting me and changing me." By the time I reached the hotel I'd decided I had to get out of the band and save my self-respect. I stayed up all night, vibrating, and called Toronto at 7 a.m. to start the arrangements for my departure.

With the passage of time and gaining of experience I can see now how back then I might have been tough to take. The Coney guys probably just wanted to have rock 'n' roll fun, away from Dixon the party pooper. My own belief system was so fixed on doing the right thing, "keeping it together," and dedicating myself to being great, that it may have been almost intolerable at times to be around me. I can get pretty overpowering when I fixate, and I'm sure I seemed sanctimonious and just not much fun at such times. I simply didn't know how to be any other way. I thought I was doing a good thing because "somebody has to be serious around here." Hoo boy, I could have done with some lightening up.

A band is not designed to last a long time. A true band is an impossible four-way marriage, and the strains eventually get to people. As so often happens when you're busy doing the work, all we felt after a while was constant pressure: "Do more, sell more, be bigger! It's still not enough!" We would gladly have complied, too, if someone had given us a little proper direction. Some bands are savvy enough or schooled enough or well-managed enough to turn the game to their advantage. That wasn't us, or it wasn't me at least. All we had was music training and an eagerness to please. It wasn't enough to carry us through the fire.

Coney Hatch had more impact than we realized at the time. I can't say that we were "ripped off" in the style of the cruel music biz stories we've all heard. I can say that we were neglected in some important ways and not given the kind of steadying big-picture guidance that would have helped us rise above our childish concerns. But Coney Hatch got a fair shot. After that, it's what you do with it. By the end, my time with the band had been just under five years. Despite the frustrations, the experience was an incredible education and also, in retrospect, the greatest confidence-builder possible. It convinced me that, yes, I belong doing this. At the time, though, my biggest thought was often *There's something about all this that I don't quite get.*

HIGHLIGHT REEL

As the years have gone by, my happiest lingering memories of Coney Hatch have tended to be of behind-the-scenes, funny, or private moments. Maybe I assume the public moments are already known to lots of folks, but people have reminded me recently that they want to hear more about the big milestone events and how it felt to me to be in the middle of them. Those moments are the rewards that a performer can cling to forever after enduring the difficult and stressful times.

There have been so many of these milestones. The sheer exhilaration of finding out that Kim Mitchell was interested in working with us kept me up half that night, speculating, marvelling, and giggling to myself. It was like we'd bridged the gap from the wilderness to an enchanted domain in one step. We were in awe that a guy who was so famous and experienced would even talk to us, let alone help with our music. It was amazing to discover that he was mostly a regular guy, just like us. He had taken his great musical ability and combined it with a fierce drive to stand out from the crowd. Kim reached down and lifted us up to the world he inhabited. It was the single biggest step I've ever taken, and I owe him.

Playing Exhibition Stadium (the CNE) in Toronto was a sky-high thrill in spite of the sound problems. As I performed, I knew I'd been there to watch shows on that stage by Bill Cosby, The Guess Who, Chicago, and Peter Frampton, and now I was a part of that history.

In fact, so many of the famed concert facilities I'd only heard of before Coney Hatch became an expected part of our "circuit." Maple Leaf Gardens, the Philadelphia Spectrum, Northlands Coliseum in Edmonton, and the Cap Center in Washington, D.C., were just a few of them. We played sixteen of the NHL rinks as a support act.

Playing the Montreal Forum on the Iron Maiden tour was another night that stands out. During the time I lived there, I had learned that Quebec audiences were reserved in their response until you proved you were worthy. At the Forum we got the expected cautious applause for the first song or two, but as we played on, the applause and the excitement grew greater and more clamorous until it climaxed in a standing ovation at the end of our set. That was a satisfying feeling, having really earned the respect of a discriminating audience.

Another great moment occurred after an all-night drive in a snowstorm through the mountains from Salt Lake City down to Phoenix. We had taped a video for one of our songs back in Toronto before we set off on tour, but we'd never seen it. Upon arriving at our Phoenix hotel around dawn, Dave and I dragged ourselves off to the room we were sharing and, preparing to crash, I turned on the TV. There we were on MTV, Coney Hatch playing "Devil's Deck," back when MTV was new and it only played music videos. Our first viewing of our video was on the national American video channel — what a thrill!

Aldo Nova from Montreal had a huge hit with his song "Fantasy" in the same year that Coney Hatch debuted. We heard that he'd liked our album so much that he was playing it over the concert sound system at his shows before he went on. Aldo also took a shine to my song "Hey Operator" and thought he could make it a bigger hit in the States, so he recorded it on his second album. I can't say I really like what he did with it, but between the good sales of his version of the song and the Coney Hatch sales of it, I've made more money from that song over the years than any other. Besides being a good ego boost, this high-profile cover was a good early lesson in the financial rewards of successful songwriting. If I'd just wanted money, I'd probably have tried to pursue that more. (Later on, when I had my staff songwriter deal, another song I co-wrote, "Taste of Love," was performed by Jimi Jamison of Survivor on his solo album. From there it went on to an episode of *Baywatch*. That also paid out nicely.)

We flew to England to make a video for our third album, and it was so exciting to be in London for the first time. I'd always been enchanted by Britain and the things I'd seen of it from afar. I was a good little colonial boy, I suppose. As we came into London from Heathrow I watched the new suburbs give way to the older buildings that marked the historical centre of the city. It's changed since, but in 1985 it was still possible to see the scars of the Luftwaffe bombings. We stayed next to Hyde Park and explored it, and saw Buckingham Palace and the British Museum, as well as some ritzy restaurants, the Marquee Club, and the London Lyceum Theatre. (One of the scenes of that video for Coney Hatch's cover of "Fantasy" had me portray a discontented worker in a Cabbage Patch doll factory. Later that year the real toy company produced a Cabbage Patch kid with my name.)

I've already touched on another highlight, our time at Le Studio in Morin Heights, where we worked on *Friction*, but that very special place is worth a revisit here. Being there really felt like the big time, as professional as you could get. The most recent clients before us had been The Police, David Bowie, Asia, and April Wine. We heard some great gossip from the staff about the big boys, stories that I really can't divulge unless you buy me a drink. I found Iggy Pop's AT&T phone card under the bed in my room. Le Studio was almost the pinnacle of recording facilities at the time, staffed by great people and filled with the best gear. If you couldn't make a good album there, it was time to pack it in.

HMM ... WHAT TO DO, WHAT TO DO?

When I walked out the door of Coney Hatch, it was like I'd popped out of the bubble that had defined my life and identity for five years. The phone didn't ring, I had no work, and I didn't know who I was supposed to be. I was out in the cold, and it suddenly dawned on me that I'd put myself there — walked away from the dream of every rock musician. The fact is, though, Coney Hatch wasn't doing it for me.

It had stopped being fun because I'd spent so much time being afraid of making a mistake. Had my quick shift in musical style five years before, just to get the gig, proven unsustainable? Several music biz veterans, while acknowledging my talent, had said to me, "What are you doing playing heavy rock? I just don't see the similarity between you and Ozzy Osbourne or AC/DC or Judas Priest." It seemed now that in my rapid ascent some steps had been skipped and important lessons missed. It was time to go back to basics and rebuild from the ground up. So I did. After I spun my wheels for a while in indecision, it was pointed out that I needed to start making money. There followed some manual labour, some construction. I did lots of shows setting up and tearing down equipment for a sound company and then a laser light company. On some of those days I'd end up working at concert events next to sound tech/roadie types who had seen me in concert or even worked on my shows. They'd ask in genuine surprise, "What are *you* doing here?" I felt bad, as if I'd let them down.

There was some office temp work, doing one- or two-day calls to work in offices on reception desks and such. Anything to scrape up a few bucks. Trying to be practical, I took a WordPerfect course to improve my marketable skills. It was a way of hiding, I think now. We can talk ourselves into thinking almost anything is a good idea if we try hard enough.

One cold January day I was walking along Queen Street in Toronto, wondering how I would pay the rent that month. I saw an open door to a vacant store and some renovating going on. I stuck my head in and said to the man inside, "What's going in here?"

He said, "I'm opening a record store."

"Need any workers?"

"I'm looking for a carpenter."

I hesitated, then: "I'm a carpenter."

He looked me over appraisingly. "Are you really?"

I said, "Yeah, sure."

"How much do you charge?"

A little uncertainly I said, "Ten bucks an hour."

He looked me over and said, "All right, see you tomorrow morning."

That night I went to the library to read about how to be a carpenter.

I did okay, although my doorframe wasn't quite square. The door was a bit difficult to close. My best trait was willingness to work hard

During this time I was fence-sitting about what to do next. There was lots of songwriting and home recording on a Fostex four-track cassette recorder, but I was out of the loop, with no gigs and no band. The feeling of failure was haunting me. It started to look like I'd blown it through my own short-sighted actions and inability to control my emotions. My first wife, Stella, pushed me to help her get a singing career started. She had her own ambitions, and I'd made a guilt-driven promise at some point to help her put a band together.

I got involved in the process of finding her an agent and then assembling young players who had some ability and would work for starting wages. I came up with a band name for her, Chinatown Traffic. The guitar player was so young that his mom, Rosa, was not that much older than me. After Chinatown Traffic was up and running, we were visiting Rosa and her husband one night. She steered me onto the topic of what my career plans were. I guess I blathered something noncommittal, and Rosa looked me in the eye and said, "Carl, stop being scared. Stop it. Just get back out there. It's time."

Dartmouth, 1988. Ad in the local newspaper: "This week at the Crazy Horse, come see Conway Hatch with his big hit Pay Operator."

That changed my thinking because it embarrassed me. Rosa lit a fire under me, and I became driven anew to succeed. I now had a new motto: "Nothing will stop me! I'll batter a brick wall down with my head if necessary!" I would now assemble a new band, be a proper leader, teach them what to play, and even how to play it. I'd decide the image, book the shows, handle the money, load the truck with the crew, and do all the driving, all while working every day at staying in top physical condition. Those were the tasks I set for myself. Above all else, I told myself, be ready. Be ready at all times because you never know when or how opportunity will arise.

This mindset seems extreme now, but I also know that for me it had to be that way. I'd convinced myself with one of my many truisms that "the lessons you learn the hard way last the longest." My reactionary response to the things I'd experienced with Coney Hatch was almost inevitable for someone as emotion-driven as me. This was to be a complete rebound from the guy who hadn't managed the pressures effectively, but I saw this resolve as good pressure, *my* pressure. The workload did cause me to buckle from the strain more than once in the form of overwork-fuelled bronchitis, gusting toward pneumonia. It knocked me out of commission for a week mid-tour. In fact, the Carl Dixon Band had to play a night without Carl Dixon in Calgary because I was too sick to leave my hotel room. On the Monday off I had immersed myself in the outdoor hot sulphur springs at Banff, clad in only a bathing suit as the snow fell magically around my head. This exposure proved to be a great boon to the virus that was trying to fell me. I'd naively thought the springs would deliver a miracle cure. With rest and determination I forced myself back to finish the remaining weeks of the tour.

I learned a ton. I played with wonderful people who are still my friends to this day. (There was an example of my perhaps taking micromanaging a bit far when I bought each guy in my band his own bottle of hairspray for Christmas. Hey, it was an important part of the image in the '80s, plus they were always borrowing mine. It made sense to me.)

I again took a couple of singing lessons, improved my guitar skills, wrote lots of new songs, and searched for knowledge constantly. It finally hit me that all my focused efforts would only bear fruit if I made the needs of the audience my priority, made it all about them. I had to loosen up, laugh, and get out of my own way. The magic of performance is in the spontaneous moments, which can only happen when you're relaxed enough to let those moments in. It took time for this new knowledge to form into a new habit. Once I started on that path things got continually better.

Performing live for an audience was always the ultimate goal. When you have that perspective, the albums and the hit songs are just devices to get you more shows. Only the performance gives you that high of the audience response. I'm often asked, "What's it like to stand onstage in front of all those people? Don't you get nervous?"

I always say, "I don't get nervous. I get pleasantly excited."

I happen to be a person who thrives against that challenge, but it's not for everyone. If you can break through the fear barrier, the wave of energy coming back at you from the crowd is the greatest high you can ever experience. That's the addictive part of performing. Once you've felt that high, it's very hard to give it up. Performers will go through unbelievable difficulties just to feel that again.

But before I could sail off into these new challenges, the decks had to be cleared. As the eighties were ending, so were my twenties. The bad marriage had to go, and the long shadow of Coney Hatch needed to be dealt with. In the summer of 1988 I'd formed my second post-Coney band, called Rough and Ready. Whilst it showed great collected skill and talent, our combo wasn't gaining any traction on the road to rock stardom. The songs and demos I was producing with R 'n' R were met with indifference by the biz. On New Year's Eve 1989 my wife bottled me from the audience while I was singing onstage — with a champagne bottle, no less. That was a good indication that we'd reached a fork in the matrimonial road. I probably had it coming.

BACK ON EARTH

— Hilaire Belloc (1870–1953)

That year, 1989, Coney had done a series of high-paying reunion shows after
over three years apart, shows that put more money in our pockets than we'd
ever made as the old high-profile touring act. I'd been spending my reunion
earnings on trips to Nashville, New York, L.A., and San Francisco, where I
was collaborating with pro songwriters and learning more about the craft. I
was now in a serious push in my pursuit of a new record deal.

The previous paragraph could lead an astute reader to ask, "How did you
get to work with pro songwriters in those places?" It wasn't easy, and you
don't get to move in those circles without a way in. The appearance of that
doorway was another unexpected and somewhat peculiar aid to my progress.
Thus does the name Brian Brinkerhoff enter the story.

Brinkerhoff was a man I would now describe as a superfan. His passion,
verging on obsession, was to scan the credits of his favourite albums to learn
the names of the songwriters, players, and producers who were a part of making the albums. He would then research those names, find out what else they'd
been involved in and form a picture of their career to date. Connections

become apparent pretty quickly in the music business; this guy worked with that producer, who always works with this guitar player, who writes with that guy in Nashville etc. Brian soon became very knowledgeable about these things. He also worked at an office for a telephone company near San Francisco, so it became his pastime during work hours to make scads of phone calls, at no charge, around the countryside to begin building a network of contacts.

In time I realized that Brian was not as connected on a legitimate level to the music business as a manager needs to be — for that is what he now asked: to be my manager, on a handshake basis. I reasoned that there was currently no lineup of people asking for this honour, so let's see what he's got. What Brian had was a whole lot of people who would take his calls. That was enough to get me on the runway for a fresh start, but not enough to get the plane airborne.

My arrival in Nashville set the course for much of what has happened to me since. I had a hotel room at the Shoney's on Music Row in Nashville, and after breakfast there each morning I'd be off to write with somebody. Through Brian's contact list I found myself set up with some really cool people. Van Stephenson was the first and best teacher I had there. He patiently and kindly helped me through my initial nerves and uncertainty to show me how the work gets done. Van had a hit under his name, "Modern Day Delilah," and was later a member of the country group Blackhawk. I wrote four decent songs with him, including "I Believe in Angels," which came about after Van looked over my sheet of title ideas. He saw that one and said, "We'll write that tomorrow. It'll be easy to write." That left me marvelling — how could he know that?

Todd Cerney, a rare Nashville native who'd been a co-writer on some national hits; Mike Lunn, a nice guy from Nebraska who was a sort of hybrid rock-country-blues writer; Taylor Rhodes, who had cuts with Loverboy, Bon Jovi, Peter Wolf, and other rock acts: these were among the other guys I wrote with and learned from. I also came across a neat English artist named Julian Dawson in the halls at Warner-Chappell Publishing on Music Row. He was also visiting to get the Nashville experience, and we got together after hours to write a couple of cool songs together.

When I got to the west coast, I bounced between Los Angeles and San Francisco. Jack Conrad, a great L.A. writer who had cuts with Dave Mason, The Babys, Heart, Three Dog Night, and tons more, was kind enough to spend time working with me and let me kip in his spare room.

The most productive writer connection I made in my co-writing travels, though, was Brett Walker, from Norman, Oklahoma, and then living in Long Beach, California. He was working hard at his craft and dedicated to "making it." Brett had no previous track record to speak of, but we had complementary styles and compatible personalities from the first day.

Some people say it takes friction and conflict to spur creative juices, but I find that draining. I'd rather work any day with somebody who is pleasant and has a sense of humour. Tension or ego on display can make the process unbearable.

Brett and I began working quickly on an idea that followed one of my perpetual themes, which is, "Let's take off outta this place and get to someplace else, anyplace, 'cause it's gotta be better than where we are." Escape fantasy is at its root, I know. "Run Reckless" was written quickly and sounded exciting. We got together soon after and wrote another good one called "Taste of Love." The story bears telling. Both Brett and I were red-blooded young males who liked girls very much but were a little bashful about laying that desire out blatantly in a song lyric. We tended to be a bit "nice" in our writing approach, and we were looking for a way to maybe put a bit more macho posturing into our rock songs. How to break out of the polite, small-town, good-boy upbringing we shared? I had an idea.

I'd heard something once about a David Bowie recording session, I think at Le Studio. Bowie had been reading the ideas of a French artist who believed in the power of "randomness" — that by removing your intention from a creation, getting out of the way, it could then take on a new and unexpected power: the way the universe wants it to be. On one song Bowie employed the "cut-up" concept made famous by William Burroughs, taking the lyric sheet he'd written for the song and cutting each line of the lyric from the page into a paper strip with a pair of scissors. He then tossed all the little strips of paper into the air and reassembled them in random order with glue on a new page. The song was thus performed and appeared on the album in this way.

I thought this was brilliant. The most interesting part of the story to me was the notion that you could be liberated from the same old way of telling a story, that everything didn't have to follow in strict sequence. You could jumble what seemed like the logical order and create a new order. As Supertramp said in "The Logical Song," "One, two, three, five!" Why can't five come after three? Who's getting hurt if you put it there? Shed the straitjacket. There are other ways to do things if you just open up to the possibility.

With the Bowie story informing my thinking, I became certain that there was a way for Brett and me to overcome our shyness at telling a girl that she's hot in the bold ways we'd always avoided. The subconscious was the thing, it seemed to me, so I convinced Brett to sit with me in the California sunshine with a yellow legal writing pad and try the following method.

I'd write one line — could be anything — about this imaginary girl to get us started, and then I would pass the notepad over to him. He had to write the first thing that popped into his mind in response and then pass the pad back to me. I would also write the first response that popped into my mind. I'd pass it back and he'd do one more, and then we had a four-line verse. It didn't matter if it made sense; that was the point.

It felt good, like we were getting somewhere. We kept going, back and forth, for over an hour until we had eight or nine verses and were worn out — so mentally tired that we couldn't tell whether anything was any good. We agreed to break for lunch and not judge anything until we'd been away for a while. When we went back, we were delighted to find that we'd achieved exactly what we'd hoped for, saying things that our normal logical approach would never have permitted and creating some nice word images that came from a different type of thinking. We selected the best three verses and had ourselves a dandy little song that we called "Taste of Love."

I felt like this partnership had promise, and so did my "manager," Brian, who was very excited by the new songs. Brian started making plans about setting up the next stage, i.e., forming a band, doing a showcase, getting a record deal, and going straight to the top. You know, the normal strategy of the time. He called me almost every day, letting me know about the group of players he had contacted to form a band around me and Brett, encouraging me to put together more material and making plans for me to come to California again. One time he put me on the phone with a young A&R guy at Atlantic Records' L.A. office, name of Kevin Williamson. Kevin knew me from my Coney Hatch days and had been a fan. He was happy to talk to me, encouraging but vague, but said I should let him know how things progressed. Hungry musicians hear that as an invitation, almost a promise of future interest. I sure did. "Foot in the door and more," I was thinking.

Next, Brian flew up to Canada to see me perform and started "correcting" my stage moves and my performing style in the dressing room. It was a bit like Max Norman's lesson to Coney Hatch on how to have more attitude. I didn't mind. I figured he was trying to help, had a few beers in him, whatevs.

Then things started to unravel for Brian and me. He told me and Brett in one of his "manager reports" about the great interest he'd created at Atlantic Records for the project and that we should start preparing the band. Atlantic was ready to put up cash, maybe five thou, for our band to rehearse the new material in L.A. and then perform a showcase for the company at the end of the prep week. From this, unless we blew it, we could expect to sign a deal. This was how everyone was getting signed, he said. Plan for September, he said. Get ready for the big time!

Well, how could we not be interested? We made tentative travel plans as Brian continued to give us glowing reports of his "great talks" with Kevin. It was confusing, though, because we still didn't have a firm date as September arrived and marched along, and our "band" was losing cabin pressure for lack of a firm plan. One day, after a couple of weeks like this, Brian called, a few drinks in, and started to complain that things were a little less certain about the date of this showcase now, and maybe we should just slow down the plans a bit. Kevin wasn't sure that we could make this work or that *our* commitment was really there. Afterward I realized that this was the prep call to get me ready for a later one with some variation of the message, "You won't believe it, but everything fell through."

I hung up and thought about what Brian said, and it didn't make sense. If there was any doubt, perhaps I could call my new friend Kevin and assure him of our commitment. Together we'd pin something down so the chance didn't slip away. I called Atlantic L.A. the next day

"Hey, Kevin, it's Carl Dixon. How are you?"

"Oh, good, Carl, good. How are things for you?"

"Great, man. I'm pretty excited about this showcase you're planning for us with Brian, and I was just hoping we could pin something down on that."

Silence for a second, then, "Uhh, showcase?"

My heart beat a little faster. "Yeah, you know, the showcase you and Brian have been discussing for the new band I've got going with Brett Walker ..."

"Carl, what are you talking about?"

I felt like I was falling down the rabbit hole.

"But ..." I felt my face getting hot, "haven't you got a plan going with Brian Brinkerhoff to finance a trip for me down there to rehearse the new band and do a showcase for Atlantic?"

"Carl, I promise you I have never discussed any such thing with Brian. I don't know why he would say that. I like you and I like your music, but I don't have the budget to do something like that."

Fury was making my mouth dry and my head light. Somehow I rallied enough from my humiliation to hear some hope in Kevin's words.

"This is all very weird here, Kevin. Look, is there anything that does make sense that you *can* find a budget to do?"

I give Kevin credit; he rallied right back with me.

"Well, I like the music I've heard. I could maybe find a thousand dollars to cover a plane ticket for you and a motel for a week so you can do more writing, just see how it develops."

"I'd be happy to give that a try, Kevin."

"All right, Carl, call back in the morning. I'll clear this with my bosses and we'll set it up."

I hung up in disbelief. In the following days I made something out of the opportunity, playing it as it lay, but I was overtaken by a feeling of betrayal, that my "manager" had lied and manipulated my feelings. I was absolutely seared by that experience. After I blasted Brian Brinkerhoff, I disengaged from him and have never had a manager since. Now I like to say that I'm self-mismanaged.

I told Brett the story and he was equally shocked. Unfortunately, the next writing sessions with him had a changed feeling. We agreed that I should fly down right away to do more work, but it was like Brett was feeling territorial now that there was a real record company involved, like he was suspicious that I would try to dominate, and his paranoia seemed to come to the fore when we went together to Atlantic to meet Kevin, who reached out immediately to greet me with, "Hi, Carl. Great to see you." Brett permitted himself to be introduced, but then as soon as Kevin was out of earshot he hissed, "How did he know you and not me?" I explained that Kevin knew me from my Coney Hatch career. This seemed to worry Brett more.

I don't blame Brett for his feelings. Maybe I did come on stronger than I realized. It was just much more difficult to write together at his place that week, once the record company was financing us. I wish it had turned out better. We got two songs in a week, which is piss-poor productivity, and I left his studio most days with a headache from the tension and edginess. One of those songs, "One Good Reason," is the opening track on my first solo album, and the other may yet turn up somewhere. I liked Brett very much, and I wish there'd been a better result.

CHANCE WALKS INTO THE ROOM

So the week in Los Angeles came to an end and I was in the offices of Atlantic Records, playing the tapes of our new material for Kevin, when Molly Kaye from Almo-Irving Publishing heard the music and asked if she could sit in. Then she said, "That's really good. Are you signed to anyone?"

I replied, "Not yet. That's what I'm working on."

Molly gave me a business card, asked for my number and said, "Send your stuff to me at my New York office. I'm really interested." My knucklehead side took over soon after and I forgot all about her because she wasn't offering a record deal, which had been my sole focus for five years. Unfortunately, Atlantic was also able to resist the temptation to sign me and Brett. Kevin offered his regrets and wished us luck, and suddenly the whole thing seemed to have fizzled. Now it was back to reality: I'd fired my "manager" Brian, my L.A. partnership with Brett was in limbo, and I had to find the next month's rent with no more Coney Hatch reunion gigs in sight. Oh, yeah, and my wife had finally left me.

About three weeks later my phone rings, and it's an annoyed Molly.

"Carl, where's that music you promised to send? I've been checking for it every day. Did you forget about me?"

I suddenly realized I was blowing it.

"Uh, no, Molly, it took me some time to get settled, and then I got really busy for a while. I'll send a tape right away."

"Well, make sure you do this time, because I'm looking for a staff writer for my New York office, and I can't wait forever."

This led to one of three major moments in my life of surrendering to the universe.

My return from that trip had been followed quickly by the collapse of my long-troubled first marriage. I think the trouble had endured because I wasn't able to stop being me. At the same time as I was finally sending out those tapes to Molly, I was shuffling around my empty apartment, wondering how to stay solvent.

I was once again searching for suitable work that would pay enough to keep me in rent and peanut butter sandwiches. When you choose the arts as your profession, it requires your full commitment. When times get tough and you need to make ends meet, you have to stick with low-commitment jobs. The autumn of the empty apartment saw me start teaching in a music school, working as counter help in a ritzy coffee shop, and doing TV extra work. The three jobs combined still left me dangling on the edge of making ends meet. My cat Nigel and I were both getting skinny again.

Meanwhile, I had engaged Gene Masson, a New York attorney, to talk to Molly about whether a deal could be struck for my services. The negotiations had been slow, tedious, and to my mind very uncertain. I was in the third month of working my three jobs, and it was not looking good for making the December rent.

One night as I lay in bed, exhausted, the phone rang. It was my mother. She had called to let me know that she and my father had discussed at length where my life was headed. I was now thirty-one, and they had decided that I was wasting my life in this crazy music career and must give it up immediately. They could no longer emotionally support or encourage me in this direction. It was time for me to wake up, grow up, and change my path before it was too late. I was shocked, but I managed to mumble, "I understand. I'll think about what you've said."

As I lay there, hungry and tired in the dark with only my cat for company, I recognized that I must be at low tide when even my parents no longer believed in me. My mind sorted through my mother's words, my experiences, and my hopes and dreams of a musical future. I finally said aloud: "I know that I have worked as hard as I possibly could and tried my very best always. I've fought through many obstacles, sacrificed stability and security, and persisted long past the time when almost everyone I know has given up on music. If giving the very best I have in me isn't good enough to make me succeed, then I just have to accept that it's not meant to be and find another path for my life. I now surrender to the universe." I really said that, and then soon afterward I fell asleep.

The next day at the coffee shop, I was in a foul mood all day, wondering what life held for me. Service was not exemplary at the counter that day. I trudged back to my apartment after the shift and checked my messages.

"Carl, this is Gene in New York. It looks like I've got a pretty good tentative deal in place with Molly for you to be a staff songwriter. Call me right away."

I almost fainted, then leapt and shouted, "Ha!" Just like that.

The deal was a beauty, more money than I'd ever made in my life, a guaranteed paycheque in U.S. currency mailed every two weeks from New York, plus a signing advance of ten thousand dollars. All this was in exchange for my agreement to write songs under their direction and to give them shared ownership of existing songs that they liked. Of course, the train had already been set in motion to that station for a number of weeks, but I couldn't help believing that surrendering my fate to the universe that night and setting my own will aside for once was the change that let the universe do with me what it wanted.

Strangely, my mother didn't share in my joy at this outcome. She felt it was just another temptation that would keep me on the road to destruction instead of getting out of music like a sensible lad. My father refrained from commenting. Parents worry so much.

STAFF? THOUGHT I'D DIE!

So now I'm a songwriter for hire, the "rock guy" for the New York office of Almo-Irving Music publishing. The idea was that I should get in there and cross-pollinate my talent with that of as many other writers, and especially recording acts, as possible. That meant I had to employ all the tricks and skills I'd picked up in my travels over the previous year and a half, just to look like I knew what I was doing.

Music publishers make money by having their songs performed on records and then collecting the royalties, known as "mechanicals," from record companies who release them, and "performance" royalties from the radio plays. When a publisher signed somebody like me, it was a gamble. They wagered I would write enough good/great/hit songs during the term of my contract that any resulting recordings would make back what they'd paid me plus a profit. Writers are assigned a quota of "credits" that must be met within the year to meet the terms of the contract; one song written fully by me earned one credit, a co-write was a half-credit, and so on. I had to produce twelve credits to meet my quota. My biweekly paycheque was called a "draw," an advance against future royalty earnings. Either Molly really liked me or Gene Masson was a good negotiator, because my deal also gave me a ten-thousand-dollar travel allowance, which was to allow me to travel to New York or L.A. or wherever they thought I should go to work, and the costs wouldn't come out of my draw. Pretty sweet.

With Molly Kaye in New York for Billboard to publicize my signing to Almo-Irving. Molly is record biz royalty through her father Chuck Kaye and grandfather Lester Sill.

The way things turned out, the only real success that resulted came from the first song they liked from me, "Taste of Love." The buzz among the song pluggers was "Wow, this sounds like Def Leppard meets Aerosmith," and Jimi Jamison did have some success with it. Aside from that one, there weren't many takers for the Dixon sound. I worked with lots of different bands and other staff writers all over the place, and maybe seven songs found their way onto albums, but none were big royalty generators.

The problem was I was still trying to get a new album deal for myself, so my eye wasn't strictly on the ball. It was not actually my bliss to be stuck behind the scenes as a writing guy, even at a good rate of pay. My bliss really demanded that I be in front of a crowd, where I could feel the buzz. Still, I thought I had time to figure things out. All the experienced staff writers told me the first year is just spent learning the ropes, and you shouldn't feel scared that you'll lose your deal.

Some of the bands I was matched with didn't really want to work with me. They resented that their label didn't think they had a hit song and that a "pro" had to be called in. There were a few sessions like that late in the year. I understood that — we were the same way in Coney Hatch — but it still wasn't fun to navigate.

The biggest change in my relationship with Almo-Irving and Molly Kaye was after I met my future second wife. I was nuts about her, to the annoyance of Molly, and one fateful weekend near the end of my contract I flew home for her birthday. Molly had ordered me to stay in New York for three more days in case some work turned up. I didn't listen, and that didn't go over well.

Around this time the bills were tabulated on my travel budget, and it came to light that I had blown past the ten-thousand-dollar mark by almost another ten thousand. I had thought the office was keeping an eye on it and they would stop me when the budget was gone, but it wasn't so. They let me just keep running up a tab. That didn't look good on Molly as the office manager, and the bosses in L.A. were telling her that her New York office was spending too much money.

The combination of my recent "insubordination" and seemingly spendthrift ways meant that I was vulnerable. Thus, in what would be one of the crushing shocks of my life, I was informed that my deal would not be renewed.

COME ON, YOU, GET UP!

The shock of being released from my position had a bad effect for weeks. I couldn't think straight or do much of anything. I really was blindsided because I'd been so secure in the belief that I'd have the first year to figure things out. My old Alvin Shoes friends invited me to play with them at their New Year's Eve show, just to help me get over it a little.

It was obvious I needed a new source of income. My confidence was down and I was way out of the loop. My goal of recording a new album, the thing that had led me to the publishing deal, seemed farther away than ever. Even though I had all these new songs from my songwriting activity of the previous years, I didn't know what to do with them.

Some friends welcomed me into their bar band, and it was like starting over yet again — working for eighty bucks a night. All the musicians on the bar circuit thought this was normal, but a lot of them had regular jobs, and for them the band money was just gravy and a laugh. I couldn't believe how bad the pay was, but I tried not to be a complainer. One night we divvied up the take at the end of the show, and it was $62.50 each. I went home depressed and thought, *This can't go on.*

I resolved the next day to institute a new "hundred-dollar rule." If the offer wasn't worth at least that much to me personally, I would refuse to play. I had to draw a firm line if I wanted things to improve, and I further had to believe my talent was worth at least that much, or why was I doing this at all? It was actually scary to take that position, for there was a real fear that I wouldn't end up with any work at all. It turned out that once I'd faced my fear, I overcame it. I only had to turn down low offers a couple of times, and my decision to hold firm seemed to have magically altered my place in the universe.

In the short term there was still ground to be retaken in my campaign for world domination. Now that my publishing deal was done, my eternal ambition to record a new album hove into view again. My last efforts had led me into the publishing contract, and now I just didn't know what to do with all these songs. I called my friend Jack Conrad in L.A. I was sure that with his experience and contacts he could at least steer me in a good direction.

He drawled, "Well, Carl, grunge is taking over at all the labels out here. All they want to sign is Seattle-sound bands. I think the best thing you could do is try for a deal in Europe, especially Germany. They still really like the heavy melodic rock thing there. Yeah, try Germany."

I thanked him for his advice and was keen to act upon it, but I did not know a single person in Germany. Yet I put out a message to the universe, a wish that something would connect me to Germany and open a new door of opportunity. I guess that sounds like a prayer. I kept busy building a new life with my second wife and preparing for the arrival of our first child, daughter Carlin. Thoughts of Europe were pushed to the background.

Amazingly, within a month or so after the conversation with Jack, I received a letter out of the blue from a man in Germany, Martin "Frenschi" Frankenburg. He told me he'd been a fan for years and asked whether I was considering doing a new album. Martin operated a music import service, which meant he'd often fly to Canada to buy up boxes of albums, which were a lot cheaper here than in Europe. He'd then carry and ship the records home for resale at a fat profit. Martin wanted to become an independent music label and back his own horse in the race. Just what I'd been looking for.

I wrote to express my interest and we agreed to meet on Martin's next trip to Canada. We roughed out a budget on a notepad at my kitchen table, and that's how I finally had the opportunity to make my first solo album, *One*. In time a second investor came aboard, Canadian Eric Wilson, who had a similar background to Martin and likewise wanted to get into the record business. In a restaurant in Toronto we agreed on a name for the partnership: Interplanet Music. A glorious future was envisioned in which they'd be the money and business guys and I'd be the producer/overseer for this and future projects. The best-laid plans of mice and men ...

With songs mostly written and ready to go and investors lined up, music personnel would be assembled from the various groups I'd worked with. I'd be producer, guitar player, and vocalist. In some cases I was also keyboardist and drummer. Whatever it took, just get it done.

I remember telling Ed Stone, the recording engineer, that my ambition was to make *Led Zeppelin I*. By that I meant something as startling, as powerfully great, and as attention-getting as that record. It was not a bad thing to hold up as my standard. Working to a tight budget meant there'd be little rest until the project was finished. Ed Stone and I slaved over the thing. In a span of thirty days there were only a couple of days off; at one stretch it was sixteen days straight of very long hours.

Billy Carmassi on drums and Tim Harrington on bass was the bed track band with me. Lots of guests pitched in. Steve Shelski played a couple of blazing lead guitar tracks; Andy Curran sang some backing vocals, as did Mark Santer, Mike Shotton, and my ex-wife Stella, to whom I'd also promised a spot if I ever did my solo album. A couple of young singers called the Jessicas, Misses Benoit and Palmer, helped with some gospel-ish vocals. Dan Leblanc and Howie Bertolo added nice keyboards and all that, stirred together "in the rock style," made *One*.

We had a nice studio party at the end of the sessions and lots of my old friends came by to listen. Everyone expressed their liking for the music, and then someone pointed out that this would be my first album to come out on CD. That reminded me; I didn't even own a CD player, so I'd have to buy one just to listen to my own album.

* * *

There were some business assumptions going into the project that didn't hold water. The plan was to make the album as great as we could on an indie budget and then pitch it to labels in Canada for a national release. Surely with the contacts and the reputation I possessed, there'd be somebody interested in a kick-arse rock album from Carl Dixon?

To pique the labels' interest, I went out to radio with my own promo campaign conducted from my kitchen. It worked quite well too, because rock radio programmers really liked my new stuff. They set the opening track, "One Good Reason," spinning on rock radio from Newfoundland to British Columbia. A couple of other songs got great regional airplay. This did not sway the record company people. I couldn't figure it out. A quality album by a guy with past success and current radio action — where's the problem? It got frustrating.

My perspective was that I had cooked the dinner, set the table, and carved the roast. Now all they had to do was light the candles and carry the food to the table. Actually, that outlook was turned on its head by a guy at Sony Canada who explained why they weren't going to sign me: "We figure you're doing so well on your own that you don't need our help. We'll pick up someone who needs us more." Oh-kaaaay....

After a few weeks of excuses or limp explanations, I realized there was no room at the inn for this baby. Radio was fading too because they weren't willing to keep playing a record that didn't have a label backing it. The conclusion was inescapable: to have sales success, you needed to have a solid distribution chain in place that would put your album where people could find it.

Why does there gots to be so darned many lessons to learn?

* * *

Of course, an album must be accompanied by a band to play the music live, so I assembled yet another Carl Dixon Band. Some friendly agents helped me get an initial three weeks of bookings, including a run of shows opening for Alannah Myles. Having the same players who made the album seemed *de rigueur*, so Billy Carmassi agreed to fly up to play drums, joining Tim and Howie. Mike Hall from the Killer Dwarfs came in to play lead guitar, even though he was a little miffed that I hadn't gotten him to play on the album. We made a pretty impressive sound together, pounding out the *One* music and a few of my Coney Hatch selections.

There wasn't enough money to sustain it, though, and with no distribution for the album, no excitement was building. Billy flew home after three or four weeks. To keep things alive, I asked Mark Santer to join, and he immediately strengthened the band with his powerful playing and great backing vocals. But we were just running out of shows.

In those days we didn't even think of selling albums at the shows; we thought it was hokey. A proper band only offered their albums in stores, right? Not at the T-shirt stand or side-stage, like beginner kids. Dumb, dumb, dumb. Sales would probably have been strong at the shows if that squeamishness had been gotten over.

The European side of things proved more interesting. Martin Frankenburg had found a company in Bavaria called Long Island Records, yet another music import company that hoped to branch out into being a record label. There's a sucker born every minute, I guess. Long Island was owned by Erwin Sonderbauer ("Sondi"), and he partnered with Martin to get my album noticed in Germany, at least. They took me to radio stations and record stores and put me together with a band called Sinner for some appearances. This was before the record came out in Canada, and it still seemed like the sky was the limit for *One*.

While *One* was falling from the sky like Icarus, I found a program from FACTOR (the Foundation Assisting Canadian Talent on Recordings) that provided tour support grants to Canadian performers who had records released in foreign territories. I qualified, and the paperwork was completed to get me quite a bit of money to support a full-on tour. Various performance places in Germany and Switzerland were booked. We sure had some fun. Though we proved our mettle at every show, the destiny of my *One* album seemed foretold, alas. It was not to be a sales success.

* * *

A few years followed during which I tried to keep a flame sputtering on recording projects, but I also had to get serious about working as often as possible, wherever possible. I had a band called Joe Cool that played cover material and also a couple of other bands, gigging somewhere every single week. The young family I'd begun made me realize there was no more room for messing around. Babies had to be fed and clothed; it was time to get serious. As I frequently have done, I put a ton of pressure on myself not to let them down and ended up giving myself repeated acid reflux attacks at times from stress.

During this time I took up a suggestion from my mother and went to see some people about the possibility of ADD being an element of my character. It had long been a point of puzzlement for people who knew me: "Carl seems to have it all, so why can't he get it together?"

I didn't want any candy-ass excuses for the inconsistent results in my work, but a questionnaire about ADD symptoms with multiple-choice answers suggested that I likely was one of those impulsive, hyperactive, distractible misfits. I had thirteen out of seventeen "yes" answers on the questionnaire, when just seven yeses would have been a strong indicator.

The diagnosis was tough for me to accept, and I rejected it for a long time. However, I knew that acceptance could help me understand myself better, and being armed with more knowledge would allow me to function better. I even tried the Ritalin prescription thing for maybe a year until they became "the pills that make Daddy yell" to my little girl. I was stupidly going too deep on the things. Three tablets daily of four hours' value each was the dose, but in my anxiety about working hard and getting better results, I started taking four a day. It wears your nerves down quickly. Ritalin is a stimulant that basically scoots you along the thought pathway and doesn't permit your distractible impulses to win all the time.

My initial experience with this medicine was probably not that different from the stories you hear of people's acid trips during which they saw the world clearly for the first time. By then I was in my mid-thirties, and as the Ritalin hit my system, one realization after another dawned on me, answers to mysteries that had never made sense to me before — inexplicable events that I was doomed to repeat because I didn't understand them.

The realizations all pointed to my own role in the things that had gone badly or unwisely. A string of poor decisions, driven by emotional impulsiveness, now crossed my mental screen like a parade of scenes from a fool's life, and I broke down weeping after enough minutes of this sad spectacle. There was no way around it; I was the author of my own defeat time and again in the opportunities life had placed before me. The highly charged nature of my emotional responses to things had acted as a repellent to many people, and I had not understood this.

The habits of a lifetime are not changed overnight, but at least I had a better understanding of myself. After I stopped the Ritalin, I hoped the self-knowledge would stick with me enough to do better in future, but backsliding to my inherent nature at times was inevitable. The leopard does not change its spots. It continues to be my great challenge to manage the "quick to fill up" side of me so that I don't rattle people or hurt feelings. My loved ones in particular have had more upset than they ever should have from the times I failed to manage myself better.

* * *

Perhaps what I needed wasn't a drug but a friend. Back in the summer of 1992, while the plans for *One* were developing, I met a man who has been a big help to me ever since. Pat " Whitey" Stapleton was an NHL great with the Chicago Black Hawks in the '60s and early '70s. His play in the 1972 Canada–Russia series cemented his reputation as one of the great players of his time.

Pat's sons were fans of Coney Hatch, and the boys dragged him along to take part in one of our weekly Sunday pickup hockey games in Scarborough. I was Pat's defence partner that night, and it was a great experience having the coach and teacher next to me on the ice and on the bench. He and his wife Jackie came out afterward with everyone for the obligatory wings and beer feed, and the man just exuded wisdom and kindness. I made a point of staying in touch, and to my surprise Pat was receptive. We'd speak from time to time, and Pat always had helpful observations. He became a mentor to me.

There was a low point in 1996, during which I started to believe that there was no future for me in the music business. I had spent the previous couple of years doing a lot of hardscrabble gigging around the bar circuit, logging many miles and many hours to achieve a bare subsistence-level income. I now had two young daughters, and the weight of responsibility for their well-being sat heavily on my shoulders.

This concern led me to sign up for a course on Saturday mornings for teaching English as a second language. I had reasoned that I liked English and I liked teaching, and my dad had been a teacher, so maybe this would be a tolerable new career choice. It was distasteful to think about, but I was trying to force my square peg into that round hole out of fear that I was on a treadmill to nowhere.

Miraculously, in the midst of this crisis, Pat Stapleton called to check on me. I don't know whether it was through a sixth sense or by coincidence, or maybe a little bird told him, but the timing and content of this call put my life back on track. Pat asked what I was up to, and I tried to sound happy and convincing as I told him about my concerns and my decision to take this course for the good of my family. Just keeping options open, right?

Whitey was quiet for a moment and then said, "Well, that's okay. You can do that, but I wonder if it's the best choice for you. Have you heard the story of the acres of diamonds?" I admitted that I had not. Pat related the tale, as told by the motivational speaker and writer Earl Nightingale. The gist of the story is that a farmer travelled far from home in South Africa to search for diamonds in hopes of getting rich, when they were right under his nose the whole time on the land he had abandoned. He just wasn't seeing them.

"Do you see what the story is getting at?" he asked.

"I think so," I replied hesitantly.

"The point is that you've spent many years building up your skills and contacts and talent in the world of music. Your chances of success won't be as good if you walk away from all that and start over in a field where you have no skills, no contacts, and undeveloped talents. You just need to see the diamonds around you in a new way, and build something out of your acres that you've already got."

Pat followed up with me the next few months and became more of a mentor than I've ever had. He sent me an audio copy of Nightingale's *Lead the Field*, which went into great and helpful detail of advice and lessons in life.

I applied the advice, and from that expansion of my awareness, fear converted to hope and everything changed for the better. Pat would often call me and say, "What are you listening to?" and remind me of the importance of the kind of messages we hear each day and how they shape our thoughts. He taught me about being able to say "I'm perfect" and believe in it, no matter what other people might throw at you. I wish for everyone reading this that they could have a Pat Stapleton arrive in their life at a time when they are afraid and uncertain of which is the way.

It took eight or nine months until the next big event in my career came along, and I was happy that I had overcome my own doubts and persisted. In the years since that time when I feared I had no future, I've experienced many of the best rewards of my labours.

THE NIGHT I JOINED THE GUESS WHO [SORT OF]

It was the autumn of 1997, and I was feeling on the upswing from six months of renewed energy and conviction. Pat's advice had turned me around and kept me in the game.

How did I come to be a member of The Guess Who?

Jim Kale, the original bass player, had kept the band going through the decades and the constantly changing lineups after the glory days with singer Burton Cummings were finished in 1975. Kale even registered the band name under his ownership for a little extra security. Smart — that move made him millions over the years.

He preferred to keep the band Winnipeg-based, as it had always been, and that led him to hire a keyboard player from Winnipeg. I'd worked with Leonard W. Shaw ("Lewsh" for short) in Toronto on some writing and recording back in the 1980s, and when The GW needed a new singer in 1991, Leonard had recommended me.

Now one morning in 1997 over breakfast I said to my wife, "I wonder what's going on with The Guess Who. I haven't heard from Lewsh or a thing about the band in years. I don't even know if they're touring anymore. Maybe I'll ask around about them." I moved on to the next thought and filed that away in the back of my mind. The next day the phone rang and it was Lewsh.

"Hey, Carl, what's going on?"

Hands up, who likes The Guess Who? Leaping to conclusion in Vegas.

"Not much, man. Where are you?"

"I'm in Idaho with The Guess Who."

"Well, that answers my next question. The band's still on the go, then?"

"Yes, and that leads me to the point. Are you interested in singing for the band?"

Terry Hatty, a singer they'd taken on in 1991, had tired of the grind and submitted his resignation.

"Yeah, I could be interested."

"We're doing auditions by tape. We'll send you some instrumental tracks from our show. You record your vocals over it, and then send it back to us."

This I did. I was later told by Garry Peterson that I sounded so much like the original recordings, they thought it must be Burton Cummings playing a joke on them.

The return call came.

"Well, the boss likes it. We're playing in Fort Myers, Florida, in ten days. Can you fly down and meet us there? You can meet everyone and have a look at the show, maybe do a promo photo."

This was pretty exciting. I'd grown up loving The Guess Who and had even seen them play once when I was fourteen. To me and many other people they were Canada's Beatles. It seemed that a door had opened for me once again, and I was determined to make it work.

✳ ✳ ✳

I boarded a plane on Friday and was met by old friend Lewsh at Fort Myers airport. He was friendly but seemed a little nervous. I soon discovered why. Boss-man and bassist Kale was sitting in the lobby bar of the hotel. He'd evidently been drinking for some time in anticipation of my arrival.

I'd last met Jim six years before, over a pleasant lunch in Toronto. At that time Lewsh, fairly new to the band himself, had submitted my name as a possible lead singer. Jim had been well dressed, polished, and impeccably mannered as we discussed the gig. At the end he reached for the bill and said, "Don't bother trying to wrestle me for paying the tab. I've been playing bass for many years and you'd lose a wrist-wrestling match." Jim declined to consider me seriously for his singing job in 1991 on the grounds that I looked too young.

Unfortunately, that well-spoken, temperate gentleman Jim I'd lunched with in 1991 had somehow declined or devolved into the 1997 bellowing fool who lay in wait. It's astounding what alcohol can do to people.

As soon as I entered the hotel Jim jumped up, approached me with arm extended as if to shake hands, then instead put a dancing hold on me, one arm around my waist and the other thrust out and holding my hand in his as if preparing to tango. He forcibly waltzed me around the lobby while loudly singing some profane gibberish. I was trying to be a good sport and just go along with this eccentricity while gathering my wits. He then reached down for a grab at my crotch, which certainly surprised me.

I think I hollered, "Whoa!" and reached down to protect my parts, at which point he bestowed a kiss right on my mouth. I jumped back in utter bewilderment, of course restrained from popping him a good one in the teeth because of the potential boss–employee relationship I was there to explore.

That was when Lewsh intervened to drag me away toward the check-in desk. Jim followed us and altered his manner for a moment to managerial mode. He told me to be available for a band dinner that evening. He then returned to his drink but continued to call out little abuses across the lobby. The last I heard was when he jumped up to yell, with hands cupped to his mouth, "Carl Dixon is a fag!" as I made good my escape behind the closing elevator doors.

I slumped against the elevator wall and managed to gasp out, "What the hell was that?"

Lewsh looked very glum. "I was afraid this would happen."

He showed me to my room and told me that everyone would be meeting in the lobby at eight to go to dinner.

I spent some quiet time trying to discern meaning in these events and failed to find any. Events had hardly begun, as it turned out.

By eight I had cleared my head somewhat. I wanted this to work. Kale, Lewsh, Dale Russell, and Garry Peterson were assembled in the lobby. We introduced ourselves but there was no time for idle chat. Kale was still being loud, but at least his verbal abuse was no longer directed solely at me. He had decided to play leader tonight (uncharacteristically, as I later learned) and was hurrying us out the door. We were to walk a quarter mile up the road to the restaurant. Kale's hyperactive loudness continued as he tried to marshal us into a military formation and then marched himself, army-style, shoulders back, chin out, arms swinging, as he got way out ahead of us, hollering "Ah-leff! Ah-leff! Ah-leff-right-leff!" like a drill sergeant.

I had my doubts about the way this new job possibility was shaping up. I wanted to take the moment as comical but it was just so manic, and I couldn't help noticing the wary and dispirited looks on the faces of my fellow travellers. Dale Russell, who always did his best to manage Jim and be his buddy at such times, trotted ahead to join him and likely also to ensure that Kale didn't arrive unaccompanied to deal with the restaurant staff. Garry and Lewsh said little beyond innocuous pleasantries as we walked at a more measured pace. We were all trying to act like this was just normal rock 'n' roll stuff, but the tension was palpable.

I later learned that Kale had said to Leonard on the night before my arrival, "You know what Carl gets tomorrow, don't you, Leonard?"

"No, Jim, what?"

"He gets 'The Moo-vie!'"

"The Moo-vie!" was of course Jim's term for letting it all hang out, every foible, wrinkle, and flaw, to see if I could take it before we decided to go forward together.

So, we get into the restaurant entrance and events begin to unfold rapidly now. Jim is already playing the bon vivant, getting every head in the place turning. The hostess is taken aback but trying to laugh it off as she leads us to a table. Jim attempts to dance with her. She escapes.

Menus arrive and Jim insists that everyone must make wine selections. Lewsh and Dale are trying to keep things light while Garry is alone opposite Jim, his face a set, inscrutable mask. I'm trying to read the body language and verbal cues around me to appropriately compose my own deportment, but it's futile. There's just no way to tell whether this is a calamity brewing or just their normal mode of being together. I was completely at sea with these strange men.

Suddenly Jim jumps up and announces that he's going to inspect the kitchen and ensure that the chef knows how to make a certain dish he'd like to order. We watch him disappear through the swinging doors. Kale's gone a good long while, and we attempt to hold normal getting-to-know-you conversation. Now the restaurant manager appears at our table to ask, through a forced smile, "Could one of you please get this guy out of our kitchen? It's against health regulations, for starters." Lewsh, as tour manager, goes off to reel in his boss.

All back at the table now and the wine having arrived, Jim attempts to call to order a business meeting. Garry, red in the face, is holding up his menu as a barrier to Jim and is staring intently into it.

Jim: "Okay, let's get this meeting going. Garry, put the menu down."

Garry: "I'm fine here."

"Put the menu down and participate."

"I like the menu where it is."

Jim exploded, "Put the goddam menu down, or I'll …" and with that Garry pushed back his chair, got up, and walked out. Kale spluttered and fumed for a second then pushed his chair back and stumbled off after Garry. Lewsh and Dale exchanged looks then said, "We'll be back in a minute," and also fled the table.

In a flash I had become the sole diner at my "Welcome to The Guess Who" dinner. Politeness, as well as a certain amount of shock, proved stronger than my curiosity, so I stayed put. Thus, my knowledge of the next moments is based on the account Leonard and Dale offered me when they returned after five or ten minutes, and which Garry later confirmed.

Jim caught up to Garry in the parking lot and hot words were exchanged. Jim asked how dare Garry defy him. Garry asked Jim what the hell was he trying to do, showing up drunk and misbehaving and possibly scaring the new singer away.

Jim asked Garry (approximately) if he was questioning Jim's leadership. Garry confirmed that he was. Jim grabbed Garry by the collar of his nice expensive new shirt and tore it. Garry saw red, picked Jim up, and body-slammed him to the pavement, wrestler-style. He kept Jim pinned for a bit as they struggled and yelled. Then the twenty-five-year-old restaurant manager appeared and found the two old men rolling around in his parking lot. He ordered them to get off the property.

Garry came to his senses and got up. In his upset and embarrassment he turned and stomped back to the hotel. Jim jumped up from the pavement to holler after him: "You're fired, asshole! You hear me? Fired! Have a nice mortgage, asshole!" Kale then disappeared into the night to find more drinks.

Leonard and Dale returned to the table to find me waiting in bemusement. "Are we still having a meeting?" I wondered. They shook their heads with sad smiles of resignation and sat down to tell me the tale. I believe we tried to eat, but there wasn't much appetite.

The discussion turned to the next night's show and how it could possibly go forward. I told them that I played drums, certainly nowhere near Garry's standard, but in an emergency I'd be willing to fill in.

"What about that photo shoot for the new promo we'd planned?" I ventured.

"I'll have to tell you in the morning," Lewsh said. "I might be booking a plane ticket to get Garry out of here when I get back to the hotel."

That night I retired with some conflicting thoughts. Should I get out of here first thing in the morning also? I was no novice. I'd been at the music game for twenty years and seen lots of things. Never anything quite this loony, though.

I was also running through Guess Who songs in my mind, trying to remember drum parts in case Garry really was shipping out in the morning.

* * *

The morning came and cooler heads had prevailed. The photographer was waiting downstairs as scheduled, and we were already late. We put on our rock costumes and went out to the parking lot to begin shooting stills. Kale had evidently either been out all night or slept on the lawn, because he turned up unwashed, with greasy hair, wearing a stained, baggy old track suit and sporting a red welt under one eye. Garry must have winged him. Improbably, a promo shot was later selected from that session in the parking lot, showing us sitting on a curb and squinting into the morning Florida sun, some of us the worse for wear.

More improbable silliness awaited. It was off to the Fort Myers beach for more photos, Kale and Peterson not speaking, but I was evidently off the hook for playing drums that night.

There was a crazy "endorsement" connection going on that afternoon that had been set up by Dale Russell in another of his attempts to work The Guess Who name to advantage. His endorsement coup to date had been to chat up a Serengeti sunglasses rep during a plane ride and score an endorsement of those expensive shades. He'd tried to get Taylor guitars to buy in on another occasion, but they declined. This day we were meeting a start-up company called American Motorcycles. American was intending to compete with Harley-Davidson for the "hog" motorcycle market. Dale met these deep thinkers on a plane and convinced them we'd be a good endorser for their promo campaign. They had brought prototype bikes down to Fort Myers and set them up on the beach next to the Gulf of Mexico. There were promises of free motorcycles for all of us in exchange for our celebrity blessing. I was thinking, *These guys can't possibly realize this isn't the original band or that I'm the singer who hasn't even agreed to join yet.*

I also hadn't ridden a motorcycle in my life and didn't intend to, so my supposed endorsement wasn't worth a hill of beans. Yet we went through the charade of posing on these hogs and trying to look "biker-ish." Somebody maybe stood to benefit, and I wasn't going to spoil it.

In another example of the general assumption that I was a shoo-in to accept the singing job, Jim insisted via Leonard that I attend the afternoon sound check and be ready to shoot "promo video." The idea was to get good value for the expense of flying me to Florida by getting video of "the new singer" to circulate to potential buyers of next year's shows. To me this wasn't a good idea because I'd had no rehearsal and was pretty rattled. That didn't stop them from getting me onstage to play "No Sugar Tonight/New Mother Nature" with them with a videocam pointed at me. I have mercifully never been exposed to the resulting video.

We adjourned to await the evening show. I still had not met Terry Hatty, the singer I was to replace; he'd ducked sound check. That night, Terry arrived backstage in his show attire. I'd been warned his image was odd, but I hadn't imagined just how garish it was until I saw it. To me, a neutral observer, his image was meant to say: "I don't want to be here."

He ascended to the stage, the show began, and I was appalled at what I heard from The Guess Who. The famous songs had been twisted and shaped by these players into low-res reinterpretations. It was like when jazzers take a standard tune, "play the head," and then make their variations. These men, who'd never written a charting song themselves, deconstructed the successful writings of the old Guess Who and showed how they would have done it. Quote: "Everyone knows that 'Share the Land' is just a bad rhythm and blues song!" No respect.

Every organization is a reflection of the man at the top, and Kale used the popularity of those songs and the band name as cash cow for many years. They made each performance a free-for-all. "You have to let people be who they are" was his mantra. Kale wasn't a fool. He took pride in his work ethic, which was about the things he could control. He never missed a show, never missed a payroll, didn't annoy the buyers by asking for too much money, willingly drove thousands of miles in a van to get to shows, and stayed away from home for months on end. The quality of the product did not concern him. He stuck with things he could manage.

All this I was able to infer from the things I'd seen and heard in those first twenty-four hours in Florida, yet I was still on the fence.

When the show was over I had much to ponder. Terry Hatty introduced himself, and he was very nice. We went back to the hotel and had a long chat in his room. He proved to be a smart, caring, and very decent man. In fact, he took the time to explain how I might be able to make this job work, even as he himself had decided he could stay no longer. Terry was a man of deep religious convictions and after six years had decided that he just couldn't hang with the Kale-man anymore. Terry took almost a fatherly approach with me that night, and I felt the goodness in him.

The next day I flew home with much to think about. It had been a rattling experience overall. On the other hand, the opportunity came with a much bigger platform than the one I currently had, and Kale had assured me in a lucid moment that "the singer dictates the approach to the music." There was also the prospect of a regular good paycheque.

I continued to agonize for a few weeks, so I asked my friends Jack Richardson and Pegi Cecconi for their professional opinions. Jack had known Jim from his days as producer of all The Guess Who albums. He told me Jim had always been the favourite of himself and his wife, especially for his manners, and that in his opinion there was still a good, honourable man inside Jim. Pegi looked at it from a practical perspective: "Why don't you just go and try it and make some money? If you don't like it, you can always quit."

Thus persuaded, I jumped in. Rehearsals began in February 1998, and I had to hit the ground running. As soon as I arrived in Winnipeg on a Thursday, I was informed that the band had accepted a last-minute offer in Florida on the coming Sunday. We would have Friday to rehearse and then get on a plane Saturday.

So there I was on a stage at Hallandale Horse Track, suddenly thrust upon the world as the singer of The Guess Who with one day's preparation. We were so short of material that we repeated one song and launched into a version of "Some Kind of Wonderful" to fill out the time. Somehow it went over well enough to get re-bookings at Hallandale, even though I was still in confusion over the band's odd song arrangements.

When we got back to Winnipeg to resume rehearsals, I immediately ran into resistance over my attempt to get everyone to "play it like the records." It was suggested if that's what people wanted to hear, then they should stay home and listen to the records. It was my belief then, and remains firmly so, that the audience comes to "hear" those happy memories that play in their heads when they hear the old songs. They don't want to hear rewrites, interpretations, or jams on the old tunes. As a performer I believe it's my duty to make the audience my priority and serve up what will make them happy. I don't expect them to follow where I lead, if that's not what they're seeking. I'm not there to educate them or challenge them with my own esoteric "outside" tastes. Don't lure an audience in with a famous band name and then mess with the music they're expecting to hear.

So, off we went together for two and a half eventful years. In that time I performed and produced a new live album for the band, containing all the old hits. I also got a much-needed boost to my confidence and was reminded that yes, I belonged.

"I WAS THE DEVIL'S ACCOMPLICE"

My first ride on The Guess Who merry-go-round came to an end in May 2000, when the original members decided to come together for a very profitable reunion. I had no hard feelings about it; if they wanted to get back together, then it was a good thing for them and for all the fans out there — fans like me.

In the aftermath I made my second and third solo albums, played with April Wine for four years, and launched the solo acoustic performance part of my career. In that time The Guess Who reunion lost momentum, and Jim Kale called me in mid-2004 to gauge my interest in returning to sing for his Guess Who. The action began again in November 2004, and the band launched into a higher-paid and higher-profile career than I'd ever seen. Everything was getting bigger and better with each successive year up to the time of my sudden exit.

My second ride with The Guess Who was far from smooth at the beginning, though. The Burton Cummings loyalists were upset that their boy was out of the loop again. In this age of YouTube, it wasn't long before footage of our ersatz GW appeared, which invariably attracted withering comments by the score. My own website was bombarded with hate messages from a dedicated band of Burton fans, unkind personal attacks meant to make me feel unwelcome. They hoped to scare me away with taunts and abuse in the hope that their Burton would be restored to his throne. I hate to admit it, but some of it hurt, though I mostly forgave them because they knew not what they did. Burton had caused his own exit, not me. There was, however, one abusive guy who got me so mad I was ready to drop the gloves with him on the main street of whatever town he lived in (he wouldn't reveal who he was) — a cage-match rumble for the ages. I forgive him too.

Detractors can rarely damage a performer's career, but sometimes they can make you wish you'd never popped your head up from the gopher hole. It boils down to how tough you are. Can you grow a rhino hide and keep going?

For my part, I saw an opportunity if I returned to the lineup. Burton was so rich he didn't have to work. Not everyone had that luxury. I took it as my role to bring that great music to audiences everywhere and honour it by playing it just like the records. That's what made most people happy — but you can't please 'em all.

* * *

Jim Kale has been vilified and excoriated by many Guess Who fans, especially over the last ten years. I personally don't hold a grudge. To me, he's one of my life's lessons.

Kale holds the belief that he is indestructible, that it would take an Act of Congress to kill him. A gypsy palm-reader once told him he had the longest lifeline she'd ever seen. He swallowed that notion whole, without chewing. The man has been guided by that certainty, conducting himself as if it's written in the stars that he will endure no matter how much he punishes himself.

And punish himself he has. Every nutso anecdote you may have heard is probably true. Gargantuan amounts of drink and drugs, outlandish attention-seeking behaviour; the stuff of legend is contained in the Kale story.

There is usually self-loathing at the root of such behaviour. This weakness can be expressed outwardly as bravado, twisted vanity, and hubris. "Look at the amazing resilience and power of my body. I am no mere mortal; I am exceptional! No matter what I do to myself, I still bounce back."

Kale believes he understands "real life" in a way that clean-living people like me never could. I would return that the sunny side of life is just as "real," and wallowing in the muck will never give you a glimpse of it. Kale's choices rarely let in the light. I wish he could get there.

The demonization of Jim by a segment of Guess Who fans is misdirected anger. His simple act of registering the name under his ownership ensured his own continuing survival as well as employment for dozens of musicians. The fact is, none of the other original members wanted to be The Guess Who at that time. Burton had walked out in 1975 to pursue solo fame. He also walked away from all the partnerships' debts and obligations, leaving drummer Garry Peterson holding the bag as the last remaining original member. When a band suddenly stops playing, there are all kinds of bills and unfinished business to resolve.

Randy Bachman, for his part, was still riding high from BTO's massive success. Kale asked the others if they minded his using the band name to go out and make a living; nobody objected. He asked some other former members, now out of work, to join in with him and give the unit credibility. Some did. Peterson likewise was invited, but, as he told me later, when he saw that first collection of unrepentant party animals in action, he politely declined.

Fans of "the real GW" want to blame Jim for the treachery of trademarking the name. Several points to make here: 1) Kale was in the band for five years before Burton joined; 2) Better Jim owning the name than some former manager or some opportunistic lawyer with no connection; 3) Burton purchased ownership of the band's publishing catalogue without notifying his former partners. Huge unshared financial benefit flowed to him as a result.

There is blame enough to go around in almost any story of old bands not getting along. The joy, energy, and hope we hear in the music of a band's early career really is the cry of youth. The idealism is what captivates young listeners, and that feeling lives on in their hearts. It's triggered again as a fond memory when the songs are heard years later. The songs may be frozen in time; musicians and bands are not. Just like everyone else, they face reality, disillusionment, and changed priorities. If a group gets through to success and makes a hit, that music forever evokes the powerful emotions of that generation's younger days — the days before the audience, like the musicians, had to make compromises and concessions to life's realities. This is why fans got excited when The Guess Who reunited and bitter when the reunion fizzled out. They wanted to clutch those old feelings tightly again and bring the band along with them into the dark unknowable future as a reminder of what we all once were.

On the big stage with The Guess Who, 2007.

For Kale-haters who may be reading this, I will say that he is not the devil. He would never have started up the band anew and called me back in, nor would Garry Peterson have agreed to leave the reunion, if not for Burton. True story.

After going great guns in 2000 and 2001, The Guess Who reunion tailed off somewhat in 2002 and then did just one performance in 2003. For Peterson this trend was already worrying because he had staked all on continuing to work steadily with the reformed GW. However, he heard in 2003 that Burton didn't feel like working much in coming years. Garry's survival instinct kicked in. Hard. He'd already been bankrupted once by Burton's unilateral decisions.

Jim was also pushed to action. Business people tried to squeeze him into signing over the band name to Burton. Initially he decided to submerge and wait them out, like the frog at the bottom of the pond. The stalemate went on uncomfortably long, however. One of Kale or Peterson called the other to discuss options. The self-described "bat-boy and water-boy" determined that their best and only chance lay in combining forces under The Guess Who name again and getting back to work. There was no other choice.

Garry now took a prominent role in the business, which was all to the good. Jim was for the moment a spent force. Peterson was crackling with energy and good ideas, and it was honestly a relief to me to have him in the leadership role. I wouldn't have re-upped otherwise.

Nobody was a villain in this scenario. Burton was doing what he thought was best; the others responded by doing what they thought they had to do. I merely boarded the train as it was leaving the station.

THE NIGHT I JOINED APRIL WINE [SORT OF]

It's another funny story, the one about how I became a member of April Wine. My history with the group had been mostly from a distance. I was excited to hear their first single, "Fast Train," on the radio when I was eleven or twelve; excited because they were another fast-rising young Canadian rock band, and we had so few of them then. I was repulsed by the cover of their first album, a photo of two gnarly feet, red-stained as if they'd just been trampling the grapes to make the "April Wine" contained within. Who comes up with these hokey ideas? (The band later liked to joke that those were Anne Murray's feet.)

Two years later April Wine played my high school on their third album and with a few more big hits. All I remember was the pre-disco-era mirror ball they hung over the stage. Through the following years I watched and listened along with the rest of Canada as our homegrown heroes from Montreal grew more successful and famous. The hits kept coming in rapid succession and April Wine became somewhat godlike in stature. I never actually saw them play during their glory days and was never moved to buy any of their albums after that first one. I don't know why.

When I moved to Montreal to play with Firefly, stories abounded of the ways in which the Winers were flying high. Such stories were an incentive to those of us on the bottom rungs of success. The knowledge that guys like them, who inhabited that magic kingdom, lived in the same town and walked the same streets meant maybe we could get there too.

Firefly even jammed one night with Brian Greenway, April Wine's lead guitarist, at the venerable Maples Inn in west-end Montreal. We had a week's booking there and Brian was at the bar, ever ready to play a bit. He even seemed to know a little about our band, which was thrilling for most of us. Our drummer at the time, however, George, found it completely intimidating to have Brian sit in with us and refused to play in case he made a mistake. I took over on the drums because I wasn't going to let the opportunity slip through my fingers. For all any of us knew, it might be the closest brush with fame we'd ever get. The jam was thrilling and I considered it one of the highlights of my time in Montreal.

Later on, when Coney Hatch was rising, we were told several times that we might open shows or do a tour with April Wine, with whom we were often compared, but it never came about. In the mid-1980s April Wine broke up for about seven years and then reformed. It was during their reunion period that I finally started to open some shows for them with both my own band and a reunited Coney Hatch. One concert in Buffalo stands out in my memory as the loudest, most punishing musical assault on my ears and my body that I'd ever experienced. It was a foreshadowing of things to come.

In early 1998 I had begun performing with The Guess Who, and that kept me in the U.S. most of the time until the job ended in May 2000. Sometime later in the summer of 2000 I got a phone call from Kenny Schultz, April Wine's tour manager. He'd followed my career and had been present for some of the shows I'd opened for them. Ken had a proposal for me. How would I feel about possibly becoming the fifth member?

There were several reasons for this. First, the band was completing a new album, which had been almost five years in the making. They were confident that the new release would carry them back to the top of the charts, and they wanted their live show to live up to the musical richness of the new material. This meant they'd need to add keyboard, guitar, percussion, and backing vocal parts beyond what the four original members could cover onstage. Ken knew I could do that.

The second reason was a bit more, um, delicate. April Wine had reunited to great hoopla in 1992, commanding hefty appearance fees as everyone clamoured to witness their return. The excitement had seemed to fade a bit as their reunion continued, though, and the band's desire to work constantly had the adverse effect of gradually driving their price down. This of course lowered the amount the band could pay themselves, and as in any other business, the individuals started to feel the pinch. The only member of the band who was insulated from the dwindling lifestyle was Myles Goodwyn, who as the writer of almost all the songs continued to receive handsome royalty cheques.

Myles had apparently upset the rest of the band on occasion by cancelling shows when he didn't feel well. The fact that he could afford to do it, and they couldn't, made them start to think it would be good to have someone who could fill in for Myles on such occasions. Kenny suggested that maybe I could be that guy. Whether the idea came from the management level or the other Winers, I don't know, but it was felt they'd be making a good business decision to protect themselves. (Luckily, it never came to that. Myles was an absolute trouper during the four years I played with April Wine.)

Anyway, Kenny couched all these ideas in "maybes" and "what ifs." I told him I'd consider the job, depending on what the pay looked like, when the time came. He felt they were maybe a couple of months away from having the new album done, and so he'd call me then with an offer. All very nice.

About eight months went by, in which time I did a number of gigs and recorded a new solo album. After so long with no news, I assumed April Wine's members had either changed their minds or found somebody else, but in February 2001 Kenny called again to see if I would still consider the job. After getting over my surprise, I told him that of course I was flattered to be asked, but I really needed more information before I could commit.

He said, "We have a show next Friday night in the Orangeville Arena with Colin James. Why don't you come out and meet the guys, see the show? We can talk about the big western tour we have coming up in April."

Concert day arrived and I drove an hour and a half through a snowstorm to Orangeville. The arena was laid out for the concert in the usual Canadian arrangement of floorboards covering the ice surface with a stage set up at one end of the oblong.

I found Kenny at the soundboard at the rear. "C'mon, I'll bring you back to the dressing room to meet the guys." I was a little excited as we entered the conference room that was serving as their backstage quarters. This was the famous April Wine, legends since my youth, about to discuss the idea of me joining the band.

Kenny led me in without knocking, and there they were: Myles Goodwyn, Jerry Mercer, Jim Clench, and Brian Greenway. All were in various stages of undress or pre-show preparation. Jack Daniels was an important, nay, *essential* part of those preparations that night and every night. It came to me again as we were introduced that they weren't as big as they looked in photos or on TV, and they were all ten to twenty years older than me. Kenny introduced me and they claimed to remember meeting me before. It was friendly enough but a little cautious.

Now, my main reason for being there was to discuss terms of employment, namely how much and when, to judge whether there was a deal possible. I wanted the job, but only at the right price. Getting a "feel" for the band and the current state of the show was secondary; I figured I could make just about anything work by applying effort and goodwill.

I chatted a bit with each guy but was looking for an opportunity to zero in on Myles since Kenny had said he was the decision maker. Cheerfully, he asked me, "So, how do you feel about a long tour out west?"

"Sounds fine to me. I like lots of shows."

"Yeah, we'll be leaving in about six weeks, and we'll need a couple of weeks of rehearsal in Montreal to put the new show together. Have you heard any of the new album yet? I'll get Kenny to send you a copy."

"Uh, that's great, Myles, thanks, but I was hoping we'd have a chance to talk about the details here tonight."

"Hmm? Oh yeah, no problem."

Suddenly Kenny reappeared to announce, "Hey, guys, Colin James has the guys from The Odds playing in his band, and they really want to meet you before the show. Is that okay?"

Myles: "Um, sure, for a little while, I guess, but let them know it can't be for long 'cause we're getting ready."

The Odds was a band from Vancouver that had a few cool songs on the radio. In a moment they were upon us and worked the room like awestruck fans. I was still standing near Myles, so when they reached him he introduced himself and then graciously included me by saying, "Oh, and this is Carl Dixon, our newest member. He'll be joining the band in a few weeks for our western tour and to help promote the new album."

I was stunned. Was Myles misinformed that I'd already accepted the job, or was he using a psychological ploy to influence my unmade decision? A beat too late I extended my hand to acknowledge the introduction. In the same moment I hoped that my silent acquiescence wouldn't be considered a *carte blanche* acceptance of whatever terms they had in mind.

I was still mulling over the meaning of the incident as showtime arrived. I wished the band "good show" and followed Kenny, who was also the soundman, out to the tech riser in front of house. I managed to say, with what I hoped was a mild note of rebuke, "Kenny, Myles thinks I've already joined. He just introduced me as the new member of April Wine!"

"Ah, don't worry about Myles. He's just confused. He's a muso, remember? Ha-ha-ha."

The house lights went down over a throng of happy Orangeville party people. They were well fuelled with alcohol and smokies and the expectation of a very good time with one of Canada's all-time great recording acts.

Jerry Mercer counted in and BOOM, the show began. I say "BOOM" because the sound levels were so loud, harsh, and pulverizing that the sound did not resemble music so much as it did bombs going off. Only fearless listening and familiarity with the band's hits could enable you to distinguish what song might be taking place behind the roar.

At the sound desk Kenny was swearing, hitting things, and frantically adjusting controls on every piece of gear in an attempt to get the beast back in the cage. The beast was too big.

And the audience? The smiles faded, the raised arms fell, and before long the poor buggers were in full retreat. Many fled to the back of the room or even outside for sonic safety. Duty-bound as I was to stand my ground and "check out the show" of my possible future employers, I sympathized. Watching them stream past me, fingers plugging their ears on either side of pained grimaces, I couldn't help thinking of demoralized First World War trench warfare soldiers, retreating in shock and disarray from an artillery barrage.

The band members themselves seemed worn, dispirited, and colourless, as if also trapped in this assault but helpless to stop it. Maybe it was partly my expectation of how I thought they should appear that led me to feel let down. What April Wine was really trapped in was their belief system. The two guitarists had Marshall amps blasting on 10, the bass player had powerful speakers pumping out massive, indistinct low frequencies, and the drummer had the equivalent of his own PA system mounted at his back so as to hear and "feel" the sound of his drums above the roaring, smothering guitar sounds. Added to this was not one, not two, but three different vocal monitor systems to enable the singers to hear themselves clearly. Ninety percent of this amplification was aimed at the audience's heads and was deafening in itself. The big sound system beside the stage is supposed to mix the various sound sources into a pleasing balance and then boost that balanced pleasantness up another level in volume above the stage sounds so as to overcome them. Sometimes, with some bands, on some nights, when we talk about boosting a clean mix up louder than the stage sound, we are talking about the impossible. To be the soundman for April Wine at that time, with the levels they were producing, was almost to be the equivalent of that fellow from Greek mythology who was condemned to be chained to a rock and have a raven come eat his liver each day for eternity.

The belief system trap was that the guys believed the loudness was an integral and defining part of "their sound," that their music and image would suffer without it. To be quieter or more controlled would be to compromise or to soften unacceptably. It might leave them prey to some unnamed bogeyman, waiting to pounce at their first sign of wimping out with age and make them admit they could no longer take it … admit that the way they did it when they were twenty-seven no longer made sense at fifty-five or sixty … admit that their focus on their own needs didn't necessarily make the audience happy.

April Wine wasn't unique in this. Many bands who've endured for a long time get "stuck in a place," fearing that if they let the methods slip or change from when they were at their peak, everything will inevitably decline and all remaining vestiges of stardom will slip from their grasp. I went through it for a time in my way after Coney Hatch. It's hard to avoid those thoughts if you liked your success and you want to keep it. Success, however, like happiness, is for the brave. Fear chases them both away.

At some point Kenny kindly found me some earplugs. Eventually he surrendered to the onslaught, stopped blaming the room and the system, and let the beast have its way. I was struck by how little entertainment value the scene held. Onstage there was little movement, no smiles, and no effort to make the night special. Only Jim Clench, who always dressed well, had any colour in his attire. The others were in shades of black or grey. It was a sombre ensemble.

Naturally, my initial reaction was to start thinking of a way to politely excuse myself and head home before any more entangling discussions could occur. Somehow, though, as I watched, I began to see a role for myself that could help me and them. I convinced myself they needed me.

I would bring enthusiasm, a colourful image, and a joy for performing that might spread. I would honour these men who had accomplished so much before I was even out of high school and bring the best of my skills to faithfully playing their amazing catalogue. In return I would learn a lot and I'd have the right to say I was once a member of April Wine. Provided the price was right, of course.

The show came to a merciful conclusion and I followed Kenny to the stage, where he and the crew set about swiftly removing April Wine's gear to make room for Colin James. It was debatable who should have been headlining the show, but April Wine were notably free of ego when it came to such things. Rather than argue about top-of-the-bill status, they were generally happy to go on first so they could get to bed earlier.

After giving the band a decent interval to clean up and discuss things in private, I got back to the dressing room to resume our face-time. The first spark of the new role I'd imagined for myself in April Wine was quietly smouldering in me now, so I was keen to find an opening to press my cause and clinch the deal. However, the room was promptly invaded by a brace of fans and friends of the kind every band builds up over a long career. All the Winers were taken up in conversation.

I turned my attention to Myles as the man I should be parleying with and asked him a couple of times if we could talk. "Yeah, sure. Just give me a couple of minutes." He had people to chat with and there was packing to be done.

The room gradually emptied until it was just the two of us. As Myles folded his pants into a valise, I stepped forward and said, "So, Myles, I was a little surprised at being introduced as the new member of the band tonight, but I'm glad you feel positive about it. I'm thinking that we need to talk about the business arrangements before the deal is settled."

Myles responded quickly. "Oh, no, no, no. I never discuss that kind of thing. I leave all that stuff to Kenny. You need to talk to him."

"Really? I thought he told me you were the guy."

"No, no, go find Kenny to discuss money."

"Well, okay. Is he still here?"

"He's probably out back, packing up the truck. If you hurry you might still catch him."

I had lingered for more than an hour, only to encounter this new twist. Myles left to jump into the Lincoln Town Car the band always rented, while I went, chagrined and a bit annoyed, to search for Kenny. I found him deep in the box of the five-ton, arranging the gear in a tight pack.

"Hey, Kenny, have you got a minute?"

"Just hang on. I'm throwing some cases around in here."

After five more minutes of crashing, banging, and swearing, Kenny jumped down from the truck, sweating and panting. "What's up, buddy?"

"Look, Kenny, it's getting kinda late here, and I really need to get some idea from you of what the pay scale is for the job, so I can make a decision."

Kenny blinked and then said, "Oh, no, no, I can't talk about that with you. You need to see Myles about that. Maybe you can still catch him."

"He just sent me to see you!" I exploded. "Myles told me that you're in charge of this stuff and he never gets involved!" I was even yelling a bit, I think.

Kenny took a step back and looked me up and down. "Really? He said that?"

"Yes, he did!"

Still a bit loud, me.

"Okay, okay. Let's calm down," he said, taking in a breath. "I'll tell you what we can do. It's already pretty late. Now, I've got a number in mind that I can pay you. Why don't you go home and decide on your number over the weekend. On Monday morning call me and we'll compare our numbers. Is that okay, buddy?"

This approach was a new one on me, and it stopped me in my tracks. After the long night, the confusion and delays, and the emotional ups and downs of the evening, I was a bit spun.

"You really can't tell me anything now?"

"No, let's do it this way. I think it'll work out."

"Okay, then. Thanks, Ken. Talk to you Monday."

I started the drive back home through the now-blinding snowstorm. Creeping along the dark highway, I slowly began to boil. It had been a crazy night and was not, on any level, what I had expected from Canada's sometime heroes. I wasn't ready to surrender to the universe on this one.

Saturday morning, Mr. I-Mean-Business calls Kenny. I give him my number along with my opinion of the silliness of the night before. It turns out that he was allowed to go up to a certain pay level without consulting the band. My number was higher, so now we're in a negotiation. At least I have the ball in play, so I can live with the delay of him talking it over with the band.

Come Monday I get my number; they've found a way to justify it. I'm now the new fifth member of April Wine.

I joined at the start of 2001 and spent the first year with the band in the unaccustomed role of sideman. We had rehearsals at Jerry's house on the West Island and I stayed with him. The guys all smoked wherever they went, indoors and out, and the smoke was hellish as we went through the show in the space above Jerry's garage. I ended up standing by the open window between every song to get fresh air. In all we spent two weeks at it, and I couldn't wait to get the hell out of there. We prepared six or seven songs from the new album, titled *Back to the Mansion*, anticipating that it would take the charts by storm. On tour those new songs were dropped from the show one by one in favour of the old hits. The year progressed and the album didn't.

Our first show was notable for a few things. One, it was just outside Toronto near the Woodbine racetrack, so my wife and friends could come to see what I'd gotten myself mixed up in. We left on a tour bus for eight weeks out west at the end of the show, and I had my goodbyes in the parking lot. Two, I learned that night how very cautious and nervous Myles was about the show. Even with all my years of experience, he didn't trust me to play the parts properly on about eight of the songs, the ones that we hadn't rehearsed quite as much. He ordered before we went on that I was to leave the stage and not play on those songs. I felt a bit embarrassed having my people see me keep leaving the stage for a song and coming back on for the next, then off again.

Third, our big night to debut the new album with the new band lineup was interrupted by a power failure, about five songs in. The building went dark, the show was stopped for about forty-five minutes while somebody monkeyed around in the basement, and a fair number of people went home. It was not a good launch for *Back to the Mansion*, but sadly, it was a good indicator of the prospects for the album's success.

At first it was odd being set up onstage in the back row where they keep the drummer. I set about proving my worth nonetheless, and by about four weeks in I'd managed to convince Myles that I could be trusted to stay onstage for almost all the songs. People began to refer to me as "the keyboard player from April Wine" as the tour went on. Being so much younger (and looking younger again than I really was) made for some funny misconceptions. People started to say, "How nice! Myles has hired his son to be the keyboard player." That got him irate a few times. When introducing the band, he took to saying, "… and on keyboards, guitar, backing vocals, and percussion, Carl Dixon! And no, he's not my son, okay?"

We began making a good sound as the band tightened up. I kept referring back to the old albums to bring in vocals and instrumental parts that the band had either forgotten or didn't think could be done, so the music gained in depth and texture. However, with the onstage din only slightly more under control than that first night in Orangeville, the band couldn't really hear much of the details I was adding. Myles admitted later that he'd hardly heard anything I'd done all year except for my backing vocals, which he liked. At least Kenny was bringing my work out front in the mix. Sometimes it was hard to accept the reduced role, but most times I was able to quell that feeling and remind myself, "At least I'm working, and I'm part of another great band and their great music."

✴ ✴ ✴

On a long ride home from Minnesota when the western swing ended, I stayed up half the night playing guitar and singing to entertain the band and crew for our "tour-end party." Kenny was watching me appraisingly and the wheels started to turn. He said, "Wouldn't it be great if we could use you as our opening act doing this solo show? It would make our lives easier for set-up and tear-down every night too."

For a few more months that idea went no further, but I continued to think about it. I also wasn't sure if they would renew my contract into the second year. Their new album had not topped the charts. When Kenny called me in January, he said the band was very happy with me and would like to keep me on. There was only one problem: I was making more money than the other band members, and they needed me to take a pay cut. I said, "Okay, I'll take your pay cut if you can get me those opening shows you talked about." It was a win-win. The band saved two hundred a week from my salary, and I added a thousand to fifteen hundred a week extra to my pay from doing the opening shows. I also got great exposure across Canada and the States. That led to lots of work later on for me on call-backs.

Money aside, I had the pleasure of performing as a member of this renowned band, and it was educational to play a supporting role to some legendary musicians. I must stress that I really got off on playing the April Wine song catalogue. I took pride in referencing the original recordings and restoring the proper parts wherever possible, just as I'd done with The Guess Who. I made the music as strong as I could with my added backing vocals, guitars, keyboards, and percussion, positioned on a riser next to Jerry's drum kit. The role of backing musician was one that I took on with all I could give. Maybe I wouldn't have been so happy with it if I hadn't had my solo opening shows to get some spotlight for myself.

At the start of year three I couldn't resist calling up Kenny to tease him. "Isn't it about time for us to discuss my annual pay cut?"

Life in April Wine settled into a pattern that stayed more or less the same every year: around March, tour the Maritimes for two or three weeks; April to June, out west in Canada and the U.S.; summertime, to various festivals and special events all over the place. Autumn and Christmastime we'd run around Ontario and Quebec. The second year, with me adding my solo opening show almost every night, I was kept very busy while building my confidence and contacts.

Back to the Mansion hadn't achieved the anticipated sales results, and the group naturally was disappointed. We toured the country, got radio play, and appeared on television, but the ball was dropped somehow. Tensions ran high at times. The band had all kicked in portions of their wages over the last five years to finance the album, and the money had mostly gone to Myles, the producer. The shared sacrifice was not leading to shared rewards. I began to realize that all that shared history hadn't improved the April Winers' opinions of one another and in fact that was their main problem in some ways: too much history. Having *too many* original members, all with long memories, could result in very subjective or bitter interpretations of new events.

Now, they always treated me well, and Myles was almost always respectful and cool with me, as opposed to some of the more difficult-to-handle moments I'd seen him capable of providing. I mostly felt bad for the band that they couldn't seem to get along better. In a just universe those men should be getting joy and satisfaction in return that was equal to that which they'd given so many listeners over the years.

I did my best to fill the role I'd first envisioned, of bringing energy and positivity. No amount of positivity was going to change the group dynamic, which seemed carved in stone: Myles hated Jerry for some reason, Jimmy was a fear-based life form, and Brian was uncertain which end was up. They are each in their own way nice people, and I saw the good in all of them. They could be a somewhat toxic brew when stirred together, though, and this robbed them of happiness. It was probably up to Myles, as the leader, to either fix this or rise above.

In early 2003 we recorded a concert for the release *April Wine's Greatest Hits Live 2003*, a two-disc document of the show as it was then. A credit to the band's playing and Myles's production, it also finally captured Jerry Mercer's famous drum solo for posterity. Once again the band had a new product to promote. At the same shows I recorded my *One Voice, Two Hands* solo acoustic live album, and the two albums made from those productive nights have both done fairly well.

* * *

In April Wine the tour bus life had rules — lots of them — to which I had to adjust. They mostly originated from Myles. Far from the popular image of the rock band tour bus being some kind of drug-fuelled, orgiastic debauch-on-wheels, this band's bus was all about staying cozy and clean and getting lots of rest. The bus driver told a funny story about how the band Blue Rodeo once refused to accept the use of a tour bus that April Wine had just returned. They were sure the bus would still be polluted with the evidence of "all the groupies and partying." Hilarious. My years with them were long, long past the days of being a chick-magnet band, and drug use never occurred the whole time I was with them.

I always had a top bunk, being the youngest and nimblest. Myles had decided that air conditioning set very cold was a necessity for sleeping,

Photo credit: Dave Gruggen

Unused promo shot from 2004. Left to right: Carl, Jim Clench, Jerry Mercer, Myles Goodwyn, Brian Greenway. Jimmy said, "The guys in our old photo looked like they could beat up the guys in this photo easy."

so I normally had a toque and a sweater on under extra covers. The back lounge was reserved as "the library," a quiet escape space. Many long days crossing the country were spent in silent reading or minimal chat. Nobody was permitted to fall asleep in the front or back lounge, as Jerry liked to do in front of the TV, or they'd awake to find they'd been pranked.

We were permitted to hang damp stage clothes briefly for drying, but they were not to be forgotten or they'd end up in the freezer. Shoes, socks, and underwear, if left untended or neglected in common space? Into the freezer they'd go. Jerry was often the recipient of this attention. One night in Quebec City he'd dropped a pair of gaunch on the bus floor while changing for the stage and wandered away. Myles, in his ire upon discovering this, made good on a long-standing threat. Jerry returned to the bus after the show to find his dropped underwear going up in flames on the pavement. He had the good grace to laugh about it.

Lateness was not tolerated. On one of the rare occasions that Myles spoke harshly to me, it was because I'd kept the bus waiting five or ten minutes for departure on two days running

At least the music felt authentic, as opposed to my first Guess Who experience. April Wine might have lost a step over the years, but they still played with conviction. Business was gradually slowing down over the four years, and I was genuinely surprised each January when they said I was included in their plans for the coming year. In mid-2004 I had gotten exploratory phone calls from Jim Kale and Garry Peterson, inquiring about whether I'd consider a return to The Guess Who. There were good prospects for the group financially in the wake of the reunion tours with Burton Cummings and Randy Bachman. I told them I'd do whatever made the most sense for my family.

They went off to work out their plans while I embarked on what was in some ways my most enjoyable year with April Wine. We had played in every Canadian province in the first six months of the year when we hit Prince Edward Island on July 1 for a Canada Day show with Hootie and the Blowfish. There was some inspired musical meshing and big shows. In spite of my growing affection and acceptance of their "little ways," I'd already seen signs of the direction in which things were headed.

There had at one point been talk of us doing a new April Wine promo photo that would finally show me as a member of the band. After a half-hearted attempt at a photo shoot on the afternoon of a show in Oakville, the "new promo" idea was shot down and quickly abandoned. They'd done a couple of shows where they'd left me behind as non-essential in order to cut larger pieces of the pie for themselves. They didn't see why this should bother me. They started to "forget" to book me a hotel room once or twice.

In the midst of this uncertainty Kale and Peterson got back to me with very certain plans about getting The Guess Who show back on the road, including me if I wanted it. I called Stewart, April Wine's tour manager (Kenny was gone by this time) to see what he thought. Stewart cautiously replied, "I would say if there's an opportunity out there for you to do something else ... you should probably grab it." He wasn't saying, he was just saying.

My time with April Wine ended in a wishy-washy sort of way. There was a string of dates booked in one week, pre-Christmas '04, three shows in all. Come the Monday, I hadn't heard anything yet from Stewart about travel arrangements, scheduling, etc., so I called him to find out.

Stewart hemmed and hawed for a bit and then finally came out with it: "Look, the guys want to know if you'll stay home this week, not play. They'd like to divvy up your pay between them so they have more money for Christmas."

"Absolutely not," I retorted. "No f**kin' way!" I added for emphasis. "They can't tell me on Monday, the week of, when it's too late for me to book anything else. It's not right. You can't do business that way."

Sort of exiting the same way I'd entered with Kenny four years before.

"Okay, okay," Stewart said, backing off quickly. I don't think he felt good about being put up to this dirty job. "I'll tell them you don't agree and that's it. Be in Owen Sound about four o'clock on Wednesday."

So I played those last three shows. The band never said a word about it and acted like there was no problem. Nobody mentioned the future. No goodbyes, no thank-yous, no handshakes, no "F**k off, Dixon." Just ... silence. Geez, I hate when things end that way.

Weeks went by, 2005 began, and I started to get wind of April Wine shows without my involvement. Luckily for me, the plans for my return to The Guess Who were in motion; we'd done one test show in late 2004, and rehearsals would soon begin in Winnipeg. I decided to take on the task myself of bringing the April Wine chapter of my life to a close. I called Myles at home one afternoon.

"Hello?"

"Hi, Myles. It's Carl."

"Oh...." Hesitation. "How are you?"

"I'm just fine, Myles. I decided to call you today to fire myself since nobody from the band has called to fire me."

Brief pause. "Well, I wouldn't call it 'fired,' exactly, Carl."

"I'm not sure what to call it, Myles, but I understand that I'm not in the plans. I just didn't want it hanging there unresolved and unspoken."

He sidestepped that. "I thought you were going with The Guess Who again. Isn't that still on?"

"Oh, yeah, I'll be fine. I just want to say thanks and good luck. I thought one of us should say something."

"Yeah, okay, Carl. Good luck, then."

So off they went while I resumed singing for The Guess Who. In 2007 Jimmy Clench resigned; then in 2010 he passed away suddenly from lung cancer. He'd been suffering from the effects of heavy smoking for years.

In 2009 Jerry Mercer likewise withdrew his services, or "retired." We've remained friends and performed as a Carl and Jerry duo a few times.

I must thank the various April Wine road crew who made the show happen every night.

✶ ✶ ✶

I hadn't seen them play since I was in the band, but ... when a benefit show and donation fund was created for me after my accident, April Wine (at Myles's behest) kindly sent along a thousand-dollar contribution to help my recovery. I believe that, whatever their foibles, April Wine are like all of us: doing the best they can with what they've got. I wish them only good things. Myles, Jerry, Jim, and Brian were a great help to me.

MUSIC SOLO, YOU CAN'T GET UNDER IT

I've had a great deal of success with my solo acoustic shows. The ability to show up and entertain with just my voice, my acoustic guitar, and a sense of humour has led to many bookings in theatres, clubs, arenas, and casinos as both headliner and opening act. As a one-man show, I've played weddings, hockey banquets, Christmas parties, après-ski parties, charity auctions, corporate parties, radio shows, and just about every other kind of event you can think of.

One Voice, Two Hands, the live CD of the solo show, has been my bestselling solo album. "World's smallest rock band, right here!" is what I like to say onstage (when I remember). Yet, for all that, I can't say that it was ever one of my goals as a young, aspiring musician to someday get rid of the other guys and stand on a stage alone.

It came about almost inadvertently. I was in Halifax in 1985. Coney Hatch was headlining three nights at the Misty Moon, and Larry Gowan was opening the shows for us. He had just released his second album, *Strange Animal*, which was to propel him to star status in Canada, and it was already clear that he wouldn't be opening for Coney Hatch for long. We shared the same management, SRO, and they had arranged for Larry to get on the bill with us so he could break in his new band. He had strong material, a dramatic presentation, and a video that was already in heavy rotation. He had the buzz going.

After the second or third night's show, I was walking back to the Lord Nelson Hotel through the snowy streets with Mike Tilka, one of the SRO managers. We were discussing Larry's confident and flamboyant style, and Mike said, "You know, he's just got that thing in him where he can grab people's attention and hold it. He doesn't even need a band. You'll never be one of those guys, Carl, that can sit and entertain a crowd by yourself."

I reeled in shock for a moment, that my *manager* was saying this to me. I said, "Really?"

He elaborated: "Nah, you're just not that kind of performer. You could never do that." I held my tongue and trudged along in thoughtful silence the rest of the way. One of those thoughts was *Oh, yeah? The hell you say!*

Here I was, thinking I was the singer and frontman of a recording act positioned for international success, and my manager was telling me I couldn't entertain a crowd. He was right in one way, though; it wasn't much on my radar to "entertain." I was completely focused on the proper execution of the musical tasks, but that didn't mean I could "never do that." I could get there.

In the short term his talk only added to my concerns as we embarked on the promotion of our third album, *Friction*. My tendency toward perfectionism had always been part of my character. That's okay when things are going well, but when we encountered mounting difficulties on the *Friction* tour, it led to my putting huge pressure on myself. I believed I had to sing every song perfectly every night, and if I ever made a mistake, we were all *finished*. Several times in those next months I broke down sobbing under the strain. I probably should've tried drinking. I didn't, and eventually the self-imposed pressure caused me to flame out and quit.

The sting of Tilka's words stuck with me, though. I wanted to prove him wrong, prove I could be that "entertainer" who could please a crowd through personality as well as musical skill. I kept my radar up for chances to try.

Meantime, a period of research and post-debacle analysis ensued. I've always read voraciously, and one of the things I read in that post-Coney, licking-my-wounds period was a biography of Sammy Davis, Jr., of all people. He had a vaudeville background prior to his Hollywood fame, and a lesson he shared from that experience was that showbiz success is all about entertaining folks, and that playing or singing a "perfect" show has nothing to do with it. The job is to make the audience feel it is part of a unique, special night that isn't just a rote re-enactment of something that's been done many times before. The entertainer has to be open to the moment and to the unexpected, and especially to the people who are in attendance on each night, because every audience is different. The part that really stuck with me was when Sammy said something like, "If one leg falls off the piano and it nearly collapses, you keep playing and keep things going with a smile on your face, and people will walk away talking for ages about the amazing piano player who somehow kept playing even when the thing fell down on him!"

The point is, they'll feel they were part of something special. If the performer gets in a snit and is thrown into a tizzy because conditions aren't perfect, he/she spoils it for everyone. That can lead to a short career as an entertainer. That passage in the book had a huge impact on me.

Around that time my attitude began to change completely, and I began to say to myself, *It's far better to shoot for being great than for being perfect. There's only one way to be perfect, and there are so many ways to be great.*

I went forward with eyes open for opportunities to become that kind of performer. About four years and many adventures later, I saw a chance. A nice drummer from Montreal, John Bouvette, was doing a weekly gig in Toronto at a bar near Yonge and Eglinton, sometimes solo, sometimes as half of a duo. I knew John from a short-lived attempt I'd made at starting my first Carl Dixon Band. He went on to be *les batteur* of Frozen Ghost for many years but kept himself busy during downtime with these little gigs where he'd sing and play simple acoustic guitar — very pleasant. I wandered in to find him doing this one night. I think I sat in for a song, and then he asked me if I'd play with him for the full night next time because his usual partner wasn't available. The pay wouldn't be much, he warned, but it would be fun. Wings 'n' beer would be on offer.

I was thrilled and scared. I don't think I'd ever played music for an audience without a full loud band around me, so this would be the most exposed I'd ever been.

My first wife, Stella, with whom I was by now engaged in a somewhat tense relationship, received this news coolly. She was still bartending at a strip club, making lots of money. She'd also been pressuring me relentlessly to get serious about making a better living and getting a real job, and started drawing hard lines about what was hers and what was ours. Looking back at it now, I'll admit freely that I was a moron when it came to understanding the real world.

This opportunity for me to take a chance and grow as a performer was not exciting to Stella. In her eyes it was nothing more than an opportunity to take another dumb step in the wrong direction. Fair to say she was a bit jaded by now with my career struggles and with paying our bills too many times from her jobs. It may also be that she felt the gig was unworthy of the rising-star musician she thought she had married.

The day of my little gig neared, and the wife bugged me about it more and more. Finally, the night of, she played her trump card. She wasn't coming, she wasn't giving me a ride, and she wasn't lending me her car. There was no middle ground. Soon I was wobbling out on my ten-speed bike, acoustic guitar case across the handlebars, in the rain, with my dearest screaming after me, "Fine, go and suck ass for twenty-five dollars! But you're an idiot!"

I had the last laugh. It was thirty-seven dollars (plus beer and wings). Hah!

I owe John. That night got me started. So what if I'd played all those big places with Coney Hatch, made those albums, been on radio and TV? I wasn't there now.

❋ ❋ ❋

I still had a feeling there was something about all this just-a-man-and-guitar business that I didn't get, but at least I was moving closer to *something*. I did the gig with John a few more times and enjoyed the relaxed mood he created. The supporting role I played to his singing and the lead role he threw me from time to time made me feel free and easy. I saw new possibilities and a way out of the same old approach.

It wasn't long before I had the confidence to try to find my own gig as a solo performer. The opportunity appeared in Keswick, north of Toronto. A bar owner named Lloyd Lang was opening a new place. I'd befriended him through playing with bands at his old place, and he mentioned he was looking for something to book for regular Wednesday nights. I said, "I can do it." A few weeks prior to that, I wouldn't have considered myself a candidate. That led to almost two years of playing solo just about every Wednesday night. Decent money too. It was the next level of apprenticeship in my craft as I learned about pleasing an audience, relating to them as individuals, and just relaxing about the whole thing. I did lots of song testing and probing the limits of how a song can be made to work with just the voice and the acoustic guitar. It was my mission to find the unexpected thing, and Keswick was a good place to try out ideas. I learned that for my show to work the way I liked, I needed to concentrate on the rhythm and on keeping a strong beat going on the guitar — to think like a drummer.

On one summer Wednesday night I pulled up to find Lloyd's latest promotion idea scrawled on a big chalkboard at the front door: "Tonite! All-you-can-eat spaghetti, 99 cents!! Plus Carl Dixon." I had truly arrived.

Those many nights of practice at Keswick stood me in good stead years later when I launched my solo opener for April Wine.

DENOUEMENT

It's taken me a couple of tries to relate the story of my crash in Australia. Certain aspects look very different to me now than they did when I began writing. I have to believe that it's all been for the best.

The big difference between now and the time I began is in the knowledge I've gained about choices made by my former wife. Rather than using this book as a platform to self-indulgently rage against "the ex," I will content myself with sharing facts of the story. I will refer to her as "E." because I now cannot bring myself to use her name in affiliation with mine.

As I've since learned, E. resolved secretly to leave me in 2007. The reasons for this are not clear to me, but simply put, she was unhappy. That spring I'd made the *faux pa*s of mentioning her rapid weight gain. Naive perhaps, but I hoped to stimulate a little discussion about how we could spend more time together, doing fitness things; maybe I'd even be thanked for speaking up. I wasn't. (Ladies, I hear your groans. Look, I'm famous for being a nice guy but not always a bright guy.)

My concern was received badly, and E. chose to turn her affections away from me. Resentfully embarking on an alarming crash diet, she felt justified in pursuing other men now because I'd hurt her feelings. I think justification really means finding an excuse later for something you knew was wrong.

Other men were pursued, and caught, with me none the wiser. That evolved into her need to get away from life with wonderful me, again "justified."

When the adventure in Australia for our daughter's TV show came along, E. was already planning her escape from our marriage and family life. She used our daughter's role in a sweet little children's show as the getaway vehicle to a new life.

Unfortunately, E. failed to inform me of these ideas. On my two visits to Australia to reunite the family, I was met with her criticism, skepticism, and coldness. From each trip I returned to Canada very low, in deepening sadness and confusion, mystified by the rejection and almost wishing I hadn't gone.

After stewing in this unhappiness for a while I decided to ask for a short time off from The Guess Who. I would make a third visit to Australia, use it to remind my wife that I was a good guy who was completely devoted to her and our family, and whatever the problem might be, we could overcome it with love and commitment. The idea consumed me. I would fix this.

The Guess Who leaders saw the state I was in and granted me compassionate leave, even though it cost them many thousands of dollars to shut down for two weeks. I gratefully made my travel plans because I was determined to make a difference in the outcome of my marriage and my family's future. It was not in me to suspect or even imagine that something sneaky was going on in Australia. Cheat? My wife? Oh, no. Our commitment was too strong for that to ever happen.

This was my illusion, my blind spot. The power of my determination was not sufficient to overwhelm the power of E.'s hurt feelings and hostility. The adulterous path she'd pursued empowered her to decide she didn't need or want me any longer.

So … CRASH! Irresistible force, me, met immovable object, E. Something had to give.

They say energy never dies, it just takes a different form. The energy in my effort to get my marriage back on track transformed just so after the crash. It first went into the mammoth task of ensuring the survival of the organism, me. Then came the slow revival to as wholly restored a creature as medical expertise and the human will would allow. (Guardian angels and divine intervention are thought to have had a role. I'll buy that.)

E., the immovable object, also changed after the crash, perhaps from guilt or maybe just plain human compassion. It wasn't from love, because her perfidious ways continued while I was in a coma and long, long beyond.

E. had an escape fantasy, and I went and spoiled it by getting myself in that stupid car crash. Now she was stuck with me.

All who know me know what my marriage and my family meant to me; it was paramount. I lived for being a good father and a good husband and spoke about my wife and daughters everywhere I went.

I included them in the nice perks of my job and was deeply involved in their lives and in being caregiver for the girls when I was home. My desire to be a good provider drove me ever onward to greater accomplishment and reward. I didn't smoke, drink, gamble, or take drugs. I was faithful and loyal as a dog to my wife. Every penny I brought home was turned over to E., the CFO of our little company. In every way I could dream up I made the world magic for my children. That I could be disliked by any of my loved ones was inconceivable to me.

In the months and years that followed my crash, as I worked to resume my life and restore the Dixons to wholeness, I was resented, mocked, and betrayed by my partner. She wouldn't love me but she wouldn't leave me.

Many unsavoury episodes unfolded that wrecked my beloved family. The secret life E. was pursuing only accelerated in pace the longer I held on unwittingly to an illusion.

After six years like this I found the first of much shocking evidence of the truth. Despite my efforts even then to rise above the pain and hold on, things unravelled rapidly. Now that dream is over, as if twenty-two years never happened. The kindest way I can sum up is to say that we didn't have matching belief systems.

> "How does all that disappear? The hurt is all that shows you
> were ever here...."
> — "More Than a Memory," Dixon/Walker

I go forward now into a wiser and happier third act of my life. Real love and honesty unexpectedly came to me in the form of a lady from (get this) *Australia*. My Helen, who is age-appropriate for me yet extraordinarily youthful, is of a similar temperament to me and we are a perfect match in beliefs and values. Great joy is already ours. Into the future we go....

Now back to our story.

THE SMACK-DOWN

"Acceptance is not submission; it is acknowledgement of the facts of a situation.
Then deciding what you're going to do about it."
— Kathleen Casey Theisen

In the consumer society we inhabit, we are all encouraged to be completely self-indulgent, deny ourselves nothing, and pursue pleasure in every category of experience. There are appropriate times for those pursuits, and they can be balm for the soul, oil on troubled waters. More often, though, we're smarter, wiser, to do what we oughta do and do the right thing, even if it's difficult.

In life there's always the element of the unexpected — and you can't really get ready for the unexpected, can you? It's like Bill Cosby's old routine where, after the young Bill commits a domestic offence, his dad says, "You go to your room, young man, and get ready for a whuppin'!"

"Now, how," Bill says, "do you get ready for a whuppin'? Do you sit in the corner and whimper, 'No, Dad, no, don't do it'? I mean, how do you get ready for a whuppin'?"

Now, it seems to me, any whuppin' that gets laid on you will certainly require the best strength of character you can muster. What if you have no practice at stepping up? What do you fall back on if you've always taken the easy way out? You learn how to step up if you always *make the effort* to step up.

Do what's right even if no one's looking. Honour your commitments and keep your promises. Live up to the best in yourself. It's just a decision, in the same way that doing the wrong thing is a decision. It's a habit, so that your life just stays on that good path and you hardly have to think about it. A helpful motto that I learned to live by as a travelling musician, faced with temptation more than most people, is "Always behave as if your wife and kids are watching you."

It may seem corny or old-fashioned, but I'm here to tell you that, if I hadn't made those decisions and built up those kinds of good thoughts in my life, I would not be here today.

The unexpected will sneak up on you and just arrive one day; that's why we call it unexpected. Here's my story of the unexpected.

✳ ✳ ✳

So it's April 2008 and I'm humming along pretty good, thinking that I've got this thing all figured out. I'm making good money with The Guess Who, basking in the adoration of fans, taking care of my family, my wife doesn't have to work, and things should be ducky. Then one day I'm in Melbourne, Australia, driving back to the countryside after a recording session for a TV series called *Saddle Club*, in which my younger daughter, Lauren, is starring, and BOOM! Lights out.

I wake up in the critical care unit of the Alfred Hospital, unable to move. My wife, E., is there to greet me after a nine-day vigil of waiting for me to emerge from an induced coma. It takes me a while to absorb her explanation of what's happened, but the evidence makes it undeniable. I've been in a terrible car accident and sustained a list of injuries as long as my shattered arm. More than fifty separate injuries from the moment of impact, any one of which would have sent me to hospital. So many injuries that it took years for them all to be disclosed.

During my drive to the rural town of Daylesford, I'd been feeling anxious about running almost two hours late. I had planned a romantic dinner for that evening with E. to soothe bad feelings. When I got lost in Melbourne's rush-hour traffic, and with time ticking away, I got myself in a bit of a state. Little memory remains to me of events once I finally got on the proper road out of Melbourne. It was my wife and kids, the police, and some witnesses who filled in the story.

In Australia they drive on the left side, as in England, steering wheel on the other side of the car and everything. Now, we had a relationship with the Canadian consulate in Melbourne because of my daughter's TV show, and they told us later that eighty percent of their time is spent helping Canadians who have car crashes because they forget for a moment what country they're in. I'd been doing fine with remembering this difference for hundreds of miles before that night, but I can only assume I was distracted by my anxiety about being late for dinner.

I later learned that the scene of the crash was about an hour out of Melbourne, and a few minutes past where I exited the major freeway. It was a dark evening on a country road with no streetlights and no other cars around to remind me where to drive. I was on the wrong side of the road approaching a blind curve in my little rented Toyota as a big SUV suddenly came around the turn in its proper lane. The police later calculated that I had about one second to react; the other driver about two seconds. The other driver attempted evasive action to avoid a head-on crash by steering hard for the road shoulder, but there wasn't time. Instead his big SUV drove right up the front of my small car at a forty-five-degree angle and then right over me.

A witness who'd been following me said that I'd spent about a minute driving on the wrong side after I'd pulled off the freeway. I must have gone on automatic pilot because my worries took over.

So the SUV went up one side of me and down the other, then rolled after landing. The driver, to the best of my knowledge, suffered a broken leg and a severe scalp wound as well as some lesser injuries. After my car was crushed down on top of me, it spun around several times before coming to an upright stop. I was as mashed and broken and bleeding as it's possible to be without being killed. The lady in the car following me stopped immediately to rush over and help, and I gather it's a good thing it was dark or she might have fainted on the spot at seeing my injuries. I was semi-conscious, babbling, completely in shock. By unbelievable luck the next person who happened along was a nurse-midwife, and she took over my care, though it was impossible for her to get at me. The crushed car had me trapped inside, as well as pinning down and shattering both my legs. All the nurse could really do was keep me talking and perhaps stop the blood gushing from the wounds she could reach. My head had taken a good whack, so it was swelling, and my face was ripped apart, with my right eye crushed and bleeding. My right arm had numerous deep cuts, a dislocated elbow, and a torn-up forearm with exposed fractures and missing bone, probably hurt in an attempt to shield my face.

Emergency crews responded quickly, but I was stuck in the wreck in that condition for an hour and a half before the crew could free me with the Jaws of Life. The officer on the scene rated my consciousness as five or six out of ten during that process. He and other witnesses also rated my accident-victim condition as the worst they'd ever seen. A helicopter had been called in to airlift me back to a Melbourne trauma unit, and when I was finally freed from the wreck, the ambulance attendants wheeled me on a stretcher to the chopper. The police officer told me he asked them what my chances were, and they shook their heads and said, "No hope."

Meanwhile, back at Daylesford, my wife had started packing a bag and calling in backup care for our daughter Lauren (our elder daughter, Carlin,

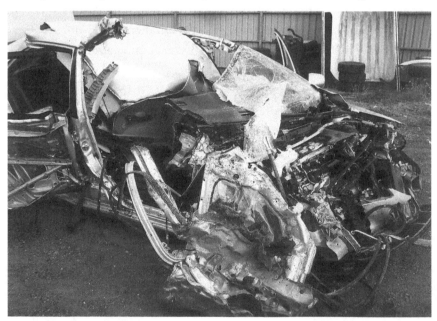

Photo: Carl Dixon

Improbable, but true: the Toyota after I was done with it.

was in Canada). This is spooky because nobody had called her yet. One of the emergency-response trucks had driven past the house in Daylesford with lights and sirens going, and she somehow knew it was for me. She started calling my cellphone repeatedly. It had been removed from the car and was out on the road, ringing away for a long time. When the police finally picked it up and rang back to the house, my daughter took the call just as the friends arrived. My wife borrowed a car to race to the scene, only to find the roads cordoned off for miles around. She came across a policeman and learned that I was already in the chopper. He gave them a high-speed escort to the freeway to Melbourne. It was clear that he wanted to help them reach the hospital before I died.

They reached the trauma unit of the Alfred Hospital as the specialists were consulting over my unconscious body. She was directed to a quiet waiting room, and after a few minutes doctors arrived to present her with my wedding ring. Not a good sign. They then asked that my daughter Lauren leave the room. My condition was extremely grave, they said, and they weren't sure they could save me.

E. looked in on me as I awaited surgery. My body wasn't forming enough platelets to stop the bleeding; I was continuing to lose blood so fast that it was pooling around me and spilling to the floor over the edges of the tray-type thing I was lying on. That first night there were some twenty-five doctors from the various specialties standing around me in the room, consulting to determine a strategy.

The first ER doctor and nurse came to tell her the news of the overall damage and that the patient might in fact die from his injuries; they advised that various teams representing my injured sites, each with their own specialty, would come and see her.

As promised, Vera, an orthopaedic surgeon, arrived a short time later. Representing the ortho team that would be working on me, she explained what they had to do and got a signed consent form in order to start work. Vera went into greater detail than the first two from ER. She explained the severity of the breaks and the damage caused and added that she didn't think they could save the right arm. The left leg was looking doubtful as well. E. told Vera that the man she was treating was special; he was a gifted musician, not just a hobbyist, and this was his life. Vera and the team would work hard to save anybody's arm, E. said, but Vera had to know how important this arm was. This arm defined a man. Not only was it his livelihood and only source of income, but the arm and what it enabled him to do was his identity. She knew that Carl could still write, sing, and play guitar with one leg, but he needed that arm.

At this point her bottom lip was quivering and eyes filled with tears. Vera reached out to hold her and whispered in her ear that she understood and that they would do their very best to save my arm. When the surgeon pulled back from the hug, she had tears in her eyes.

Various doctors trotted into the waiting room with prognosis reports after that. It was uncertain whether I would live through the surgeries. Not a surprise if you consider the list of injuries they were treating: blunt trauma to the head, crushed right eye and broken right orbital bone, face lacerations, cracked C7 vertebra, collapsed and bruised lungs, liver lacerations and internal bruising, dislocated and shattered right forearm with exposed fractures and missing flesh, multiple deep lacerations to the upper arm, multiple fractures of the right thigh and the left knee, exposed fractures in the left shin with missing bone and flesh, lengthy deep gashes to both legs and multiple broken toes and fingers. Amazingly, though, none of those dire predictions came true. Soon the doctors, having made a plan, each took their turn on me. The bleeding finally slowed enough that the surgeons were able to get to work. An initial nineteen-hour round of surgery was followed by a break of a couple of hours and then another seventeen hours.

Sometime during the early stages, my blood pressure, which was being regulated, dropped to zero. Panic ensued. They thought they had fixed it, and then it soon dropped again. This happened four times.

It turned out that my blood pressure was dropping repeatedly because the pressure-regulating medication wasn't actually reaching my system. The tube carrying it, one of about a dozen plugged in to me, had got pinched somehow and the flow was blocked. Some bright light figured this out by checking the connections. Just like a sound system problem: check the cables first.

My skull was swollen to such alarming dimensions that they elected to drill a burr hole (named for the sound the drill makes) just behind my right forehead hairline. They shaved a narrow swath on my scalp, leaving the rest of my chest-length hair intact. At some point E. came along, saw this, and said to them, "Oh my God, why did you do it like that?"

"We thought you'd be upset if we cut off all that beautiful hair."

"Well, he looks ridiculous. Buzz it all off to match! It'll grow back."

A bit later they came and offered her a plastic bag containing all the shorn hair, caked in dried blood and brain matter, as a souvenir. She declined.

The hole thus created in my skull had a drainage shunt with a long tube to draw away the fluid causing the swelling. The hole also offered the perfect location to implant an electrical activity sensor right onto my brain. This enabled the doctors to see on a monitor screen that my brain was still quite engaged in the business of keeping Dixon alive. They had no way of knowing how much function would remain, and the odds were high that brain damage would compromise my life if I survived. The electrical impulses at least showed that I wasn't a vegetable beneath my stillness.

E. was still reeling with the uncertainty of everything on that second day when a different pair of ortho surgeons turned up to explain what they intended for my shattered left shin bone. "We'll take a piece of bone from his hip, plus a piece of stomach muscle to fill in for the tissue that's been lost, then we'll use a titanium plate to back the broken tibia, add the hip bone piece into the shattered area to make a graft, then a patch of skin from his thigh to cover it all up. Whaddya think?"

E. took this in and responded, "My goodness, I hope he's going to survive after all that work you're putting in!"

One of the surgeons replied, "Do you think we'd be going to this much trouble if we didn't think he was going to live?"

My wife and daughters attended to me each day of my coma, gathering around my left arm since it was the only part of me not too damaged to touch. My swollen, broken head and limbs were at least still attached, but to my babies in particular the macabre figure before them was not their daddy, their "superman." My head was so swollen that my nostrils were stretched taut across my face, image-defining long hair buzzed right off, feet and right hand swollen into big blocks of meat. The girls bravely endured and hoped for my safe return to their world of consciousness. A large part of my children's innocent belief in a world of orderliness and predictability was shattered in the process. It had to happen sometime, I guess.

GREAT HALLUCINATIONS

At first I was too numb to fully comprehend how badly I was hurt. The doctors told E., "He's had enough painkillers to stun two elephants." As a result, when I started to come to, I experienced some outstanding hallucinations. In the last day or so of coma, about nine days after my arrival, my family saw me begin to twitch, make hand gestures, and try to remove the respirator. These were all unconscious moves. I was busy with some very convincing dreaming. In one dream I was sitting in an oddly furnished Mediterranean-style room with the musician Ben Harper. We were discussing musical choices for the radio station we were both helping, and we couldn't agree on the right approach. For at least a week after the coma I was pretty sure that I'd been working with Ben Harper in the recent past, but I couldn't determine how I knew him. I've actually never met him, but I was later reminded that the engineer with whom I'd been working in the recording studio on the day of the crash was named Ben. I'd dubbed him Ben Harper in my mind as a mnemonic.

Just prior to waking from the coma, or at least what seemed to be just prior, I was in northern Ontario in a walk-in medical clinic filled with Native Canadians like the ones I grew up with in Sault Ste. Marie. There were old and young there, all waiting to see doctors. It was on the highway near Espanola in a small plaza of storefronts. People came and went in pickup trucks, and the scene felt so familiar. From that dream place I woke from the coma to find my wife looking down at me and speaking in slow, soothing tones. "Hi, Carl ... hi, baby ... hey, Carl, it's me...." I struggled to focus my vision on her as if through a fog, a dark-haired angel looming over me, backlit by hospital lamps. There was no "Am I in heaven?" moment. I didn't even know I was hurt or that I was seeing through just one eye. It felt like waking from a dream.

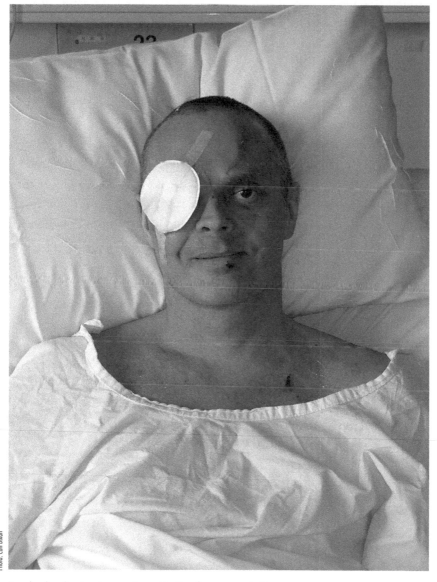

Photo: Carl Dixon

Dazed and confused, trying gamely to smile. Out of coma, now what?

She told me where I was and that I was badly hurt. In fact, she had to tell me about five times before it registered. After a moment of reflection I asked, "How's the other guy?" My concern was based purely on what I'd just heard, as I had then and still have to this day no memory of the accident. Post-traumatic amnesia (PTA) is the medical term. "Nature's mercy," I call it. Carlin (somehow) was there with her, and that helped me to stay a bit grounded while I wrapped my mind around the shocking news. Also, as David St. Hubbins said in *Spinal Tap*, "If I wasn't so heavily sedated, I'd be feeling this quite a bit more."

My voice was so hoarse and my throat so dry from the respirator tube, which had just been removed, that the relief of a cool drink was foremost on my mind. I managed to croak out as my first request (to my daughter), "Honey, can you get me a beer?"

In fact, I kept insisting on it. A cold beer after playing hockey always felt so good. When the beer wasn't forthcoming, my request turned into a demand for "a double, or a triple!" This desire was completely out of character. My wife was at some pains to convince the nurses I was not a drunk. In the next minutes, as the orderlies prepared to transfer me out of intensive care, I was certain that some nurses had turned into waitresses for a noisy rock bar that had materialized just outside the doors to my room. I could hear much barroom chattering over loud music, and the sound burst in whenever the doors swung open. I was wondering why the hospital would sponsor such an activity in close proximity to the critical-care patients. The waitresses kept coming back to load up with drinks from the bar, which was in a corner of my room, before rushing out again into the swirling noise and smoke. Only semi-conscious, I was splashing through choppy waters of the inland Sea of Memory, a narcotics-filled inept swimmer with no shore in sight. Much more interesting stimulus response was to come.

* * *

I learned much later about the frantic arrangements that had been made immediately following my crash. Carlin, my first-born girl, had actually been in Canada at that time under the temporary care of Jenny, a family friend. I'd been meant to head from Australia to Biloxi, Mississippi, for a single Guess Who show and then return home immediately to resume being a parent. Instead, Carlin got the news that I might not be coming home at all. Newspaper reporters started calling her for updates on my condition, and she fielded their questions with poise, although her heart was breaking. Then Carlin and Jenny had to scramble to catch a flight the next day out of Toronto to Melbourne. There were delays en route and they missed their connecting flight in L.A., which left them stuck there for an agonizing night.

Carlin is an experienced traveller. She took charge of arrangements and made things as comfortable as they could be, but it was still an exhausted girl who finally arrived in Melbourne to gaze upon her father's comatose, ravaged form. Unsurprising, then, that she swooned with the shock.

Each night thereafter E. and Carlin had to make the trek back to Daylesford to sleep briefly and then get up to return to my side. Lauren came after work when she could after returning to the *Saddle Club* set. With her slender form she was able to slip in behind the electronic life-support gear, closer than anyone else. There she'd speak quietly into my ear and tell me secret things, even though I was unconscious.

Eventually I was transferred out of intensive care and installed in a temporary bed in "acute care." The ward was actually a bit over-full, and I was placed in the centre of a kind of common room, which had a number of doorways around me to patient rooms. With the influence of the narcotics I formed a bleary first impression of being on a raised platform with a great space in front of me. I slipped in and out of consciousness, troubled intermittently by the new knowledge of my injuries and hospital patient status.

A young male nurse on his inaugural shift was in charge of me in the ward that first night. Among my hallucinations was a feeling that my bed was on an upper level of a large gas station/convenience store, and cars were pulling up outside a large plate glass window. Customers came and went, and there was a checkout counter with a scanner and a computer. I became convinced that the nurse had intentions of draining my bank account via the new universal price code the doctors had somehow installed in my arm. (That would be from my drugged impression of the incredible scars that I was seeing for the first time.) I was sure he'd brought the checkout scanner to my bedside and removed my credit card from my wallet. In the midnight gloom I saw and felt him running the scanner and the credit card across my forearm, and the devilish glee in his expression as he was stealing my funds really started to bother me.

After a day or two I was moved to my own room in a corner of the acute care unit, which had a window with a very bleak view: a hospital rooftop wasteland for me to contemplate day and night, with two chimneys perpetually belching smoke. Too reflective of my hellish state, I felt. The hallucinations continued unabated in my rattled mind. By day I was fairly lucid (I thought), although moving shadows still often looked like creatures to me, and new information had to be repeated frequently because I wasn't retaining details well. At night, however, there were some serious auditory illusions. Each night I heard the sounds of what I took to be a closed-circuit radio station that serviced only the wards in the hospital. It operated into the wee hours, playing strange music or bizarre spoken programs. I can still remember a song that sounded like German- or Dutch-accented English sung over slow, early-'70s-style rock: "Hands! ... Hands! ... A Polly is a bird that will never ever let you down ... and even if he did, he will never let you drown ... Hands! ... Hands!"

One night they broadcast disco night — infuriating. Another night featured a lengthy discussion between a female call-in show host and a woman caller to the radio station. I listened in irritation as the host managed to convince the caller to come down to the station so they could possibly love each other up, but when the caller arrived seconds later there was some performance anxiety problem that brought the radio show to an argumentative halt.

In the mornings I would complain to the nurses and my family about this crazy loud radio station operating in the night. They all claimed there was no such thing. Now I'm not sure which is the greater marvel: my odd imaginings or the fact that I can still remember them so clearly.

An impulse to make a song out of this very strange time crept over me, and I dictated some lines to E.:

> *I got hit in the head with a flying car,*
> *Never did drugs, never had the time,*
> *But now I see that morphine is fine.*
> *Got strong lungs used to hold air to sixty,*
> *Had a machine do it for me,*
> *Got me fifteen in a minute,*
> *I'm a bionic man.*
> *My hip bone connected to the ... shin bone.*

There were some lines in there about the maddening and frequent PA announcements to the hospital staff for a "code blue" alert or other code colours, along with a note that I should use the sound of electric shock paddles as a drumbeat backing this "song." These dictations were all the product of my addled wits in the first days of coming out of my coma and unhappily discovering my new limitations.

A massive head injury can make you edgy, irritable, and irrational. Your emotional sensors get scrambled, crushed, or cut. A regret I feel to this day, even though I couldn't help doing it, is that I'd get agitated by the energy of certain people. Sadly, Carlin was one of them. The poor thing was trying to be bright and chipper around her sidelined daddy while suppressing her own fear and heartache. I, on the other hand, got wigged out when she'd visit and kept insisting she be shooed away. I don't think I was very nice about it, but then I was out of my mind. Carlin was baffled and hurt, but she's the most forgiving person I know. As the weeks went on, she became a trusted helper in the dressing and caring for my wounds.

Days passed in a semi-dream state. I started to acclimatize to my surroundings and to understand that I was extremely injured. My left arm was one of the few parts of me left undamaged, and a look down allowed me to contemplate an unlovely collection of stitches, sutures, and staples, numerous scars from surgeries and gashes, swollen and broken hands and feet, and seven or eight drainage bottles attached to two horrendous wounds. In addition, the doctors had helpfully inserted a catheter to ensure a managed urine flow during my coma and on into the first weeks of consciousness. All this was viewed through my one good eye, the right one having been crushed in the accident.

I had long bed-ridden days to contemplate this turn of events. From a life spent in action, fitness, and high-energy output, constantly seeking to improve myself, my knowledge and my results, I had now been brought to a helpless standstill. In less than a minute's distractedness and about two seconds' massive impact, everything changed. I was unable to use any limb except my left arm and couldn't even turn on my side without the help of two nurses.

My helplessness also affected that most mundane and basic of human requirements, the emptying of the ballast tank. I was permitted to begin light solid food soon after coming out of the coma, which led of course to the creation of light solid wastes. I was unable to leave my bed and so the bedpan was brought to me. I even needed help to arrange myself on and off that. The whole thing was humiliating, and I was embarrassed for myself and sorry for the nurses. Did they really accept it as part of the job or did they resent me and loathe me for my filth? The thought was unbearable and I chafed against my helplessness. I kept asking to have my bed moved closer to the bathroom, or at least to have someone help me in and out of the bed because I was sure I could get there. I was not accepting the truth of what it meant to have two recently smashed legs. This obsession soon got me into a bit of difficulty.

As part of the nurses' rounds, they checked on me every two hours in the day and several times each night because of the severity of the wounds. At 11 p.m. they'd rouse me from slumber, then again at 1 a.m., then once again at 5 a.m., after which I'd get a break until breakfast. I'd spend my nightly solitude brooding over my limitations and mildly objecting to the sleep disruptions. On a couple of nights I wriggled along and down the bed, using my good left arm for leverage, trying to plot how I'd get myself off the bed and over to the bathroom. I knew it would be difficult, but I thought if I could get myself free of my remaining wound-drainage bottles and catheter, I'd stand a better chance. I worked out how to detach the drainage bottles (now down to four) but couldn't manage the catheter at all. I later learned that there is an internal inflation device to keep it lodged inside your bladder, but I hadn't dared ask anyone about such details for fear they'd suspect that I was up to something. I therefore set about tugging on the thing, feeling the internal stress and pain but pressing on in the belief that if I could stand a little discomfort, I'd soon be free of the intruder and closer to my objective. My will to withstand the pain gave out before the catheter did. Good thing, too.

The following daytime I told my wife about the failed removal attempt. Appalled, she convinced the medicos that I no longer needed the device, and they agreed to remove it. Poor E. became an unwitting accomplice to my scheme. That achieved, I was now free to contemplate my escape attempt. At lights out that night I pleaded with the nurses to skip the 2 a.m. routine check so that I could get some badly needed sleep for once. I had befriended them and they thought I was a sensible guy, so they reluctantly agreed.

I lay there in wait that night, contemplating the hours to come and the success I'd had at shifting myself down the bed on previous nights. Tonight would be the night, and if I could prove I was able to do this on my own, then I would please and amaze everyone and regain a bit of independence. It would not surprise me to learn that this is the way crazy people think.

I wriggled and squirmed my way down to the end of the bed. I had now been out of the coma for almost two weeks, and my unhurt left arm was the key to anything I hoped to do. Once at the foot of the bed, my useless legs dangling over the end, I sat and reviewed my plan. There was a visitor's armchair against the wall, about three feet from the end of the bed. I knew my legs shouldn't bear any weight, but I calculated that I could reach the chair with a good push-off and my feet need only touch the floor for an instant. Rolling carefully over on to my stomach, I let my legs slide off the bed toward the floor until my hips were over the end and my toes grazed the carpet. I held this position for a time while gathering my courage and re-gathering my strength. After a long pause I realized the moment of decision had come. It was either act now or wear myself out in holding the ready position.

A deep breath, then touch down on my toes — a bit more pressure on the legs than I would have liked — and push! I fell across the space between and, by God's grace and a good aim, ended up slamming down into the padded armchair.

It had seemed in my addled mind that this kind of back-first landing was a fairly safe risk because my back, shoulders, and buttocks had been spared from injury by the frontal assault. What I didn't know (or had forgotten) was that liver lacerations, bruised and collapsed lung, and a fracture to the C7 vertebra had occurred. Luckily I hadn't knocked anything loose upon impact with the chair. For the moment I sat there, giddy with my successful crossing, and told myself, *Aw, I took worse hits than that every time I played hockey.*

The adrenaline wore off as I continued to recover. My plan had been based on the idea of leveraging the chair, once I was in it, closer to the bathroom door and then somehow taking a couple of quick steps while leaning on the wall to make it to the toilet. This idea now looked like fantasy. I did pull the chair along a foot or so by grasping the end of the bed, and then I sat there in the gloom.

The pain of that brief touch on the floor told me that further strain on the legs was not an option. My determined drive toward independence was now stalled. Reason won out, and I finally shifted into reverse, seeing that the only option was to get back to the bed and accept my lot. The nurses would soon come along and help me back, and though I'd be embarrassed at being caught, I'd get over it. Of course it was with horror that I remembered I'd insisted they stay away for the night so I could sleep. A groan escaped my lips, which was then followed by the realization that I'd have to find my own way back or spend the night in the increasingly uncomfortable armchair. A very long time, perhaps an hour, passed in alternating denial and acceptance. At the same time I was hoping that the nurses had fibbed and would turn up at any moment, but no such luck. Time spent on screwing up my courage led to more time spent on focused self-talk: *You can do this. You can do this. Just don't rush and be stupid. You can do this.*

The first attempt wasn't committed enough. My left arm, the sole means of locomotion, didn't push hard enough, and I collapsed back into the chair. At something like 3:30 a.m. I had to regain my focus and gather my energy for what must surely be my last gasp. Deep breath in, push up on my left arm, and heave forward! Again there was more pressure on the broken legs than had been prescribed, but I made it onto my front torso at the end of the bed and grabbed the railing with my one hand. I pulled myself up the bed, with just that left hand, with what felt like the last reserves of my strength, and then slowly crawled to safety at the head of the bed. Thoroughly chastened and now no longer under any illusion about the extent of my injuries, I fell into deep sleep for the rest of the night.

Next morning the nurses noticed some disarray in the room, but I managed to talk my way out of that. However, when my wife came along, I confessed all. Secretly, I think I hoped to be admired for fighting heroically against the odds. E's eyes grew wide as my story unfolded, then narrowed. Uh-oh. When I got to the end of the tale, she promised me through barely restrained fury that unless I swore on my life that I would never do anything like that again, she would immediately arrange to have me strapped in with powerful restraints every night. I saw her point and swore the oath.

It's interesting that, even with the body so broken and damaged, the mind still pursues the same thought pathways built up over a lifetime, with no acknowledgement of the altered physical reality. My habit had always been to believe that I could overcome anything through my own force of will.

✳ ✳ ✳

The midnight escape attempt had been ridiculous, and I recognized that now, but I still felt a powerful desire to get out of that bed and out of that room. Change the view and get some fresh air. It was almost mid-autumn in Australia, with the same overcast and blustery days that accompany a northern autumn, but the idea of being out in the air seemed like heaven to me.

The nurses were sympathetic, and in fact there was a medical directive from someone in charge that I should be moving toward normal functioning as soon as possible. They announced that the "Pink Chair" would be made available for that purpose. I imagined some sort of gaily decorated wheelchair. After some delays it was brought into the room, and what appeared was surprising. It looked something like an upright pink vinyl couch on wheels, with a seat set in to keep the patient's weight off his legs. The arrangement was similar to being stretched out flat on a board, strapped in, and tilted upright.

It took two nurses and my wife to transfer me carefully off the bed and onto the Pink Chair. A nurse came along to supervise as my wife, two daughters, and a family friend wheeled me down the hall to the elevator. After overcoming my fear and surprise, I started to feel a little self-conscious. It occurred to me that being secluded until that moment also meant I hadn't faced the world yet in my broken, mutilated condition. I felt dubious about the image I was presenting: bandaged, stitched, helpless, swathed in oversized clothing to stay warm, and strapped onto this moving platform. On the one hand I saw myself like the famous Jesse James death photo, propped up in the street in his coffin for passersby to gawk at. On the other hand I felt like Frankenstein's monster, held by restraints to the lab table with the evidence of medical atrocities hanging and fluttering from almost every location on my body. The drainage bottles hanging off the wounds on my limbs added an unusual aspect to the presentation. I suspected I might be a tad conspicuous.

When the elevator door opened to disgorge our party into the crowded main floor lobby, my suspicion was confirmed. We made our way across the atrium toward the courtyard, and many people stopped and stared in surprise or pity at the macabre spectacle of Dixon passing by in the Pink Chair. It got so obvious that Carlin yelled out savagely, "Take a picture, people. It'll last longer!" We got through the mob scene, and the girls pushed me in my odd device out into the afternoon sun.

What a feeling! A return to the real world, the natural environment around me at last after weeks inside. The warmth of the sun on my face, the outside air, even an occasional chilly breeze — all were like kisses from angels. I watched my daughters twirl and laugh in the sunshine and felt my spirits rise. I was euphoric as E. went in to get me a "flat white," the ubiquitous Australian coffee drink, and continued that way as I sipped and chatted about whatever topic I could muster.

All too soon the magic spell wore off. Full-body fatigue and the slight nip in the air brought me back to earth. The Pink Chair was turned round and wheeled back through the madding crowd, but this time I closed my eyes and tuned it all out. Spent from the effort and the emotional strain, I gratefully accepted the return to my bed and slept through supper and into the night.

There were a couple of these excursions, and they clarified for me the extent of the change in my circumstances. A few weeks before I'd been an energetic jet-setting entertainer. Now it took all my strength just to be roused for a Pink Chair outing. Very sobering.

SURRENDER ... AND DRIVING FORCE

The knock to my noggin in the collision had been a doozy, but I hadn't been knocked completely silly. I now reined in my thinking to surrender to the universe and acknowledge that I had some physical limitations — not giving up, but not being in denial any longer either. The pain-management drugs in my system had to be having an impact on my reasoning ability, so I began weaning myself off them. I wanted a clear head.

After several weeks of rest and treatment at the Alfred Hospital, I apparently had progressed enough that I was to be transferred to the good folks at the Epworth, a physiotherapy hospital. I was still pretty helpless, and drainage bottles were still hanging off my wounds. The skin graft on my smashed-and-rebuilt right forearm was not healing well; in fact, two holes refused to close up, where you could see the tendons inside when the bandages were off. My shattered left leg was likewise not healing well, and I was continually reminded that they still didn't know if the salvage operation was going to take. The skin graft was still held on with staples over the complicated bone graft, metal plate, screws, and soft-tissue transplant treatment they'd used to stick me back together. I was scarred with angry red welts from head to toe after all the stitches and staples had been removed, just prior to my departure. My left arm was still the only limb of use to me, and I still couldn't get out of bed. On the positive side of the ledger, I was out of the life-or-death stage.

They needed the bed for new cases. For my part, I wasn't heartbroken to leave. I said goodbye to the nurses and the meal attendants who'd been caring for me as I left the Alfred on a gurney. I'd return for specialist appointments, but the change of scene seemed a good sign, if a bit scary.

My first night at the Epworth they put me in a shared room. My initial skepticism about this decision, after the solitude and quiet of my private room at the Alfred, soon proved to be well founded since my new roomie was a Hungarian man of about seventy who grumbled loudly about everything and stayed up most of the night with the TV playing loudly. It was nothing personal against me; that's just who he was. The head injury I was nursing made me sensitive to noise, so they couldn't have landed me in a worse spot. After two nights like that the sympathetic nurses found me a bed in the head trauma ward where I could escape my unwitting tormentor and things were vewy, vewy quiet. Here I lay in wait for the next assault by the surgeons.

My surrender in the fight to keep my right eye was one of the toughest decisions of my life. I had pangs of doubt for ages afterward, second-guessing my eventual choice. This was the only decision about treating one of my major injuries for which I'd been conscious. Every other bashed-up bit of me had been assessed and acted on in the first forty-eight hours. Those crises I'd sailed through in a coma, blissfully unaware of the horrors that my body was enduring. But when it came to my vision loss, the true extent of the damage would only be known if, and when, I returned to consciousness. Only then could I tell them how much of the world was still lit for me.

Now, what any fool could see immediately on my arriving at the Alfred was that I'd had a mighty whack to my face, consistent with a Jeep SUV driving over me at high speed. My right orbital bone was smashed, a deep gash ran across my right brow and down into the eye socket, and a second deep gash had made a torn flap of the cheek below. Cuts below my other eye and across my nose, as well as a torn upper lip, made an easy-to-follow and colourful map of the Jeep's progress across my face. Just to add interest, my head filled with fluid and swelled to the size of a basketball, straining my nose, cheeks, and eyelids to near bursting. I'm told my features were unrecognizable. Even so, aside from stitching my face back together, it was felt by the attending doctors that in the light of so many worse injuries to deal with, my smashed eye had to be left until later.

My return to consciousness after ten days delivered me into confusion and fear, but it also began the resolve that I was going to be healed in all respects. It was la-la land for me when I was first told the news of my injuries, so addled was I with anaesthetics and painkillers, but from the start I was determined.

Many parts were potential write-offs, but I just didn't believe any of them would go that way. This is why, even while seeing the gauze patch over my eye and being told of the awful damage behind it, I wouldn't give up hope of my sight being restored. The damaged eye ached as it tried to move in tandem with my healthy left eye. Even though the nurses and my family were careful in their choice of words to describe it, I knew there was some very ugly stuff hiding behind that bandage. My hope remained undimmed because each day, as I lay in that hospital bed, I was convinced that I was seeing points of light. They seemed to be getting in around the edges of the bandage; surely that must mean that with time and healing I'd end up with two good eyes.

Specialists of all disciplines were visiting several times weekly to check on my progress. The ophthalmologists were a couple of well-dressed young men with great haircuts; they had a very pleasant manner and were a lift to have in the room. My girls called them "The Cute Eye Doctors." The CEDs were not very pleasing in their diagnoses, unfortunately — the only flaw in our otherwise top-drawer friendship. They gently informed me that the damaged eye, if left in place too long, could leak toxic fluids as it decayed and deteriorated, fluids that could cross over and blind my good eye. *Cross-contamination* was their term for it. It sounded like they were talking about something dead, and I was still convinced the injured eye was gonna be okay. The surgeons, however, were greatly concerned and scheduled a procedure to remove the mangled eye.

This news came to me during the time when I was still so weakened and injured that I could barely move around in my hospital bed. At the same time I had enough sharpness and high-function thinking to be a danger to myself, as evidenced in the bed-escape fiasco. The impending removal of one of my eyes got me in a very agitated state, which intensified as the surgery date drew nearer. I became convinced that nobody had ever given me a proper eye exam. The images of light that I believed I'd been seeing must mean there was still hope. Accordingly, I made it known the day before that I intended to cancel the surgery. My wife took this news calmly enough while in my presence. Soon, however, she excused herself from the room and ran to phone the doctor who'd scheduled the thing, Van. Our first-name basis with the doctors was a nice touch during the continuing crisis; no standing on formality for the Australians.

"Van," my wife said in rising panic, "you've got to get over here and talk sense into Carl. He wants to cancel the eye surgery."

We always found the doctors in Australia to be really good people who showed every sign of caring about their patients. Van had given my wife his cellphone number for just such emergencies, and she had caught him at the other end of Melbourne at a clinic where he worked. He jumped in a taxi to the Epworth to talk me through the crisis, but the afternoon traffic was very heavy, and he wasn't going to get across town in time to see me before I could cancel the surgery. I was certainly proving to be a wilful, difficult patient.

Until then I had avoided any glimpse of the damage to my eye because I didn't want to believe it was done in. If I didn't see it ruined, then I could still pretend the problem wasn't real. Now, on the eve of dealing with this remaining big problem, I was balking, and it was an immovable Dixon who refused to just meekly turn up tomorrow to have his eye cut out. I was adamant that I needed to see an optometrist for a proper and thorough eye exam, right now, because I still believed I could recover. Van, stuck in a cab in Melbourne traffic, frantically called the optometry clinician down on the first floor of the Epworth. This doctor agreed to stay after normal hours and give me an emergency eye exam. He spoke to me calmly about my concerns and set me up at the scanner, which isolated each eye and tested my good eye first. He then turned the light on my damaged eye at three different strengths, giving me every opportunity for hope. I saw nothing. That's when I finally surrendered.

Next day I was put under. They removed my eye and I was rolled back to my room at Epworth. The pain was excruciating when I awoke, as if I'd been hit in the head by a car all over again, but they kept me in quiet and dark as much as possible. It was saddening to know that I'd had to surrender. On the other hand, with all the traumas and injuries I'd already absorbed, I was able to resign myself to it. I'd lost the battle to win the war, really. The loss of my eye now became just another obstacle to overcome and work around.

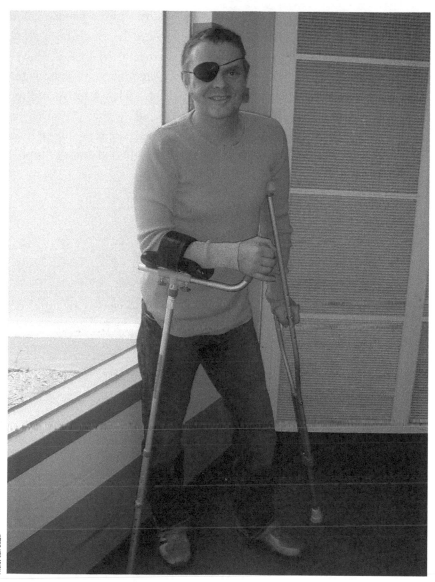

First day without wheelchair at Epworth.

There was an eerie aspect to those first post-op nights. The quiet space they gave me to limit stress and disruption was in the head trauma unit, where some very damaged people resided. There was one man they called "The Midnight Walker." He had a tumour or something, that was putting pressure on his brain cells and causing problems. He had the unnerving habit of appearing in other patients' rooms at 2 or 3 a.m. with no pants on, and after a confused verbal exchange he'd proceed to use their bathroom. Most of us were in no position to resist his entry — twice in my case, at least — and the hospital staff felt he was harmless, just a bit disruptive. Nobody felt the need to sound alarm bells over his wanderings. When a nurse told me, "That guy won't ever be leaving here; his time is winding down," I saw again that no matter how bad things looked for me, there were people right in front of me who were worse off. I had a future beyond the walls of a hospital.

MY HANDS CAN'T FEEL TO GRIP....

For the duration of the extensive physiotherapy, the incredibly lovely staff at the Epworth had decided they liked me enough to give me the nicest private room on the floor, with a beautiful view of the city and easy access to the lounge area next door. Within a day of moving in, I was introduced to the team that would be supervising my daily recovery work. At this point I was assigned a kind orderly, Andrew, to push me through the halls and across the street twice a day to the physio facility. I had nowhere near sufficient strength to go anywhere on my own. My progress was still slight, but I could at least assist in shifting myself off the bed and onto the wheelchair, no small achievement considering that my wounds were all still bandaged and not closing up yet, four weeks on.

In that physio facility it was impossible for me to fail. Knowledgeable, encouraging staff who were examples of health, strength, and wellness made for an inspiring environment. The equipment they used was simple and old-school in a way, but very effective. Twice each day, morning and afternoon, I'd be hauled over there to get to work at strengthening. This stage proved to be hard slogging, sometimes even drudgery.

My still-swollen right hand was terribly stiff, weak, and unable to close. My fingers wouldn't curl to grip. Weirdly, I could still play piano because the splayed fingers didn't have to curl for that, so Lauren bought me an electronic keyboard. I composed a few good song ideas on that thing, whiling away the hours of downtime.

My right hand was thought to have limited prospects for return to full use. Missing chunks of forearm flesh and muscle looked ugly, but worse was the loss of function and strength. Three days a week I'd see Jeremy the occupational therapist, who'd go to work forcing my fingers to bend. This job requires that the therapist have not only strong hands but a strong resolve to press ahead even as he watches the patient suffering.

Gavin, the head-man of the physios, would get me to hang from a chin-up bar, just grip and hang in short bursts, to build the small gripping muscles. There was an amazing variety of exercises to do with simple gear, ropes, and pieces of wood. As I say, old-school.

One day in the gym, Gavin had me test my recovery on a hand-strength measuring device. This fiendish thingy required you to grip round the handle and then squeeze with all the strength you could bring to bear. A gauge would give a pounds-per-square-inch reading of your hand strength. I expressed my doubts to Gavin about how I'd perform after such awful damage to my arm and hand, but he insisted we at least get a baseline measurement. Oh, all right. So, grip with stiff fingers and SQUEEEEZE, until I could squeeze no more. Gavin took the device from my hand and looked at it with a frown.

"How'd I do, Gav?"

"Umm, zero."

"Ha-ha. No, really."

"Really. Zero."

This wasn't in itself overly surprising, except I kept getting the same damn result week after week in spite of all my supposed strengthening. It wasn't until my last week there that I finally scored a positive reading — all of 8 psi! And there was much celebrating throughout the land.

The hospital offered music therapy as well. At first it was sobering to find how little I could do with my right hand, but in a short time the muscle memory started returning. Once my finger and thumb could pinch together enough to grip a pick (after about three months), I began to strum the guitar lightly. Soon the music therapist asked me if I could play The Beatles' "Blackbird" and teach her, and I was amazed to find that I could — because, you see, I never could before. (Okay, corny old joke.) Another physio, Sean, offered me a different form of music therapy by creating a six-CD set at home for me of all the Australian music that I should know about. Cool guy.

✷ ✷ ✷

On my final day at Epworth I did a little concert in the common room for the patients and doctors. It was meant to be a farewell, a thank-you, and a demonstration that I'd regained strength and independence. I also wished to quell the doubts that the staff still held about my leaving. I put on the nicest clothes I had with me and got out of my wheelchair onto an armless chair that was raised on some kind of unsteady platform. I was warned not to "rock out" too much or I'd fall off the back. The performance lasted about forty-five minutes, and Jeremy and Sean were among those gathered. It was fun to watch them both fixing their

Goodbye, nurses. Last day in Epworth Hospital, August 2008.

stare on my hand through progressive stages of concern, amazement, and then glee. On the conclusion of one difficult song that I'd gotten through successfully, they jumped up to high-five each other as if to say, "That's our hand!"

I was very happy to give them that feeling. There were so many nurses, doctors, attendants, and various other functionaries in the hospital whom I'd gotten to know and like. A few other patients were my friends, but that was less intense than the feeling I had for the staff. Even the snack-trolley ladies and the man who came around for blood samples had become part of my world during my long stay. Some nurses had become such special friends to me, and I wished I could stay connected, but it was time to go.

WE'RE ON OUR WAY HOME

It was time for my flight home. I was still on gutter crutches for short walks and in wheelchairs to go any farther. Passing through the airport to catch our flight was my first indication that I was not yet as well as I'd convinced myself. Adrenaline and willpower had gotten me out the door. Now the big, unforgiving world awaited me, and the special treatment afforded me in hospital was gone. A friend named Sandy took me with my wife to the airport in her compact car, full to bursting with the luggage and other items accumulated through our combined months' stay. Immediately upon hauling me by wheelchair along with all our luggage into the Melbourne Airport, the first hassle struck. The check-in officer, after inspecting my documents, notified us that my visitor's visa had expired during my long stay in hospital. Bureaucracy dictated that I was now in legal trouble and would have to report to immigration authorities to clear this up before I would be permitted to leave the country. They run a tight ship in Australia.

The immigration lady was made to see reason after some fifteen or twenty minutes of back-and-forth and clear this frivolous but potentially huge setback from our path. We were then set free to engage with the normal hassles of global travel.

It was tense at first because by this point, after the unexpectedly lengthy stay, we could only afford economy-fare tickets. I was in extreme discomfort in the limited space. Soon I was apparently looking the worse for wear, and we hadn't even lifted off for the long flight. I still wasn't willing to confess any problems in case someone changed their mind and made me stay. "No fear, no weakness" — that was my mantra of the time.

We were airborne when I started to fold like a cheap suit. The crew was very sympathetic, and they too had been noting my pained greyish pallor with dismay. There were two unused bunks in the first-class cabin and the crew waived the usual restrictions in an act of mercy. I moved there to fall into exhausted, grateful sleep through the night as we crossed the Pacific. New Zealand Airlines will forever occupy a special place in my affections.

The Los Angeles airport was very unfriendly. It was necessary for us to change airlines and terminals to pick up the next leg of the flight home. We had to clear U.S. Customs, and the Homeland Security officials, bless their little hearts, viewed my need for a wheelchair as a security concern. What might you be hiding, Mr. Dixon, *if* that is your real name? Pain and injury prevented me from getting out of the wheelchair to walk through their screening process. They seemed to resent this, or at least disbelieve it. The scowling "male attendant" gave me a full-body pat-down then inspected every inch of my wheelchair. They then asked me to remove my long red woollen scarf, knitted by my mother, and held it up to the light to inspect every woolly fibre. E. was holding back tears of rage and frustration at these needless indignities being imposed on me. I just went with it. I was pretty used to feeling helpless by then. Also, we were now on the same continent as home. I could almost smell it now, the way Mole could smell his long-neglected little Mole End cottage calling to him in *Wind in the Willows*.

We made Toronto late that night and stayed in an airport hotel so that my friends and family could come have a look at me next morning before our long drive home. My father was one of the first to greet me. He strode forward and said, "Ah, the man they couldn't kill. Welcome home."

Tearful reunions followed with those who loved me and had been so shaken by the events. My children, parents, sister, grandma, uncle and aunt, and faithful friends all assembled to greet me. My friend Luke, who'd called every single day from Haliburton to my hospital bed, drove down to chauffeur us back to our highlands home.

My dogs awaited me and I sat with them in the sunshine, gazing at the beautiful forest that surrounds my home, and gave a contented sigh. I'd done my time and was an unwilling prisoner of Australia no longer.

Being home brought me to a greater recognition of the change in my life. The hospital environment had been designed to keep challenges to a minimum for the patients' diminished capacity. Now, returned to my hometown, I had to face that huge difference of navigating even the simplest tasks, minus the abilities I'd had when I'd left months before. It was merely "the end of the beginning."

Freedom to come home was mine but I was also free of medical supervision. There are many benefits to living in rural Ontario, but comprehensive medical attention is not usually among them. With the decline in the public health-care system, it's bloody hard to get a doctor to take you on. In those first months I could not even get in and out of the bathtub by myself. I spent a great deal of time in my bed, with my wife bringing many of my meals on a tray. Attempts to resume normal life were well beyond me still, as I learned with a jolt just how sheltered and protected I'd been at Epworth World. So how did I manage in this largely unsupervised state? By overdoing it and taking on too much, of course.

Both my broken legs were not healing properly; the damage had been too great for my body to mend according to the normal schedule for a broken bone, which is six weeks or so. It was beyond my addled wits to take it easy, though (massive head blow and concussion, right?). I was pushing myself to get fit enough to be able to walk around, stand on a stage, and go through airports with The Guess Who again. My family needed me to get back to work, and I thought the band needed me too. I returned to doing solo gigs seven months after the crash, going in on crutches and sitting on a stool to perform. The audience was medicine for my heart; the performing was balm to my soul. There was no power, though, that was sufficient to make my legs heal any faster or properly at all.

In June of 2009, as I set about trying to resume normal life and do things like a regular guy who hadn't been torn apart, my right femur re-broke. It had never set properly to the titanium rod the doctors inserted in Australia; the break point was fibrous and "punky" from inadequate healing. Metal fatigue from my intemperate use of my limbs caused the rod to snap and the screws that held it in place to shear off. This new injury was quite agonizing, and an emergency surgery was done at St. Michael's Hospital in Toronto. The difference between my stay in Australia's hospitals and my brief sojourn at St. Michael's was like the difference between a dream and a nightmare. My surgeon was top-notch and he made a good fix on me ("I made the incision along the same scar as the last time so you'd have less of a mess on that leg," Dr. McKee cheerfully told me afterward), but the facility was run-down, bleak, and unhappy.

Again I checked out of hospital early after a blood transfusion, and three days after that I was playing drums for the swing band at the Relay for Life fundraising event, with the drums extended far out to allow for my bandaged, unbendable leg.

My other leg, with the bone graft on a shattered tibia and a knee held together with nine screws, was also showing up under X-rays as unhealed after fourteen months. The good Dr. McKee said I'd need to return in August to have that leg operated on again. He'd address the bone graft with a piece of bone taken from my other hip, possibly re-break the leg to straighten it, and replace the bent metal plate, which to date had not helped. This was all terrifying. I didn't feel weakness but I did feel fear.

There is an ultrasound device meant to speed healing in broken bones that you can buy for a hefty sum or rent more affordably. I rented that and began applying it zealously, also giving a little bit of time to the bone graft on my other leg without any real hope. At the same time an acupuncturist named Danielle Staub was highly recommended to help with the continuing post-accident difficulties. Her ministrations addressed a number of problems — for example, needles at blood-cleansing points to clear my system of the residue of all the general anaesthetics and painkillers I'd been given. That made a big difference in improving my sense of well-being. Most significantly, Danielle stimulated the *chi* points for bone healing. When I returned to Dr. McKee in August for the prep appointment to my next surgery, he discovered to his surprise that the bone-graft problem leg was now finally healed, as was the leg on which he'd operated two months before. Another small miracle had come to me.

Try acupuncture. It helps.

IT'S A MIRACLE!

People have remarked that my recovery has been miraculous. One of my Haliburton buddies had a good line. We were sitting around Walt McKechnie's restaurant on a Friday night in the autumn after my return home from Australia. It was one of my first nights out, about seven months after the crash. Friends and acquaintances came over to chat and ask about my health as I sat at a table with my beer-drinking peers. Anthony asked me how things were different now. I spoke a bit about how my self-image was assaulted by the experience. I had been pulled from the little Toyota's wreckage a broken, mangled man, gushing blood and next to dead. I recalled that weeks later my agent was almost sobbing to me over the phone that his whole world had been rocked by my crash because he had considered me some kind of a Superman, indestructible. I allowed to Anthony that this was how I'd thought of myself for many years. Anthony said quickly: "But you *are* indestructible. Look at you, you're still here!"

What had given me this "miraculous" result? The simple answer for a religious person would be that "It was God's will." That may be so, but many earthly factors had to align to help the spiritual ones. The other heavenly reference that people have offered: "It just tells you that your work here on Earth isn't done yet." I like the notion that there is much left I'm meant to do.

As I've noted elsewhere, my cardiovascular health and my physical strength and endurance enabled me to withstand the trauma. The head blow, along with the external cuts, rips, and tears, resulted in massive blood loss and tissue damage. I was at grave risk of expiring on the operating table during almost forty hours of emergency surgeries. I got through it.

The blow to my head could have addled my wits permanently. It didn't.

Infections could have set in on any one of my many grievous wounds during my long hospital stay. I repelled all invaders.

The mangling of my left leg and right arm also damaged the nerves. Permanent loss of feeling and of motor control was anticipated in those areas and others, but I've regained the feeling and motor skills almost completely.

There was internal organ damage, including lung, liver, gallbladder, and duodenum. All recovered.

Because of the fractured C-7 vertebra, it was feared that I might become paralyzed from the chest down. Instead it fused while I was in my coma so that I never knew my spine was hurt until someone told me. (It only hurts now when I spend too long writing a book.)

I note on this list only the "highlights" from among the fifty separate gashes, blunt-force traumas, and bone breaks. My point in rehashing these injuries here is that any one of them could have resulted in a major setback for the rest of my life. Almost none of them did so. A quarter-inch this way or that was the difference between my death or dismemberment, or my getting on again with life after a decent interval. Good health and clean living aided my recovery. It's measurable.

However, I don't want to be coy or misleading. I did lose an eye, there's nerve damage to my face and head, I can't close my right hand, and there's nerve damage through the right hand and forearm corresponding to the blow from a car undercarriage. The ulna (forearm) bones were shattered and flesh was ripped away to reveal tendons and jagged broken bone ends. My legs are held together with metal plates. My left knee was shattered and put back together with long screw nails; my reassembled left shin bone healed at a funny angle, collapsed after non-union for a year and a half. I'll likely never be able to kneel again. My face is disfigured. There's probably psychological damage, as some "funny" things continue to emerge from my thoughts. I certainly have suffered post-concussion disorder. My stomach bulges out on my lower left side down through the groin, a result of the surgeons' harvesting of soft tissue from my stomach muscles to use in rebuilding my left leg. There are many "awesome" scars on my hide. There's other stuff too — bits all over.

So, you see, I didn't get a free pass from the consequences of a terrible car crash. Once the game had begun, though, the one thing I could manage was my thoughts. My mantra of "no fear, no weakness" helped me gain mastery over many tough moments. What it meant was that I would not permit myself to think I was beaten or that my helpless injured state was permanent. I would meet head-on whatever lay ahead, and I'd spend myself completely in the effort of doing it well. That's how I'd lived before, to lesser purpose, so why would I stop now?

Often in life I've discovered that, while I've assumed that everyone was like me and that people mostly think as I do, it's very often not the case at all. It was with puzzlement that I saw other patients in hospital who had either surrendered to their woes or were only indifferently going through the motions. *Whaddaya mean, you don't feel like trying?*

Why go to therapy only to stare at the floor or complain about the work? The recovery of your physical wellness is the key to having all other things turn out well. Why would you not give that task every ounce of your strength? Strength and energy magically grow over time as you use them. They dwindle if you *don't*. It's no good saving up that effort for later. It's like when you leave the cap off the gas can in the summer; by the time you come back to it, it's seriously depleted.

When the doctors and therapists at the Epworth Hospital conducted an exit interview with me as I was approaching discharge day, they told me I was the most motivated patient they'd ever seen. While it was flattering to hear, it got me wondering: Why would I stand out so much among all the patients who had gone through the place, just by putting in effort? It seemed wrong. We all have things we want to do in our lives, and I didn't think hospital was where any of them were going to get done.

In essence, what I recognized was this: a simple plan had been put in front of me, and all I had to was follow it diligently. The supervising physicians and therapists at Epworth created a structure for me, just as they do for all patients; they'd given me "the how," as they say in corporate-speak. "If you follow this plan," goes the message, "you will get the results."

I didn't want to be in hospital (who does?), but I was too hurt and damaged to leave. Therefore, I needed to get strong enough and well enough to be fit for dismissal. To that end, I attended the twice-daily physiotherapy workouts for stretching, strength, and balance, and the excruciating therapy for my broken right hand that also occurred most mornings.

Now I wish again here to represent the facts accurately. There were many mornings when I wished I could sleep in longer, and sometimes I did, causing me to be a bit late for a session. A couple of times I just couldn't muster the strength. However, hospital life is regimented so that there is no escape from the morning meds, the nurses' checklists, the doctor's rounds, the breakfast lady, the tray-pickup lady, the newspaper lady, the cleaning staff, the shuttle chap to push my wheelchair, the postman, the blood-sample collector, and all manner of random visitors needing something.

The surprising variety of people with jobs to do meant that there were some days when by noon I'd had twenty or more separate visitors to deal with just in my hospital room, let alone all the people outside. I had a far more peaceful existence on the road with a rock band. In truth, the demands of dealing with the many staff could be more taxing than the physical workouts.

After a month or more of physiotherapy, though, I was taking it upon myself to get in and out of the motorized wheelchair on my own and scoot through the quarter-mile or so of corridors to cross the street for physio.

Some of the challenges of a recovery like mine are not what you'd expect. Case in point: every night the nurses had the job of giving me this nasty little needle containing a blood thinner, meant to counter the threat of blood clots from me not walking. The act of walking makes blood circulate in a most helpful way, evidently. I put up with it for a time, a nightly injection in my thigh offering me yet another opportunity to be a brave little soldier. In a couple of weeks I started to get lumps under the skin where I'd had so many needles. I was told this was normal, but I became phobic about the process. A nice nurse suggested we try it in my belly instead; she claimed to have patients who much preferred this to the leg because the belly fat helped them feel it less. Well, I was mostly lean, about 165 pounds when I got hurt, and I'd lost about fifteen pounds during my intravenous diet days, so there wasn't really any belly fat to work with. I did agree to try it, though, on her advice, and instantly regretted it. It may seem wussy after the way I'd borne everything prior, but seeing and feeling that stupid needle go into my stomach was not to be tolerated.

In fact, avoidance of the needle became a priority for me. I'd scheme to outwit the nurses who were supposed to put a ticky in the box on the Carl Dixon sheet next to "blood-thinner needle." I'd tell the night nurse that the daytime nurse had given it to me. I'd engage the nurse in distracting chat for as long as I could until they might get called away to another room and forget to come back. I'd say it had been left with me to do and I'd already done it. Oh, I was wily. Maybe they were just humouring me. To me this needle ritual was some redundant procedure, forced on the nursing staff by the liability-averse insurance companies, and I didn't intend to be a pawn in their crazy game. I got nowhere with my assertion to the head nurse that I must be a low risk for blood clots because I was so healthy before the crash. Of course I was a bit nuts, having been whacked in the head and all. Eventually the nurses caught on to my little tricks and were concerned enough to stand over me after that and make sure it got done. The pain of injection was still there, however, so finally Head Nurse Jackie offered to teach me to inject myself. She assured me that I'd probably feel it less if I had control over it and, by golly, she was right. At least initially it seemed to hurt less, but it still had very annoying after-soreness. I never stopped hating that needle.

It was with some annoyance that I discovered near the end of my stay that I'd had a little metal catch device inserted into my main heart artery during my coma that was meant to catch ... blood clots. "Why did I have to have all those damn needles stuck in me if I've already got this device to stop blood clots getting through?" I demanded.

"Precaution," I was advised. I had to get yet another surgery, with accompanying general anaesthetic, for them to put a nick in my main artery and fish the damn thing out before they'd let me leave. I've still got it in a little jar. It looks like a cluster of fishhooks, and it reminds me of the indignities of even a miraculous recovery.

✳ ✳ ✳

I can't take all the credit for the "miracle" of my outcome; other people did help, a little bit (just joking). It's like my description of the music industry: many links in the chain that runs between the musical idea at one end and the listener at the other end. If any of the people at each link in the chain don't do their part, the whole process stops dead. That's what I see in my story. There were a great many people who represent links in the chain of events that got me from the car wreck on that dark road through to the other end, the largely healed place I inhabit today.

I've noticed an unexpected effect of my car crash and subsequent strong recovery; I'm now a "feel-good" story to a lot of people. Maybe that's too flippant a description, and it does look funny to me on the page. That's what it's like, though.

Some wise people have cautiously suggested that the crash might have helped me. I see their point.

Of course to me the question of my own survival and return to health was one of compelling interest, but eventual success was rarely in doubt in my mind (as far as I can remember). That unwavering purpose I showed seems to have caught people's attention in a good way. I also have come to some hard-won wisdom.

I see the importance of calmness and keeping oneself in check. I see the deep necessity for love between people. I see how we are all connected and interdependent, and how powerful the human spirit truly is. Human energy, when harnessed, is incalculably strong.

The greatest obstacle to happiness is that person in the mirror. "I have seen the enemy and he is us." The harmful, blocking role of fear is primary in stunting our development or skewing us off the path of who we're meant to be. Small fears take on huge significance over time, until we learn to get out of our own way. The crash helped me to do that.

Things in my life that no longer fit simply fell away or are falling away. Some roles that I'd taken on repeatedly in my life I see now to have been misguided. New people who possess deep spiritual awareness and heightened sensitivity have emerged in the course of my healing journey. Other people whom I knew prior to my big event have revealed more of their depth. Still others seem to be no longer a good fit for me. It's as if I'm now attuned to a deeper vibration of existence and to the other souls in this world who also feel it. They were always there, but I wasn't ready to receive them. I didn't recognize them so readily before.

I can look back and observe with new eyes (well, eye) the "old" me, BC (Before Crash). I was not living a "bad" life. On the contrary, I had striven throughout my life to be a conscientious, responsible, "good man" as much as my lights allowed. Like everyone I had my wild times and made some big mistakes, but doing the right thing was always a high priority.

I also learned by my mid-twenties about the ideas of karma and old souls. In numerology I'm a One. It seems any wrongdoing I commit in this life gets smacked back down on my head instantly. One could scoff at this, but I felt the blows of the seeming proof enough times to get any thinking man's attention. In daily living that translated to, "I won't ever get away with anything." Then I began to notice a strong correlation the other way, between doing good, right things and having a happier life. It's positive reinforcement, if you pay attention.

There's no doubt that my father's absence during much of my youth, combined with my mother's stoic Nordic reserve, resulted in my having a certain emotional neediness. I badly hungered for hugs and kisses and to be told that I was loved. Probably that hunger contributed to my becoming a performer almost as much as my musical ability did. It's also why I rushed into marriage at an early age. No harm, no foul? (I hope.)

The point is that I had already lived for many years thinking that I was applying wisdom and good thinking to my place in the world. I didn't think I was better than the people around me; I just conveyed a certain detachment to define my separateness from the ones who bugged me. The trials of my crash and its aftermath have given me a whole new perspective on life. I now know things that I couldn't have known before that event because I couldn't even see them.

We don't know what we don't know, right? For my whole life, from the time I began to think about such things, I thought I was getting smarter, and maybe I was. But looking now at the man I was then, I believe a few unhelpful ideas got knocked out of me in that car crash, and better ones filled their place.

The physical damage I endured has been the cause of much pain, and it's made me adapt to the new reality. I've tried to make light of it by jesting sometimes that a few parts of me are gone now and they're not coming back. To this one of my clever friends replied, "Well, see, you've proven that you didn't need those parts anyway."

We have the ability at every moment to consciously choose our path. Choose wisdom, tolerance, strength, love, kindness, and all the other virtues, no matter what the situation.

In the months and years since my return to Canada, I came to realize that the blow to the frontal occipital lobe of my brain has had delayed effects. While I was still in the sheltered world of the hospital, I was able to come along at my own pace without having to deal with the often confusing and constantly stressful events of daily twenty-first-century life. The doctors ordered that I not be exposed to news of the outside world or to the avalanche of good wishes pouring in every day. They felt that such exposure could cause emotional trauma because I wasn't ready for it. They were no doubt correct. As a result, some said that period of time was "the happiest I've ever seen him." Lucky me. My strange contentment was also attributable to being forced for the first time in my life to ease off on the self-imposed pressure to succeed and build my career. Instead I now had to turn my attention to being peaceful and rebuilding my body.

Football players and hockey players who get concussions from head blows often end up with severe irritability and irrational temper outbursts. I was tested a number of times by psychologists for any memory and perception problems during my hospital stay. The results were shaky at first but soon improved greatly. The mental sharpness and personality continuity that I retained after my head blow were considered remarkable, and indeed I've often marvelled at how much I still seem like myself. However, it's undeniable that since the accident I've been more vulnerable, more emotional, and more prone to irrational anger when provoked. I believe this is driven by fear and by the *shouts,* not whispers, which I've now heard as to my own mortality.

I believe my subconscious must still harbour fear and shock over what happened in the crash, even though I have no conscious memories of the event. That latent fear must be affecting my responses to certain events in ways that I can't control.

My great hope is that these negative developments will diminish as I build new neural pathways and find a calmer perspective over time.

THERE YOU GO, THEN: GOODBYE, GUESS WHO

"Things change, the mountains do fall, and no one knows at
all where they go
Things change, the rivers run dry, and no one tells you why,
it's just so."

—"Things Change," Carl Dixon

It's been difficult for me to recount the story of The Guess Who's involvement in my accident recovery. The reason is that some painful and shocking events unfolded as things progressed. Jim Kale said much later that I brought it on myself. Maybe.

My final show with them was at a Native casino in southeastern California. What was notable on this trip was that a thaw had begun in the icy relations between Kale and me. Some three weeks earlier he'd gotten extremely drunk on the first night of our annual one-week run at Disney World. It was too vivid a reminder of the unmanageable Big Bad Jim of my first stint.

As I noted already, I was in a bad personal state from the strains on my divided family in connection with Australia. I unfortunately took it upon myself, not for the first time, to be the guy who would express displeasure with Jim's excess. It wasn't aggressive. I merely blanked him all week, onstage and off, making it obvious that I wasn't speaking to him or acknowledging his presence.

Really, I'd been frightened by the reminder of his bad old days. That trait in me, of being able to turn icy cold with someone, is regrettable and something I wish I'd never learned. It obviously stems from fear, and it has no relation to the best self I aspire to be. As a younger man I'd be ready to meet a threat with my own threat or even blows, but as a family man in my forties I wanted to take a more cerebral approach to "threats." I also had to remember that Kale was my boss, and no matter his transgressions, The Guess Who would always be *his* band and Garry Peterson's, not mine.

Since we only saw each other on weekends for gigs, I kept him in Coventry for another week or two. On that final weekend in California, however, I began to calm down and even feel some renewed affection for the old boy. We were speaking in short gusts of cautious goodwill. My impending departure for Australia was only possible because Kale and Peterson had felt sympathy for the difficult time I was having with my family being apart, and they agreed to shut the band down for two weeks so I might have more time with my girls.

"See you in Biloxi!" we said as we left each other at the airport.

My crash happened three days before I was to be in Biloxi. It was a stunning blow to the plans and hopes The Guess Who had for the future, and Jim and Garry reacted at first with shock and dismay.

When my wife called to tell them what had happened, it was all very fresh. I was still in a coma but my life signs were stabilized. My survival was by now probable, but the list of items that could become permanent disabilities was lengthy. The reports to the media about my injuries had been guarded and incomplete, so as to lessen the stress on the folks back home. She spoke first to Randy Peterson, Garry's brother, the business manager for the band. She laid out the complete story, omitting no detail so that the band could know the full impact and have as much time as possible to react before the next show.

The band brought in Colin Arthur from Randy Bachman's band to fill in at Biloxi. Colin had for years been doing a pretty fair Burton Cummings imitation in helping Randy perform The Guess Who part of his career. Unfortunately, when Colin arrived to meet the guys, he had the idea that he was the answer to their prayers and was now "in" as the new guy. His performance didn't live up to the expectations he'd created.

They moved on to the next guy on the list, Derek Sharp, with whom I'd played once or twice many years before. I was actually the one who'd suggested him. A year or two earlier we'd discussed the need to have the names of "subs" for each guy in band, guys who could fill in for any of us in an emergency. I'd found it very difficult to think of anyone who could do exactly what I did, and I certainly couldn't imagine that I'd ever miss a gig for any reason. I thought the exercise was all about covering Garry and Jim because of their age and physical ailments. Since I had to name somebody to be my sub, I suggested Derek simply because he plays guitar and sings.

They brought Derek in for the next show, and he proved to be a better fit than Colin to keep the show in business. Meanwhile, as I lay in the Alfred Hospital ICU, my body broken and my wits addled, I got calls from Garry and Jim to check on my progress. With no idea how wrecked I was, I confidently said to Garry, "I'll be back by June."

He sort of chuckled and said, "Yeah, okay."

Jim called to offer me his best wishes. "Take all the time you need to get better. You *are* the singer of The Guess Who — period. You just get better and come back when you're ready. The door will be open."

That reassurance freed me from worry about my employment future while I was busy working on my ambulatory future. I was sure I could get back to being on that stage with "my" band before too long, even though my body was so ripped apart that I couldn't even turn myself in the hospital bed. I had but one working limb, yet I believed it was within my power to quickly resume my former life.

It was perhaps inevitable that the temporary solution would become entrenched as the new reality. Derek is a great guitar player and a less-great singer, but once given the opportunity, he decided he liked the job and applied himself to it. It was probably more fun for Jim once he didn't have me scowling at him when he went overboard. The new guy got along well with the boss.

I understand now that Jim would have liked to fire me on those occasions when I stood up to him or froze him out, and it would have gone down that way if he'd been the only boss. In fact, he has said to me since, "I wanted to kick you right in the balls."

I thought I was being the "enforcer" for the guys, the one who would stand up to the monster in our midst. Guitarist Laurie Mackenzie, who signed on in 2006 and hadn't worked with Jim in the old days, would tell me, "I've heard the stories, but I just don't see him that way now. I think you guys are damaged." More than I knew, it seems.

So The Guess Who kept going and Jim grew more and more content with the new guy. Meanwhile, our agent, Randy Erwin, the band members, and the crew made the noble gesture of each giving up their pay from one show to donate to me in my time of need. I had supportive calls and messages from all of them in various ways in the first months of my recovery, most faithfully from Garry Peterson.

Then, after a few months, I noticed a change in the tone of the calls. Garry started to talk about what a great job Derek was doing, and I asked him to thank Derek for me for stepping in so capably. Garry mused aloud at some point about whether it might be good to have Derek and I share the singing gig when I was well enough to return. He hinted that Jim and Derek were getting along "really well." Although apprehension was growing in me, my reassurance lay in those words that Jim had said to me early on. If there was one thing I knew about Jim, it was that no matter what, he kept his promises. His sense of personal honour required it of him.

By the third month, the communication from the other guys was drying up. As I pushed my limits to get strong enough to leave hospital, in part because I couldn't "let the guys down," I couldn't have known that across the Pacific there was a clash brewing around my impending ouster.

My desire to be there for my bandmates was a large part of my motivation, but there were other reasons. I felt stupid that this enormous catastrophe had hit me at the point in my life where I thought I'd hit my stride, where I'd finally put it all together in a perfect meeting place of preparation and opportunity. It was incomprehensible to me that I could have lost this achievement through a moment's forgetfulness. My role in The Guess Who had meant I could finally support my family properly as a musician, an achievement in itself. There was a certain prestige attached to the job, and my family could share in nice experiences with me as a result. This must not end.

The crash could be directly attributed to one of my long-standing weaknesses, namely distractibility and impulsivity from high emotion. This was another reason for me to feel stupid and balk against the constraints from injury. Delay was impermissible, for the longer this convalescence dragged on, the likelier that unacceptable consequences would overtake me. These factors, combined with my determination, led to my part in the survival and recovery I made. Yet it seemed that much of what I was working for was slowly slipping away from my grasp no matter how hard I tried.

Looking back, I can see why Jim might have wanted me out now that he had the chance; he'd have nobody calling him out on his excesses. I was always ready, maybe too ready, to stand my ground. I could just say that I made Jim feel bad, and nobody wants to feel bad. He got me back.

Jim also thought I was too nice. He had always dreamed of using The Guess Who platform to have a band of rockin' pirates who'd travel the land looting, pillaging, and raping like a proper rock band ought to. It was a juvenile concept, but he believed in it. Confirmed nice guy Carl was no help there.

Even though he uncharacteristically went back on his word and ousted me, I can see how he got there. I didn't like it then, but I understand it now.

What shocked and hit me hardest at the time was realizing that Garry was backpedalling on his commitment to me after I returned home from the hospital. One sunny afternoon, sitting on my deck and speaking on the phone with Garry, I had called to get some clarification about my future with the band and, really, some reassurance. Garry would offer none. He was cagey, evasive, and noncommittal. I hung up after twenty minutes, now irate. There was no sense to be made of any of it, only a growing feeling that my return to the job was not assured.

I jotted down some point-form notes about what had just transpired and then resolved to call back right away and address my concerns openly. Garry avoided saying anything that could be construed as a commitment or anything that could later be held up as an admission of wrongdoing. I couldn't even get him to say that I'd ever been any use at all to them. He didn't deny that point; he just danced around my direct questions.

The tactics smelled to me like he'd been counselled on how to deal with me to protect the band from a possible lawsuit. Had a decision already been made? Garry said again that Jim liked the band the way it was now, and this fact made any discussion of my return difficult. He griped that my injuries were making it difficult for him to plan for next year, as if I had intentionally created a problem for his business.

In reality the whole discussion was moot. I couldn't even walk without crutches or a cane for another year or more. Surgery and new crises were still to come, and my energy levels would be sadly depleted for a long time.

The dramatic damage to my body, mind, and spirit was of course going to delay me going anywhere. Mentally I was ready to gut it out, but Garry saw the writing on the wall. I give him credit for being tough when he had to be.

As Garry and I spoke, I couldn't help groaning aloud as my frustration mounted. Frustration was then overtaken first by disbelief, next by dawning realization. I felt as if I were plummeting to Earth from a great height. My head was spinning, as it had at other times I'd been in shock. I raced through different scenarios that might forestall this outcome, to alter this decision made against me, but the sense of being kicked over the cliff sapped my will for the moment. There I was, gone.

Garry's guilt about giving me the Spanish Archer was crowding up against the reality of hard business decisions. He could not go against his partner Jim in favour of me, the substitute-Burton guy, in spite of our close ties prior to the crash. I had actually put Garry in this dilemma by my "decision" to run head-on into another vehicle in Australia.

✷ ✷ ✷

So the separation process began. In Haliburton I added the task of forming a response to the threat of lay-off to my daily work of mending and recovering. I was only good for a little bit of movement each day and mostly continued the hospital pattern of resting in bed between managed activities. Television was my friend, and I learned all about the *Trailer Park Boys*. Somewhere in there I had to convince myself and The Guess Who guys that I'd be ready to get back to work very soon. Talk was all I had to try to keep the gig in my grasp.

Garry's brother Randy flew from San Francisco to Toronto and then rented a car to drive three hours to meet me in Haliburton to discuss terms. The message: we might be letting you go, and you need to think of a settlement amount, but don't ask for too much. He was also having a first-hand look at me to assess my prospects of returning to stage-worthy health. I couldn't have been a very encouraging sight, but I spoke with a powerful positive attitude: I could get there.

A week or two later I received word that the band had decided to let me go and stick with the new guy. This hurt, but I took it as just another shock. Everything in my life had turned into one shocking surprise after another since those two seconds on the Australian highway. The fact that I was considered expendable under any circumstances, even broken to bits, was something I fought hard against in my own mind.

After some time stewing over all this, I decided that the only response that made sense was to draft an email to Garry, Jim, and Randy to say that I thought they were making a *mistake*, for the following reasons, and that I *rejected* their dismissal.

This got the desired response: "What if Carl's right?" Discussions and arguments on their side then resulted in another trip for poor Randy Peterson to the same restaurant in Haliburton.

This time the discussion was an exploration of the steps that would enable the GW to feel good about reversing their decision. Randy made it clear they were ready to acknowledge my value, but they needed to know that they could plan a firm agenda around my return date. I showed well, and that meeting came to a considerably jollier conclusion.

Randy presented his findings to the band, and they did indeed reverse their decision after some back and forth. Jim was reluctant but in the end agreed. I was given a hint of this good news in late November and told to expect a confirming phone call. I was redeemed and happy.

It was a Friday evening, the night of Haliburton's little annual Santa Claus parade, and I had a table reserved in Walt McKechnie's restaurant overlooking the street so I could still see the parade and not stand out in the cold in my weakened condition. As I was about to leave for the restaurant, the telephone sounded the long-distance ring. I picked up.

"Hello, Carl. It's Jim."

"Jim! Wow, hello! It's good to hear from you."

I had warm feelings about this man whom I'd been told had renewed warm feelings for me.

"Where are you?" I asked.

"Just checked into my hotel room in [wherever]. What are you doing, Carl? Have you got a few minutes to talk?"

"Well, I was just about to go into town to see the Santa Claus parade, but I can spend some time now and talk."

I should have just said yes.

"No, no, that's okay, Carl. You go do your thing and we can talk in the morning. We'll have plenty of time to talk."

"Are you sure, Jim? Because I can take time now."

Fin de siècle avec The Guess Who. Say goodnight Carl.

"No, go ahead and we'll talk tomorrow."

I never did hear from Jim the next day or for years after that. As the story was told to me, Jim was making that call to invite me back into the band, but he wasn't happy about it. He felt he'd lost the argument. The next day Jim dug in and said he wouldn't do it, that he was too old to do something he didn't want to do. Garry later told me with sadness that it reached the point where they were both talking about staying home if they didn't get their way, and Garry decided it wasn't wise to break up the band over this. Dixon: out.

My 2008 Christmas present from the band was a pink slip. After recovering from this latest setback, the more stunning for having been the reverse of what I was told to expect, I'm afraid I lashed out with a venomous letter to Garry and Jim. Already scared about the future as I was, plus physically mauled and psychologically wounded, the news that they'd changed their minds *again* made me a little crazy. I turned all my creative writing skills toward crafting a message that was meant to hurt and to hold a mirror up to what I saw as their treachery. I'm sorry I did that. Getting let go hit me hard in the place where I'd been holding on to the last hope that perhaps my accident hadn't ruined everything. Now I didn't have any certainty to return to.

I was incapable of seeing what they must have gone through to reach their decision. The doubts and agonizing over the *right* thing versus the *smart* thing were a preoccupation for those guys in the months that followed my crash. My traumatic event was also a shock to their own vision of the future they'd planned, and a threat to all the progress they'd made. The ripple effect touches everything, but when you're the stone making the splash you can't see it happening as you're sinking to the bottom. The Guess Who had to make the best decision available to them in order to keep the company going, and in the end I accept that. I sometimes miss it, though, even Kale. There were lessons I was meant to learn from dealing with him. I knew I'd miss the platform the GW provided for my skills, and meeting all the fans, touching lives all over the place. I would miss performing that music under that banner, music of which I was as much a fan as the people in the crowd.

The band made a settlement offer to me to go away, which was within their means. Disappointing, but I was in no position to refuse it or fight about it.

It kept my family going for another year. Thank you, Garry and Jim.

ICELAND IT IS, THEN

At the time of my crash I'd begun work on a new solo album. Kicking the tires on a few songs, but the form of an album had not emerged. The work was savagely disrupted by nearly having my head torn off, but as my wits slowly returned, my desire to write and record also returned.

Getting to the point where I had a finished new album called *Lucky Dog* was the measurable proof that I'd gotten back up after getting knocked way down. Hundreds of hours were spent in getting the bulk of the recording completed, not least because I was working in a weakened and depleted state for the first long while. Many hours were spent at the Haliburton studio of my friend Ian Pay, finding our way through to the end of the songs. I knew I needed to complete the thing in a good facility with an experienced engineer, and my favourite engineer is my friend Kyle Gudmundson. A search revealed he had moved to his family's "old country," Iceland.

For years I had felt the inexplicable urge to travel there, and so I made up my mind that fate had directed me thither. Kyle was set up there with a studio, so we made a deal to work together again. After shipping discs of my many recorded multi-tracks ahead of me, in August 2010 I boarded Icelandair to put the finishing touches on the project. The studio was in Akureyri, Iceland's second-biggest city after Reykjavik. Kyle arranged a bed and breakfast stay for me and loaned me his car.

After sixteen days of hard work we had the thing licked, so I headed for home. Kyle and I agreed that we had made a musical success, but the prospects of financial success for my new album were as uncertain as they'd always been. The difference this time: from being broken to pieces I'd recovered enough to complete the most mature work of my life. Having bounced back from the prospect only two years earlier of never playing or singing again, I now believed I'd laid down some of my best performances ever, and they were ready to be offered to the world.

I got home full of hope and enthusiasm from completing the project, only to find my wife unchanged in her lack of enthusiasm for me and for our life together. Her bleak view of us having any future prompted me to get completely hammered on the bottle of very good Icelandic vodka (Reyka) that I'd brought home for special occasions. I was left to speculate darkly that perhaps my surviving the terrible accident and getting up off the mat wasn't actually a good thing in everyone's eyes.

There was much torment still ahead and much to be revealed. Even the "great awakening" of my car crash hadn't brought me far enough along in personal development to make sense of things. The questions were torturous and unanswerable without more information, but what could that information possibly be? To a man who had been so set on being virtuous and living "right," what could I have done that was so wrong? The answers to those questions proved elusive, the experiences far more painful than that of having my body mangled in a car wreck. To endure and strive is the only way forward to the solace we all seek. My solace comes from my art and from the open heart that I have maintained through pursuing it. An open heart makes you receptive to the good things that can change your life. Like love.

In the final days of the making of my *Lucky Dog* album, I wrote a song that sums up what I learned from the journey so far:

"The point of this life is to get along, to make this world better before your time's gone. Think of all you still have and not what you've lost, the point of this life is to get along, and give it all you've got."

A NEW CHAPTER IN THE OLD STORY

Many unexpected events came in the wake of my car crash of 2008, but the most unexpected was the return of Coney Hatch as a part of my life. The band had been through so many splits and returns since my departure at the end of '85: short-term reunions, half-hearted reunions, cash-grab reunions, partial reunions ... we couldn't let go of each other, but we couldn't stay together either. If we couldn't commit, we also couldn't deny. It was like the indelible feeling that your first love leaves on your memory, and then trying to return to that person and that pure place after life's progress has left you disappointed: "To Feel the Feeling Again." The things we went through together in the early days of "going for it" left us forever bonded, like first love.

We each had some residual pain through the many years since the band ended, and a thought of "what might have been" haunted all our psyches. There was a sense, acknowledged or not, that we had unfinished business both with one another and with the band, a separate entity in itself.

I say "an entity in itself" because any band is a collective of the human energies that are gathered in it. The more powerful the energies focused on it, the more that entity throbs and shines with life. The whole is greater than the sum of the parts, and when you've been part of such a creature, the experience is both formative and defining for the individuals involved.

"Coney Hatch" was the name used for the gathering place where we each threw our emerging talents and abilities into the pile, and also the place where our individual hopes, wishes, desires, and dreams met and agreed to get along. In effect it was a fifth being, larger than any of us.

John Paul Jones once said, "Led Zeppelin was the space between the four of us." I understand that completely. A band is an acknowledgement of, and an agreement on, that space between.

When you're young and headstrong, you can't see that you are. You're too busy trying to assert your own beliefs of what's right. I simply didn't understand people and relationships very well then, or that people's feelings are important to getting a good result. It was my belief expressed through words and behaviour that commitment to the work and the results ought to be enough for anyone. Sure, there could be laughs and joy along the way, but *my-gawd-it's-so-tough-to-make-it-you-can't-afford-to-ever-let-down-in-any-way!*

To me back then, the loftiest goals to which our band should aspire were discipline (measured by some objective standard), self-improvement, and a certain amount of self-denial. I didn't know that most people felt it essential to have some fun in the mix. Over time I have seen that most people are right about that.

Let me establish here that I am not proclaiming that Coney Hatch was the greatest thing ever created in the history of popular music. Nor were we cruel Fortune's plaything and unjustly overlooked. There is no way of knowing what the outcome would have been if the band had stayed together. The setbacks we encountered were often self-inflicted.

I cannot legitimately say I'm sorry for quitting Coney Hatch, even as I acknowledge the consequences of that decision. I was incapable of a different choice. At that point in my life, with the best of my thinking and wisdom, leaving the band was the only response I could formulate to the confusion, the conflict and the feelings of failure and separateness that dogged me. I was pretty much on my own at that time, with nobody offering me a different message, and leaving was the best plan I could come up with. Maybe a manager or somebody influential could have changed my course with some words of encouragement, but on the other hand maybe everyone was sick of Serious Carl and glad to see me go. It seems we all thought we'd do better without each other back then, and none of us really appreciated what we had. I couldn't have articulated that idea of how we conjured the Coney magical entity back then, when I was in the midst of it all — no way. Emotion trumped thinking, as usual. Managing emotions has been my greatest lesson in this world ... which leads me to the new chapter in the Coney Hatch portion of my story.

In the aftermath of my car crash I was faced with enormous change. The Guess Who had fired me. My family's well-being was imperilled by the sudden halt to my income, while our debts mounted through month after month of my forced inactivity. The life I returned to from the hospital in Australia now looked quite different from the one I had six months before, yet — and here's the significant part — it was the people and the relationships and the feelings I'd created with the people in my life that sustained me in my time of need and through the difficult months that followed. My family and some faithful friends like Mark, Tim, Mike, and Howie came out to greet me on the day I landed back in Canada. Then along came Andy Curran, and I was so happy to see him. As he listened to me telling my story to the group, his face bore a look of compassion, but something more was going on in Andy's mind. In the weeks that followed he hatched an idea to create a fundraising concert to help me and my family in our distress.

The event was held at the Phoenix Club in Toronto on October 30, 2008. I'm forever indebted to Andy and Warren Toll for the hard work they put into organizing the benefit, and to the great guys in Brighton Rock, Helix, Soho 69, and Russ (Dwarf) Graham for performing and making the night magic. There were many others who offered to perform, and I appreciate their gestures also. On that night the seeds were planted for Coney regrowth because it put Steve, Andy, and Dave Ketchum and me in the same room together for the first time in many years. It's amazing how a near-tragedy can make us put aside small differences and realize what we care about.

From that reunion a discussion grew of how we might play together again for fun (and profit, if it was there for us). It took a long time before my injuries healed enough to allow me to consider rocking out on the big stage again. Finally, in 2010, we put together a couple of shows with the original four Coneys, and we surprised ourselves and pleased the crowds with the sound we could still make.

It had been at least fifteen years since the four of us had played a show together, and in some ways it was better now than ever. Certainly it was in no way an embarrassment, as if we shouldn't have dug up the old band after all those years. We did dig it up, yes, but we found the audiences digging us again too.

Coney Hatch tour, 2013.

"Let's do more!" Well, okay. We cobbled together a few more show offers in 2011 as everyone juggled their grown-up work schedules. These included a trip to England in October 2011 to play Firefest in Nottingham, where in a memorable performance we shone perhaps as brightly as Coney Hatch has ever done in a live setting. We rocked hard, and we slaughtered. Next morning over breakfast in the hotel I was approached by a label from Germany to do a new album.

It was a small budget, but I figured we could make it work if we prepared well and cut recording costs to the bone. Then, just as we were about to sign, a second offer came in from an Italian company called Frontiers Records. This was for the world and for more money; still not a large budget, but more breathing room to get a good album done. After much back and forth we settled on terms with Frontiers, and at this writing Coney Hatch has released a fourth album, *CH4*. That's quite an unexpected turn of events in my life, and one I'm glad I've lived to see.

To Andy, Dave, and Steve: thank you for letting me into your band all those years ago.

ACKNOWLEDGEMENTS

I offer thanks and respect to all the musicians and techs I worked with over these many years; I learned something from each one of you.

I would not be an author today but for the input of a few crucial people. My friends Brant Cook and Leandra Ruttan believed I could become an inspirational speaker after my crash left me with a very uncertain future. They pointed out that to support that ambition, it would be very helpful if I've written a book, and so I began. Leandra and Brant encouraged me through my wobbly beginnings.

Martin Townsend was my editor on the first long march to a manuscript. His sympathetic ear and steady eye brought me back on course from my frequent meanderings toward something presentable. I wrote a very considerable amount more than what appears on these pages. Mr. Townsend was my sensei.

Allister Thompson advocated for me to my publisher, Dundurn, and convinced them that my story could be a book. He then did yeoman's work condensing what was still a lengthy volume by applying innumerable judicious and stealthy cuts. Allister led me to the promised land of publishable word count. This was no easy task with someone like me who you can't shut up once I get going. AT is a very useful man with the red pencil.

Ron Dixon, my father, wrote out several pages of good suggestions for anecdotes from my life; his great sense of humour has inspired me. Ron was a writer who never found a publisher and would have been very proud to see his son, the author.

Ken Sherwood, Vince LaRuffa, Ian Pay, Randy MacDonald: Supporters in business and friendship. And Hal Hanka, enduring friendship through the years.

Thanks to the good people of the Haliburton Highlands.

I would also not be alive to be an author today if many amazing people in Australia had not given the best of themselves to save me and restore me. To all in the Ballan Emergency Rescue Team, the Albert and Epworth Hospitals, and the Victoria TAC, I thank you all forever.

INDEX